THE
WAR
OF ALL THE
PEOPLE

Also from Potomac Books

Axis of Unity: Venezuela, Iran & the Threat to America
—Sean Goforth

THE
WAR
OF ALL THE
PEOPLE

The Nexus of Latin American Radicalism and Middle Eastern Terrorism

JON B. PERDUE

FOREWORD BY STEPHEN JOHNSON

Potomac Books
Washington, D.C.

Library of Congress Cataloging-in-Publication Data
Perdue, Jon B., 1967–
  The war of all the people : the nexus of Latin American radicalism and Middle Eastern terrorism / Jon B. Perdue ; foreword by Stephen Johnson. — 1st ed.
      p. cm.
  Includes bibliographical references and index.
  ISBN 978-1-59797-704-3 (hardcover : alk. paper)
  ISBN 978-1-59797-803-3 (electronic)
  1. Radicalism—Latin America. 2. Latin America—Politics and government—1980– I. Title.
  HN110.5.Z9R365 2012
  303.48'4--dc23

                                                                    2012016051

Printed in the United States of America on acid-free paper that meets the American National Standards Institute Z39-48 Standard.

Potomac Books
22841 Quicksilver Drive
Dulles, Virginia 20166

First Edition

10 9 8 7 6 5 4 3 2 1

To my father,
who taught me that effort,
though not equal to talent,
can still be its master

Contents

Foreword by Stephen Johnson ix

Preface xiii

Introduction 1

Part I. A Brief History of Terrorist Collaboration

1 Assessing the Enemy 15

2 Checking the Record 19

3 The Wolf at the Door 42

Part II. Joining the Two Extremes

4 Revolution Makes Strange Bedfellows 59

5 The Transformation of Neo-Nazi Ideology 67

6 The Third Position 85

Part III. Step-by-Step Subversion

7 Slow-Motion Revolution 97

8 Managing the Media 117

9 Managing the Masses 133

10 Managing the Military 140

11 Managing the Militias 152

12 Exporting the Revolution 163

Part IV. Gauging the Threat

13 The Threat to America's "Soft Underbelly"   185
14 A Potential Failed State Next Door   203
15 Venezuela: State Sponsor of Terrorism   209
16 The Emerging Threats   214

Notes   223
Selected Bibliography   253
Index   255
About the Author   263

Foreword

The threats we face today are quite real. Suicide bombings in Pakistan, kidnappings in Colombia, and foiled terror plots more ambitious than the attacks of September 11, 2001, are evidence enough. Yet until they reach our shores, these threats remain largely in the mind of the beholder. What an analyst makes of them depends on connecting dots between the attitudes of states, the activities of suspected support networks, and the psychologies of individual actors. Often a good bit of interpretation is needed to bring relationships into focus to be able to predict how hostile intentions may result in a strike.

There are plenty of ways for strategists and policymakers to go wrong. Concentrating on vulnerabilities leads to a mind-set of constantly trying to fill gaps. Frankly, there are too many weaknesses for that to be practical. Trend spotting is popular because experience teaches us that criminals and terrorists tend to be copycats. Yet that can lead in the wrong direction when dealing with creative adversaries.

Predicting intentions through message and document analysis is useful up to a point, except that it is hard to know how seriously adversaries take their own words or whether they use them as cover for ulterior motives. Six years ago, Jorge Verstrynge's guide to asymmetrical warfare, *Peripheral Warfare and Revolutionary Islam: Origins, Rules and Ethics of Asymmetric Warfare,* gained attention when it was distributed as a little booklet to members of Venezuela's armed forces. Was it a battle plan or a diversion to make neighbors nervous?

Then there is media reporting, which tends to market titillating information to a sensation-hungry public. Often decision makers are forced to react to these media bursts, adding to the distortion that comes from paying too much attention to the obvious. For more than a decade, journalists and U.S. intelligence agencies alike have concentrated on reporting about the Middle East, because that is where the big stories are—to the neglect of hostile movements, terrorists, and criminals operating much closer to home.

The *9/11 Commission Report* chronicled public servants who went to extraordinary lengths to alert their agencies to glaring vulnerabilities and emerging threats, only to be dismissed or worn down by bureaucratic inertia. In the example of Colombia's war on internal terror, the intelligence bonanza found on the computer hard drives seized in various raids on terrorist camps have already been thrown out of a Colombian court as inadmissible evidence, proving that shortsighted domestic politics and legal legerdemain can be as big an obstacle to thwarting terrorism as tactical variability.

Fortunately analysts such as Jon Perdue know that the solution to ineffective threat assessment is to use a big net to take in a lot of information, then examine motifs and draw conclusions in a historical context. It is the historical context that is often forgotten or overlooked, yet it can be the most reliable predictor when it is properly understood.

One might argue with how Perdue connects the dots or dispute the interpretations he draws from the evidence. Even like-minded observers may do it differently, weighing some bits of evidence more than others. But the important thing is that historical analysis and the resulting decision making are taken into account and that reliable information gets presented. In security matters, ignorance is not bliss.

At this point in the evolution of human progress, one might ask why the United States and its democratic neighbors in the Western Hemisphere could have adversaries. Obviously the United States is a great power, and its success fuels resentment. Those countries that cling to archaic concepts of mercantilism and centralized rule necessarily misunderstand our concept of government of the people and the undergirding of the rule of law. Strides by others on the democratic path are similarly suspect and resented by those who mistakenly believe that such nations deny their heritage in order to align with what seems an alien way of governing.

Furthermore, not all countries that are advancing toward individual freedom and the rule of law have had time to move beyond simply holding elections in their democratic progress. Freedom's halting progress often fuels disappointment among some citizens who expected a more rapid rise and more immediate economic opportunities.

To be sure, the history of the United States as an actor in the hemisphere is far from spotless, and adversaries tend to recall our mistakes far more than our policy triumphs. Efforts to impose order or promote democracy have sometimes backfired, opening doors to dictatorship. But the power derived by Latin America's populists from blaming the United States for their unbroken record of failure has proven too strong to resist.

What Perdue has done is to paint a detailed picture in the here and now of hostile actors and hostile external influences in the hemisphere. And more importantly, he has done a much-needed study of the historical collaboration between the terrorist groups in Latin America and those in the Middle East and Eurasia—providing the reader with a historical context with which to more clearly analyze today's threats. For the benefit of the reader, Perdue has painstakingly overturned lots of stones, and up close the picture isn't pretty.

—**Stephen Johnson,** *director of the Americas Program for the Center for Strategic and International Studies and former deputy assistant secretary of defense for Western Hemisphere affairs*

Preface

Irgenhausen Castrum, the ruins of a Roman fort built at the end of the third century AD, lies at the top of a hill on the eastern shore of Lake Pfäffikon, near Zurich, Switzerland. It was built during the reign of Diocletian to help defend Rome's border at the Rhine from invaders. The fort's significance lies in the vivid historical parallel that it represents of Samuel Huntington's "Clash of Civilizations" thesis, where the depth of the cultural chasm between Rome and those who sought to conquer it can still be seen.

At the time the fort was occupied, Roman soldiers garrisoned inside its heated walls would have scoffed at the notion that those "ululating barbarians" camped in the freezing forests outside would ever challenge Rome's greatness. But it would take less than a century before the barbarians would rule the land, ripping the stones from the great facades and aqueducts, which they knew not how to maintain, to build their huts with the detritus of the fallen empire.

As Edward Gibbon hypothesized, despite its greatness and the quantum leap in human achievement and prosperity that it wrought, Rome fell after being pushed—but it required little force to topple what had already been hollowed from within. Rome fell when Romans lost the desire and the ability to defend it.

We have always looked to Rome to try to extrapolate lessons from its downfall in order to prevent our own. Free societies, or more specifically representative republics, are the rare exception in human history. Once established, they become the principal targets of external tyrants who must discredit them in order to retain power in their own forcibly obtained fiefdoms.

The American republic has survived the buffeting winds of war and governmental caprice to stand as the sole remaining superpower. Its principal threat is no longer from rival nation-states but from a multitude of smaller subversions. And between the larger threat of the Cold War and the lesser belligerents of today, the latter could prove to be the more formidable foe.

Our current enemies have done what we have yet to do: they have learned the lessons of our past wars and have adapted their tactics to win the next one. They are also joining forces and becoming an amorphous, cellular structure that strikes with stealth and by proxy, leaving no target at which to retaliate.

Out of necessity U.S. military planners have belatedly updated their threat doctrine to reflect the change in expectations from having to stop the Soviets in a conventional war to a more agile counterinsurgency strategy designed to counter the threat from al-Qaeda and other terrorist groups. But, as the military strategist Bernard Brodie noted, "good strategy presumes good anthropology and sociology. Some of the greatest military blunders of all times have resulted from juvenile evaluations in this department."[1] Brodie's advice applies to analyzing both the mind-set of our enemies as well as our own.

What still challenges the United States today is the pervasive lack of seriousness that prevents those agencies tasked with defending the homeland from being able to even name the enemy that we face. It illustrates a failure of will to claim the legitimacy that we have sacrificed so much to attain and an infectious self-consciousness that has no basis in realpolitik. More than any failed strategy or improper foreign policy, it is this American self-consciousness that is the topsoil for the growth of anti-American terrorism worldwide.

There is a reason that the United States has rarely had to contend with internal insurgencies of any account. Regardless of its faults, our constitutional republic has proved to be the most capable of providing prosperity and delivering justice in the history of civilization. And while this self-evident truth would make an effective weapon against the agitprop that keeps unfree minds obedient, it remains a sheathed sword in our public diplomacy.

America's involvement in war is unique in human history. Rather than a legacy of wielding unprecedented power to usurp foreign lands, our greatest transgressions have been leaving the liberated to their own devices perhaps a bit too early. And while we must accept that we cannot and should not try to replicate our success where it will not be accepted, it is foolhardy to allow our enemies to paralyze our will to fight by defining American foreign policy as some new form of imperialism or hegemony. The desire for human freedom, lamentably, is not an expansionist impulse.

The number of allies that have the will, and the capacity, to help us fight this prolonged war are diminishing. And while we can count on technological and logistical superiority, we cannot expect that alone to defeat an enemy willing to destroy himself in order that we not survive.

The ill-conceived ideologies that bloodied the world throughout the twentieth century were only earlier iterations of those that now threaten the twenty-first. And while the threat of mutual assured destruction could deter the Soviet Union, today's enemies seek to conjure the apocalypse. It has been said before in less ominous times: we ignore them at our peril.

Introduction

"The War of All the People" is the doctrine of asymmetrical and political warfare that has been declared against the United States, Western civilization, and most of the generally accepted tenets of modernity. At its helm today are Hugo Chávez of Venezuela and Mahmoud Ahmadinejad of Iran—two self-described "revolutionary" leaders hell-bent on the destruction of capitalism and what they call "U.S. hegemony" throughout the world.

Both Chávez and Ahmadinejad have systematic and well-organized plans to defeat their enemies—both domestically and abroad—and both have subverted elections to stay in power long enough to try to see them through. In October 2007 the two announced the creation of a "global progressive front" in the first of a series of joint projects designed to showcase "the ideological kinship of the left and revolutionary Islam." Ahmadinejad would promote the theme on state visits to Venezuela, Nicaragua, and Bolivia, highlighting what he called "the divine aspect of revolutionary war."[1]

Declaring his own war against "imperialism," Chávez aims to supplant U.S. dominance in the hemisphere with so-called 21st Century Socialism. And though Chávez's antics have been treated with benign neglect by successive administrations in Washington, his alliance with Ahmadinejad's soon-to-be nuclear Iran has escalated the threat to an unavoidable level. And Chávez's ability to thwart sanctions on Iran makes his bluster more sinister than just the ranting of a Third World caudillo.

It is hard not to dismiss Hugo Chávez as a madman or buffoon. He has a weekly television show called *Aló Presidente!* (Hello President!), in which he pontificates on everything from fleeting ideas on statecraft to the length of time that Venezu-

1

elans should spend in the shower (three minutes, in order to save water during state-induced water shortages). He has changed the country's official name, its coat of arms, and its flag, and on a whim he even changed Venezuelan standard time by thirty minutes, because, he questioned, "Why does the world have to follow time divisions dictated by the imperial United States?"[2]

But it would be foolhardy to dismiss Chávez as a harmless blusterer. Though Venezuela has never fought a war against another country, he is conducting an arms buildup unprecedented in his country's history. And Chávez's burgeoning civilian militias are said to be necessary to defend the country against a Yanqui invasion. However, their actual purpose, like the "enforcers" of all autocratic regimes, is to serve as a counterweight against the military and the civilian opposition that might end the leader's reign before he decides to leave office voluntarily or because of his cancer. Chávez's Bolivarian Militia, like Ahmadinejad's Iranian Revolutionary Guard Corps (IRGC) or Fidel Castro's Territorial Militia Troops, is just one further concentric circle of praetorian guards necessary for the protection and preservation of an increasingly oppressive regime. Even if he were forced to leave office for medical reasons, the militia can also ensure the continuation of a successor regime.

Castro once conceded as much when he gave advice to the Sandinista government in Nicaragua in 1988. He suggested that both the Sandinistas and the Cuban regime required a "committed . . . people's armed defense that is sufficient in size, training and readiness." Clarifying the point, Castro declared that the reason that Salvador Allende was overthrown in Chile was that he had not built a large-enough civilian militia to stop the 1973 coup that toppled his budding socialist regime. Raúl Castro, the brother of Fidel, made a similar statement in 1987 when he declared, "The war of all the people training has multiplied many times our defense capabilities; and, more importantly, it has shown us the right road to safeguard . . . our people's independence and the Revolution's survival."[3]

The Castro regime adopted the War of All the People doctrine from Viet Minh general Vo Nguyen Giap, who began publishing the military theories of Ho Chi Minh along with his own (much of it adapted from the theories of Mao Zedong) in the 1960s. Giap's most thorough examination of the tenets of a "people's war" was put forth in his book *To Arm the Revolutionary Masses: To Build the People's Army*,[4] published in 1975.

In the book Giap detailed the origins of the "people's war" theory as a mixture of classical Marxism and the early writings of Ho Chi Minh. Its use in Vietnam, according to Giap, was developed from the combination of Ho's theory and actual practice during Vietnam's native resistance against earlier invasions by the Chinese and the Mongols. Giap referenced a quote from Friedrich Engels in the late nineteenth century that summed up the Marxist relevance of a people's war: "A people who wishes to conquer its independence will not limit its methods to ordinary warfare. Insurrections of the masses, revolutionary wars, detachments of guerrillas everywhere, this is the only method by which a small nation can defeat a bigger nation, and a small army oppose a bigger, better organized army." Giap also cited Vladimir Lenin's statement that "to conduct a war, it is necessary to mobilize all the people's forces, to turn the entire country into a revolutionary bastion. . . . In the final analysis, victory in any war is determined by the willingness of the masses to shed blood."[5]

Cuban politburo member Jorge Risquet explained the concept of the War of All the People in an interview with the Cuban magazine *Bohemia* in 1987. According to Risquet, the development of the doctrine was in response to the increased threat that Cuba faced from the United States in the 1980s.

Risquet's interview was aimed at a Cuban audience and sought to propagate the cry of every totalitarian regime—that the regime, and only the regime, is the last bulwark against some phantom external threat. Risquet was purporting that it was only this willingness of the Cuban people to support the regime's defense plans that had dissuaded the behemoth United States from invading Cuba. Risquet described the doctrine:

We conceive of such a war, if one is imposed upon us, as a war of all the people. It is not a question of army against army since the United States has forces so much more powerful than those of Cuba that it could liquidate entire units with its air power. What [the United States] cannot liquidate is an entire people ready to struggle. And the experience of Vietnam demonstrated that.[6]

The mention of Vietnam refers to the perennial criticism that armies are always "fighting the last war." In Vietnam, instead of applying the necessary counterinsurgency strategy that had worked in similar situations such as Malaya and the Philippines, the U.S. military clung to the same doctrine of attrition that had been used in World War II and Korea. When asked by a reporter about how he planned to defeat the Viet Cong insurgency, Gen. William Westmoreland had famously replied, "Firepower."[7]

Westmoreland's predecessor, Lt. Gen. Paul D. Harkins, had shown a similar penchant for disregarding the niceties of counterinsurgency doctrine when responding to a reporter's question about squaring the doctrine of "winning hearts and minds" with the use of napalm: "It really puts the fear of God into the Viet Cong. And that is what counts."[8]

Commenting on his part in the war, Westmoreland later admitted, "Like most Americans who served in South Vietnam, I had at first only vicarious experience in counterinsurgency warfare. Although I had dealt closely with the local population during my service in post–World War II Germany, no earlier assignment had involved such an intricate relationship between the military and the political. . . . My colleagues and I in Vietnam were for a long time on what I called a learning curve. There was no book to tell us how to do the job."[9]

The Forgotten Doctrine

Eager to put the stigma of Vietnam behind it, the U.S. military eschewed the doctrine of counterinsurgency for many years. According to Col. Bob Killebrew, USA (Ret.), "After Vietnam, the Army just walked away from unconventional war."[10] The concept fell so far out of favor that, according to a report by Conrad Crane of the U.S. Army War College, when instructors at the Army Special Operations School sought material to develop a course in the 1980s, "they found that the staff there had been ordered to throw away their counterinsurgency files."[11]

Army Field Manual *FM 100-5*, published in 1993 and known as AirLand Battle, was considered to present the seminal doctrine on army operations, but it only contained three paragraphs on counterinsurgency. The subsequent *FM 3-0*, the official doctrine of war training at the beginning of the Iraq War, skims over counterinsurgency in only one page. It was only during the brief period of the Central American wars of the 1980s that counterinsurgency doctrine had a temporary revival among military planners, but it fell out of favor again almost as quickly as the guns fell silent.[12] The first time that the concept of asymmetric, or fourth-generation, warfare was officially acknowledged and defined in the United States since the fall of Saigon was in a 1989 *Marine Corps Gazette* article titled "The Changing Face of War: Into the Fourth Generation." It defined asymmetric warfare as a return to a decentralized form of warfare in which at least one of the combatants is not a state but a violent non-state entity.[13]

This "generations of warfare" concept, developed by the U.S. Army in 1989, delineates the changes in tactics from massed troops confronting one another in line (first generation), to smaller troop movements engaging one another by surprise (second generation), to the Wehrmacht's use of blitzkrieg in World War II (third generation). Fourth-generation warfare, now more commonly known as asymmetric warfare, describes the return to a more decentralized form of warfare, where the distinction between military aggression and political engagement is less defined.

Since then, the concept of asymmetric warfare has been elaborated upon by military and security experts, but it has yet to be internalized within much of the state security bureaucracy in Washington, although many in the Department of Defense have begun to show a much greater acceptance of the concept than other security agencies. It was the failure to thwart the postinvasion insurgency in Iraq that thrust the concept back to the forefront among military planners.

The army's official historian and later a planner of postinvasion Iraq, Maj. Isaiah Wilson III, described the situation as such: "Reluctance in even defining the situation . . . is perhaps the most telling indicator of a collective cognitive dissidence [*sic*] on the part of the U.S. Army to recognize a war of rebellion, a people's war, even when they were fighting it."[14]

The Return of Asymmetric Warfare Doctrine

In mid-2004, the national media was looking for story lines of salvation in Iraq. On July 5 Lt. Gen. David Petraeus stumbled into the spotlight on a *Newsweek* magazine cover with the headline "Can This Man Save Iraq?"[15] As in most competitive organizations, the publicity led to grumbling in the Pentagon from more senior individuals. Some officers with more combat experience and more stars on their lapels than Petraeus had felt that he was doing more self-aggrandizing than war fighting.

Nonetheless, Petraeus received orders in September of that year for an assignment that many considered a Siberian exile. He was sent to command the Combined Arms Center (CAC) at Fort Leavenworth, Kansas, putting him in charge of doctrinal development for the Command and General Staff College as well as a number of other military schools and training programs. But Petraeus didn't treat the assignment as an exile. Instead he used it as an opportunity to develop a doctrine for fighting the irregular, asymmetrical wars that had subsumed U.S. forces after the successful invasion of Iraq.

When he had been in charge of training Iraqi troops to take the place of Coalition troops, Petraeus began reading T. E. Lawrence's diaries about his frustration while training Arabs to fight in World War I.[16] At Fort Leavenworth, he would use his own experience in Iraq to reestablish this unconventional warfare doctrine and to implement it in Iraq and Afghanistan.

Petraeus had made counterinsurgency the principle study of his career and had a tough time convincing those higher up the chain of command to revive the military's interest in the subject. Throughout most of 2003, Defense Secretary Donald Rumsfeld had refused to publicly acknowledge the existence of an insurgency in Iraq, partly because of the public relations repercussions that would result.

In the fifteen months that Petraeus spent at Fort Leavenworth, he produced a new counterinsurgency manual, *FM 3-24*, the first revision since the army's counterinsurgency operations in Latin America twenty years earlier. Petraeus also invited the Marine Corps to participate in the development of the manual in order to get wider buy-in and to incorporate the broader scope that the Marines had developed in their area of operations in recent years.

General Petraeus chose as his coauthor Lt. Col. John Nagl, whose Oxford University dissertation had been about the British and American experiences with counterinsurgency in Malaya and Vietnam, respectively. The book's title, *Learning to Eat Soup with a Knife*, was taken from the same accounts of T. E. Lawrence that Petraeus had read for insight in Iraq. Lawrence, describing the difficulty that the Ottoman Turks faced in thwarting the asymmetrical threat of the much smaller Arab Revolt guerrilla force, had said, "To make war upon rebellion is messy and slow, like eating soup with a knife."[17]

Before the release of the new counterinsurgency manual, the authors invited a number of counterinsurgency experts, as well as many civil society and human rights authorities, to a two-day symposium to comb the text and make suggestions. Much of the manual's tactics and strategy were credited to the long-term work of Dr. Max Manwaring, the General Douglas MacArthur Chair of Research at the Army War College. Manwaring's thesis on the necessity of establishing "legitimacy" for the host government became the central tenet of what became known as the Petraeus doctrine.[18]

Explaining his thesis in 2006, Nagl wrote:

The soldiers who will win these wars require an ability not just to dominate land operations, but to change entire societies. . . . Decisive results in the twenty-first century will come not when we wipe a piece of land clean of enemy forces, but when we protect its people and allow them to control their territory in a manner consistent with the norms of the civilized world. Thus victory in Iraq and Afghanistan will come when those nations enjoy governments that meet the basic needs and garner the support of all of their peoples.[19]

General Petraeus had done just that in Mosul and Nineveh Provinces with the 101st Airborne Division, and when he returned to Iraq in 2007, expectations were high. The *Washington Post*, which had been an adamant critic of the George W. Bush administration's Iraq policy since the run-up to the invasion, published an article by former deputy assistant secretary of defense Sarah Sewall in February 2007 that set the bar for Petraeus inordinately high:

> If anyone can save Iraq, it's David H. Petraeus, the ultimate can-do general. Installed in Baghdad earlier this month, he's bringing in his A-team and rolling up his sleeves. The question for the history books is before us: Will he be an alchemist, fusing existing elements of a moribund strategy with his knowledge and willpower to erase the United States' biggest mistake since the Vietnam War? Or does success in Iraq require more than is humanly possible?[20]

Sewall acknowledged that Petraeus's risky return to Iraq could very well be a "no-win mission" and that it "could not only stain his professional reputation but also, ironically, discredit the new counterinsurgency doctrine he spent the past year creating."[21] Fortunately for Petraeus, as well as President Bush, who had decided to double down on the "surge" when all around him were advising strongly against it, the doctrine was proven sound.

It was Petreaus's focus on Max Manwaring's concept of establishing legitimacy that proved to be decisive. The concept had been written about as far back as the Vietnam War by Col. John Boyd in his report *Patterns of Conflict*: "Undermine guerrilla cause and destroy their cohesion by demonstrating integrity and competence of government to represent and serve needs of the people—rather than exploit and impoverish them for the benefit of a greedy elite."[22]

Boyd's advice was prescient not only for Vietnam but for most of the trouble spots in Latin America over the last half century as successive governments revolved from rent-seeking elites to revanchist caudillos with the predictability of Kabuki theater. Hugo Chávez came to power by attacking the legitimacy of Venezuela's old guard ruling elite and its "Pact of Punto Fijo," a revolving-door alliance of the three ruling parties that was seen as a way for political elites to stay in power. Yet, instead of reforming the Venezuelan government, Chávez has proved to be just the next Latin American example of an age-old system that exchanges a ruling elite for populist autocrats—both often equally ineffective once in power. And despite Chávez's recent alliances with America's enemies, he is not the first to magnify the threat to the hemisphere by allying with belligerent regimes. Fidel Castro, who has served as Chávez's mentor, brought the world dangerously close to nuclear war in 1962 in a similar alliance with the Soviet Union. But at that time the world was choosing sides in a bipolar alignment, and the gravity of the threat was generally acknowledged by all.

What makes the current threat different is its stealthy, asymmetrical nature. The doctrine has been adapted to avoid the missteps made during the days of Soviet expansionism and has instead focused on the asymmetrical advantages that unfree states enjoy over free ones. While the United States enjoys a free press, it has no equivalent to the now-globalized state-run propaganda operations that unfree states utilize to attack the legitimacy of free ones.

Moreover, when free states try to utilize multinational organizations to rein in the actions of rogue regimes, oil-rich states such as Venezuela and Libya have been able to leverage their petrodollars to buy influence in those organizations and by corrupting weaker states to do their bidding on the world stage. These regimes have also formed new alliances around "revolutionary" and "anti-imperialist" ideology in order to coordinate their efforts against the ideals of the West.

Fourth-Generation War

At a September 2009 summit of African and Latin American leaders on Margarita Island off the northern coast of Venezuela, Hugo Chávez and the late Libyan dictator Muammar el-Qaddafi signed a joint declaration that called for a new definition of terrorism. The declaration stated that Venezuela and Libya "reject intentions to link the legitimate struggle of the people for liberty and self-determination" with terrorism and threw in a nod to "the importance of countering terrorism in all its forms." Chávez told supporters at a rally, "Let's all be conscious that we are writing the new pages of history, confronting imperialism, the bourgeoisie, backwardness and colonialism."[23]

Chávez's need to redefine terrorism derived from his decision to replace the Venezuelan military's use of the U.S. Army field manual with *La Guerra Periférica y Islam Revolucionaria: Orígenes, Reglas y Ética de la Guerra Asimétrica* (Peripheral Warfare and Revolutionary Islam: Origins, Rules and Ethics of Asymmetric Warfare) by Jorge Verstrynge, a Spanish socialist and arriviste military theorist. Verstrynge's manual calls Islamic terrorism "the ultimate and preferred method of asymmetric warfare because it involves fighters willing to sacrifice their lives to kill the enemy" and includes instructions for building and detonating a "dirty bomb."[24] Verstrynge has since become a consultant to the Venezuelan army, whose members have also been forced by Chávez to recite the Cuban-style pledge: "Fatherland, socialism or death."[25]

Chávez began training his military in this method in 2004 at the "1st Military Forum on Fourth Generation War and Asymmetric War," where he encouraged his soldiers to change their tactical thinking from a conventional style to a "people's war" paradigm.[26] Chávez then had a special edition of Verstrynge's book printed and distributed to the army as its new training manual.

The "peripheral" portion of Verstrynge's title defines the type of strategy adopted by Iran of gradually increasing its military capacity through surrogates along the borders of its adversaries. Iran was one of the first "revolutionary" countries to pursue an asymmetric warfare doctrine. Since the end of the Iran-Iraq War in 1988, Iran did some modernization in all branches of its military, but it has eschewed building up its conventional army. Iran's military planners instead focused on improving its missile technology to harass its neighbors and its naval capacity to be able to cause problems in the Persian Gulf. But more importantly, Iran fortified its networks for international subversion by backing such terrorist groups as Hezbollah, Hamas, and the IRGC that specialize in peripheral asymmetric warfare. Iran used Hezbollah to prepare specialized missile crews on Israel's northern and southern borders. These "peripheral warfare" tactics practiced by Hezbollah, which fired Katyusha rockets into Israeli civilian areas, would lead to the 2006 Israel-Hezbollah War.[27]

Even before the decision was made to remove Saddam Hussein in 2003, Iran was utilizing this peripheral warfare tactic by financing, supplying, and training several Shiite groups within Iraq. Iran continued this strategy by building up a presence in Sudan, just south of Egypt, in order to support terrorist operations against the former government of Egyptian president Hosni Mubarak. It also supported anti-government groups in Yemen—often infiltrating them into the country—to enable them to threaten Saudi Arabia's oil infrastructure.[28]

Chávez has also utilized peripheral warfare methods modeled on those of Iran. In 2009 he sent letters of invitation to several mayors in the Amazon region of Peru whose municipalities lie near the area where the borders of Peru, Colombia, and Brazil meet. Although some mayors refused the invitation, several were reported to have made trips to Caracas. One of the mayors explained, "Chávez is searching for friends on the border with Colombia, probably because he considers Colombia an enemy and a threat."[29]

In this region of Peru, members of the terrorist group Revolutionary Armed Forces of Colombia (Fuerzas Armadas Revolucionarias de Colombia, or the FARC) have also forced farmers to grow coca to supply its cocaine operations, which have been displaced by the Colombian government's aggressive antidrug and counter-terrorism policies. Peruvian officials have also speculated that Chávez's entreaties to mayors in the region are designed to buy their acquiescence in the cross-border gambit of drug smuggling and coca cultivation, as well as providing a FARC refuge within Peru's border areas.[30]

Peripheral warfare conducted by Chávez also includes the use of "ALBA houses," ostensible medical offices for the poor that serve as recruitment and indoc-trination centers for his supporters in neighboring countries. ALBA is the acronym for the Bolivarian Alliance for the Peoples of Our America, a cooperative organiza-tion of the socialist-led countries of Latin America and the Caribbean. Started by Chávez to thwart the proposed Free Trade Area of the Americas agreement, it in-cludes Antigua and Barbuda, Bolivia, Cuba, Dominica, Ecuador, Nicaragua, Saint Vincent and the Grenadines, and Venezuela. ALBA houses are modeled on Cuba's Barrio Adentro program, which it has utilized for years to infiltrate spies and agita-tors into neighboring countries under the guise of doctors, coaches, and advisers to help the poor.

Chávez has also formed civilian militias that have trained Venezuelan teenagers and even grandmothers to fight the evil Yanquis from up north. "Kill those gringos!" was the war cry quoted by a reporter for the Associated Press who witnessed a mili-tia drill instructor barking at a fifty-four-year-old grandmother undergoing militia training in 2010.[31]

This type of "war of all the people," where young and old are indoctrinated to fear an American belligerence that does not exist, is a tool of control more than preparation. From a U.S. point of view, there is always a balance to be struck between strategic indifference to an authoritarian like Chávez that denies him the importance he seeks by provocation and strategic resistance designed to help those oppressed by his regime. What is given up by ignoring a tyrant's provocations is the ability to actively prevent the incremental destruction of democratic institutions that solidify his power.

The War of All the People

This book is divided into four sections. Part I covers the history of international terrorist collaboration—an essential element for understanding the current threat—and some of the failures of analysis and policy utilized to combat that collaboration.

Part II explores the seemingly unlikely collaborations between disparate radical groups that conventional wisdom assumes would never work together. It also analyzes some of the durable myths that have clouded our judgment during past conflicts.

Part III analyzes the systematic subversion carried out by Chávez and his allies under the guise of constitutional reform, how it has supplanted the conventional coups of the past, and how it presents a threat to the free world as well as to those citizens forced to live under it. Part IV examines the threats posed by the coalition of multinational actors as it utilizes our borders against us, as well as what could be the ultimate asymmetrical threat to the United States and its allies.

PART I
A Brief History of Terrorist Collaboration

1

ASSESSING THE ENEMY

As the Soviet Union was collapsing in January 1989, Iran's Ayatollah Ruhollah Khomeini sent a letter to Soviet premier Mikhail Gorbachev exhorting him to look to Islam to take the place of communism on the world stage: "I openly announce that the Islamic Republic of Iran, as the greatest and most powerful base of the Islamic world, can easily help fill up the ideological vacuum of your system."[1] What is notable is that Khomeini was not suggesting a religious conversion but an interchange of ideologies—one heading to extinction, the other growing—both intending to envelop the world.

What was once thought to be "the end of history" as Francis Fukuyama proposed, or a "peace dividend," turned out to be a short-lived respite between the epic battle against communism and the twenty-first-century threat that has arisen to take its place. And while the doctrine of mutual assured destruction prevented nuclear catastrophe before, the doctrine of the Iranian regime specifically requires desolation as a precursor to consolidation of power. As Bernard Lewis, professor emeritus of Near Eastern studies at Princeton, said, "With these people with their apocalyptic mindset, mutually assured destruction is not a deterrent, it's an inducement."[2]

To effectively combat this new asymmetrical terrorist threat, it is necessary to understand the interactions and the collaboration between regional terrorist groups and their counterparts in other parts of the world. An impediment to that analysis in the past has been the tendency among terrorism analysts and journalists to downplay or dismiss the relationships between disparate extremist groups and their connections to particular regimes. These partnerships are often treated as outliers or anomalies and receive scant attention from counterterrorism planners. This preconceived notion, when adopted by the media and the security establishment, becomes a persistent obstacle to developing and conducting a twenty-first-century counterterrorism strategy.

Having a proper understanding of one's enemies—of the motivations of those who engage in either subtle subversion or overt terrorism—is half the battle toward defeating them. Over a decade since planes toppled the Twin Towers, American and allied counterterrorism planners have not only failed to properly classify the threat but have been unable to decide what the enemy should properly be called. Maj. Stephen Collins Coughlin, USAR, an intelligence officer and counterinsurgency expert, has called this a "failure to conduct a doctrine-based assessment of the enemy."[3]

Besides the failure to properly assess the enemy, there exists an equally mistaken view of the interactions between disparate extremist organizations and terrorist groups internationally. This "burqua-bikini paradox"—the premise that culturally or ideologically distinct actors couldn't possibly be cooperating to any significant degree—has frequently been the default position of journalists, the diplomatic community, and even some in the intelligence community. These durable falsehoods seem to be more of a product of politics, or of dueling worldviews, than of conflicting results from differing analyses.

Douglas Farah, a former Latin America correspondent for the *Washington Post* and now a senior fellow at the International Assessment and Strategy Center, challenged this premise at a December 2008 Capitol Hill briefing titled "Venezuela and the Threat It Poses to U.S. and Hemispheric Security":

> I saw, in the Democratic Republic of Congo, Israeli diamond dealers selling diamonds to a known Hezbollah guy, knowing that he was Hezbollah. I documented the sale of large amounts of weapons to a Hezbollah operative through an Israeli retired military officer in Panama. These lines that we think exist where these groups like Iran well they're a theocracy, or Hezbollah, they're religiously motivated, they won't deal with anybody else—bullshit! They will deal with whoever they need to deal with at any given time to acquire what they want . . . and the idea that someone won't deal with Hezbollah because they don't like their theology is essentially horseshit. You can document across numerous times and numerous continents where people of opposing views will do business together regardless of ideology or theology.[4]

The history of international terrorist cooperation is long and complex and belies the notion that regimes and terrorist groups that use radicalized religion to gain and hold power are incompatible with those that use radicalized political ideology, despite their apparent cultural differences.

It is no stretch of logic to surmise that terrorist groups are the natural allies of authoritarian regimes. But throughout the 1970s and '80s, there was a battle in Washington between those who believed that the Soviet Union was complicit in terrorism and those who maintained that the Soviets eschewed it as a tactic. The official policy of the Soviets during the Cold War was to declare its opposition to terrorism while unofficially supporting and supplying proxy terrorist groups. But in 1970 Moscow had grown bold enough to train terrorists to overthrow the Mexican government and set up a satellite totalitarian state just across the U.S. border.

In 1970, the Committee for State Security (KGB) helped form a terrorist group called the Revolutionary Action Movement (Movimiento Acción Revolucionaria, or the MAR) that was made up of radical Mexican students attending Moscow's Patrice Lumumba University. The students were sent to North Korea for training in weapons, explosives, martial arts, sabotage, clandestine communications, and terrorism operations.[5] After training, the MAR students were sent to Mexico, where they recruited more Mexican radicals. Their mission was to plunge Mexico into a civil war and then overthrow the government. An informant associated with the group stated that they planned to turn Mexico into "another Vietnam."[6]

As was standard operating procedure at the time for Marxist terrorist groups, the MAR utilized burglary and bank robbery to get funds for its mission, stealing $84,000 from a bank courier. But the robbery also alerted Mexican authorities, and a break in the case occurred in March 1971 when MAR terrorist Francisco Paredes Ruiz was picked up on a vagrancy charge while carrying a fake passport. Under questioning he gave up the others in exchange for immunity. Mexican police soon arrested, on a variety of charges, nineteen more MAR terrorists who quickly admitted that they had received training in North Korea. Fabricio Gómez Sousa, one of the founders of the MAR, told the authorities that "no easy coup d'état was planned, but a long struggle, guerrilla warfare and armed confrontation."[7] Corroboration with other Western intelligence agencies revealed that the plot had been hatched under the aegis of the Soviets and was far more ambitious than authorities had originally understood.[8]

After the plot was first uncovered, the Mexican government moved cautiously to avoid implicating the Soviets and instead placed the blame solely on North Korea, with whom they had no diplomatic relations at the time. But when it was revealed that the Mexican "students" had traveled to North Korea via East Germany and were given fake North Korean passports there, the Mexican government had no choice but to eject five top-level Soviet diplomats and recall the Mexican ambassador to the Soviet Union. Although the Mexican government attempted to avoid the Cold War implications of such an international incident, it knew beyond any doubt that students at a Moscow university could never travel to North Korea without Soviet intelligence knowing exactly what they were doing. Moreover, other Western intelligence agencies confirmed at the time that Soviet diplomats had been directly involved with the plot.

This was further confirmed when the investigation revealed that at least fifty Mexican radicals had made the trip and that they had stopped over in Moscow for ten days after leaving East Berlin. They had subsequently made a stopover in Moscow six months later on their way to Mexico after graduating from Pyongyang's guerrilla training course. Mexican authorities also uncovered a number of payments from North Korea to cover their travel and their expenses and recruitment costs once they arrived back in Mexico.

At first the Soviet Embassy issued a pseudo-denial that proclaimed its "strict observance of the principle of nonintervention in the acts of each country." But when the evidence became incontrovertible, even with KGB disinformation trying to discredit it, the Soviet diplomats were expelled—and Moscow did not even attempt to respond with a similar diplomatic measure. It simply "swallowed its humiliation without protest."[9]

Despite the audacity of Soviet coup plotting just short of a decade after the Cuban Missile Crisis, and despite the prima facie evidence that this international incident provided of direct Soviet sponsorship of terrorism, the incident was hardly mentioned just a decade later when the Ronald Reagan administration reiterated the claim that the Soviets were sponsoring terrorism. In fact, it would take until the Berlin Wall and the Soviet Union were toppled before the evidence became overwhelming enough to convince most skeptics.

2

CHECKING THE RECORD

In 1989, amid the panic on the East German side as the Berlin Wall began to fall, the Stasi gave the order to shred and burn the millions of documents that it had accumulated from spying internationally as well as domestically on its own citizens for over forty years. The agents ripped, cut, and shredded the documents into over 600 million pieces and stored them in 16,000 trash bags that were supposed to be burned. But the bureaucrats never got around to completing the job.

Twenty years later, a group of German scientists developed a computer algorithm and optical scanner called e-Puzzler that could process the pieces optically and put them back together with vastly greater speed than humans could sorting them by hand. This has led to a number of well-known politicians, journalists, and others being fingered as former Stasi spies or collaborators. Some of those whose names have appeared have claimed that their contact with the Stasi was only tangential, that they were only questioned about mundane matters. But the more important revelations have been the links that the Stasi documents have confirmed between the Soviet bloc and international terrorists.[1]

This collaboration had already been confirmed by ex-terrorists and supporters. Monika Haas, a former Red Army Faction (RAF) member, after being on the lam for twenty years, was convicted in 1998 for supporting terrorism. Haas wrote in 1996 in the *Los Angeles Times* that when ten RAF terrorists escaped from West Germany to the East, the East German communists "gave them refuge—in exchange for long debriefings with the insatiably curious Stasi."[2] But the meticulous Stasi files filled in the gaps in intelligence that existed up to that time. The files showed that Stasi chief Erich Mielke aided Abu Iyad (aka Salah Mesbah Khalaf), the

Palestine Liberation Organization (PLO) head of security who was later killed by Israeli forces. Mielke offered the PLO weapons, and the PLO gave the East Germans information on West German intelligence operatives in Beirut in return.[3] The copious files also revealed that, after German reunification, the East German intelligence agency Hauptverwaltung Aufklärung (HVA) had "secretly aided left-wing terrorists such as the Red Army Faction."[4] On October 30, 2010, the *Daily Mail* of London documented revelations about the East German communist regime's support for Venezuelan terrorist Ilich Ramírez Sánchez, also known as Carlos the Jackal: "While the West was hunting the man responsible for atrocities all over the world, the Communist regime in Berlin was busy handing him the means to carry out more." Carlos was not only given sanctuary by the Stasi, the East German communists also provided him with weapons and "ensured the killer was feted and indulged like a dignitary from the Soviet Kremlin." Carlos "was given a staff of 75 to plot further deaths and provided with guns, explosives and an archive of forged papers" by the East Germans. He was provided with safe houses and East German experts to ensure that his phones were not bugged, and even his cars were repaired by the Stasi.[5]

Carlos, along with his terrorist partner Johannes Weinrich of West Germany, was treated the same as a member of the Soviet politburo on a state visit, according to the files pieced together by the new technology. Moreover, "at least ten of his East German entourage were privy to the terror plans he formulated while in the country," and his "relationship with the Stasi was so close that his handlers knew the times and places of planned attacks and this was information shared with the KGB in Moscow."[6] Carlos's Stasi files are so detailed that they recorded his habit of strutting around the Alexanderplatz in East Berlin while carrying an automatic weapon. The files also confirmed that the East German communists gave him supplies, support, and even accomplices "because they viewed him as an enemy of capitalism who would do much of their dirty work for them."[7]

The Stasi developed an early presence in Latin America. Its first endeavor abroad was in Cuba, after Castro signed an agreement of support in February 1960 with Soviet envoy Anastas Mikoyan. Soon afterward, the Soviets began sending arms as well as advisers to the island nation. They were primarily from the Soviet Union, but a contingent of Stasi operatives from the HVA concentrated on setting up a sophisticated intelligence service and an oppressive secret police apparatus modeled on that of East Germany. Moreover, the intelligence that the Cubans gathered from operatives in the United States was turned over to the Stasi, including a thick dossier on Ronald Reagan that was later uncovered. During German reunification, the Central Intelligence Agency (CIA) acquired the Rosenholz Files, a collection of around 300,000 HVA employee dossiers that contained the names of agents who had worked in the former West Germany. A similar set of files uncovered in Finland, the Tiitinen List, is said to contain the names of many current politicians who had contact with the Stasi. Because the list does not describe the nature of the contact with the Stasi, it has been kept classified by the Finnish government so as not to cause undeserved shame to those who might not have collaborated with the Stasi but were only contacted and rejected the overture.[8]

The recovery of Stasi files has proven that the extent of Soviet bloc involvement in terrorism was far greater than even the CIA and other security agencies had considered. Throughout the Cold War, much of the conventional media and the foreign policy establishment often dismissed reports that the Soviets were sponsoring international terrorism or that the Marxist terrorists of Europe might be intermingling with Maoists in Latin America.

Some analysts and scholars referred to the writings of Karl Marx and Lenin to show that they, and hence the Soviets, were ideologically opposed to terrorism.[9] Marx, Engels, and Lenin all professed the belief that revolution would be fostered by "objective" conditions, both politically and economically, and that only through economic crisis could a true revolution have the impetus to be politically viable. This and other tenets of Marxist-Leninist theory were often used to claim an ideological aversion to Soviet terror sponsorship.

In the early years of Marxist theorizing, the communists were often in ideological competition with anarchists who had beaten them to the punch, so to speak, as practitioners of terrorist violence—giving them a practical reason to denounce it. Lenin had similar reasons to express an aversion to terrorism in his early writings. Toward the beginning of twentieth-century Russia, it was the Socialist Revolutionary Party members, or SRs, who advocated revolutionary terrorism. The SRs were the main rivals of the Social Democrats, whose dominant members were Bolsheviks.

After the Treaty of Brest-Litovsk was signed in 1918, marking Russia's exit from World War I, disgruntled Socialist Revolutionaries assassinated the German ambassador to Moscow, Count Wilhelm Mirbach. When their attempts later that year to start a third Russian revolution failed, many were either exiled or executed. Those who remained at large turned to revolutionary violence. Most notably, former SR Fanny Kaplan attempted to assassinate Lenin himself that summer, giving him another compelling reason to denounce the practice. Writing about the SRs two years later, Lenin said:

This party considered itself particularly "revolutionary," or "Left," because of its recognition of individual terrorism, assassination—something that we Marxists emphatically rejected. It was, of course, only on grounds of expediency that we rejected individual terrorism, whereas people who were capable of condemning "on principle" the terror of the Great French revolution, or, in general, the terror employed by a victorious revolutionary party which is besieged by the bourgeoisie of the whole world, were ridiculed and laughed to scorn by Plekhanov in 1900–03, when he was a Marxist and a revolutionary.[10]

Marx's contempt for a principled aversion to terrorism belies the notion that his rejection of individualized terror signaled any ideological proscription of its violence. Lenin himself had ordered Felix Dzerzhinsky to undertake the "Red Terror" just three years prior via the Cheka secret police, the precursor of the KGB. And before the Bolsheviks rose to power, Lenin had professed a similar viewpoint on the matter:

We have never rejected terror on principle, nor can we ever do so. Terror is a form of military operations that may be usefully applied, or may even be essential in certain moments of the battle, under certain conditions, and when the troops are in a certain condition. The point is, however, that terror is now advocated, not as one of the operations the army in the field must carry out in close contact with the main body and in harmony with the whole plan of battle, but as an individual attack, completely isolated from any army whatever. In view of the absence of a central revolutionary organization, and the weakness of the local revolutionary organizations, terror cannot be anything else but that.[11]

In 1916 Lenin wrote to Franz Koritschoner, one of the founders of Austria's Communist Party, telling him that the Bolsheviks "are not at all opposed to political killing . . . but as revolutionary tactics individual attacks are inexpedient and harmful. Only the mass movement can be considered genuine political struggle. Only in direct, immediate connection with the mass movement can and must individual terrorist acts be of value."[12]

As in most theory, experimentation often breeds variation, as Marx and Engels both readily acknowledged. Marx, as far back as November 7, 1848, wrote in *Neue Rheinische Zeitung* that "there is only one means by which the murderous death throes of the old society can be shortened, simplified and concentrated—and that is by revolutionary terror."[13] In 1852 Engels wrote a series of articles (under Marx's name) for the *New York Tribune*, which included his advice on the "art of insurrection." The suggested actions of these articles would most certainly be considered terrorism today.[14]

From the beginning of the Cold War, the Soviets had always played a rhetorical game with terrorism, decrying the terror tactics that posed a threat to them while wholly encouraging and supporting activities that could weaken Western democracies. Soviet policy in the 1970s and 1980s was to loudly declare Moscow's opposition to "acts of terrorism . . . such as the murder and kidnapping of foreign citizens and aerial hijacking."[15]

But the Soviets refused to agree to the use of the term "international terrorism" because it was considered too broad and would include acts against innocents that were the stock-in-trade of so-called national liberation movements.[16] But when Soviet dissidents began hijacking planes to escape communism, the Soviet Union agreed to become a signatory to the 1970 Hague Convention for the Suppression of Unlawful Seizure of Aircraft and the 1971 Montreal Convention for the Suppression of Unlawful Acts against the Safety of Civil Aviation.

Israeli prime minister Benjamin Netanyahu, writing in 1982 on the Soviet strategy of terror, stated that "while it is true that the Soviet Union as a matter of doctrine traditionally has deplored the use of violence, . . . the Soviet Union has attempted to voice opposition to terrorist activities to which it itself is vulnerable, especially when the opposition is mainly rhetorical. . . ."[17]

He noted the case of UN General Assembly Resolution 2625 (XXV), submitted in 1970, which established that terrorism and subversion organized and supported by one state against another state are an unlawful use of force. But Soviet endorsement of the resolution did nothing to diminish Soviet support of surrogate terrorist movements "that attempt to tear down the fabric of Western society and to weaken other non-Socialist governments."[18]

Specifically the International Department of the Central Committee of the Communist Party of the Soviet Union (CPSU), the KGB, and the Soviet Military Intelligence (GRU) were the responsible agencies for supporting terrorist groups.

Netanyahu noted that the Soviet Union, via its international proxies—such as Cuba, Libya, South Yemen, North Korea, and the PLO—was able to "have its terrorism cake and eat it too, with pious disclaimers of responsibility."[19]

When the Soviet system collapsed in 1991, there was a window of time when researchers were given access to the files of the KGB. The brief but impactful scholarship that came out of that access included *The Haunted Wood* by Allen Weinstein and Alexander Vassiliev (1999) and *The State within a State* by Russian journalist Yevgenia Albats (1994).[20] That access was slammed shut as soon as elements of the KGB began to regain power in Russia under Vladimir Putin.

Other sources of information have had to come from such Soviet bloc defectors as Vasiliy Mitrokhin, Gen. Jan Sejna, and V. N. Sakharov, who smuggled files out from behind the Iron Curtain when their lives were still greatly at risk. Mitrokhin collaborated with Christopher Andrew to produce two volumes, *The Sword and the Shield* (1992) and *The World Was Going Our Way* (2005), that the Federal Bureau of Investigation (FBI) claimed were "the most complete and extensive intelligence ever received from any source."[21] The second volume documented the direct Soviet sponsorship and support of Latin American terrorist guerrilla organizations and Palestinian terrorist groups. KGB defector Sakharov revealed that the KGB had tried to set up terrorist cells in Saudia Arabia and other Arab states in the Persian Gulf, as well as in Turkey, since the early 1970s and had tried to infiltrate and control Palestinian terrorist groups. The KGB also established its own contacts with the Irish Republican Army (IRA) via the British and Irish communist parties, as well as the Marxist wing of the Official IRA. Using Libya as a cutout, the Soviets also provided arms to the IRA.[22]

The CPSU's International Department was tasked with controlling the policy of the world communist movement. From 1955 to 1986, Boris Ponomarev was the chief of this department, which became the premiere Soviet agency for fomenting and supporting international terrorism.

Under Ponomarev, the CPSU founded the Lenin Institute, which trained communists from Western and Third World countries in psychological warfare and propaganda and in guerrilla warfare. Seeing the potential of "liberation movements" and "anti-imperialist" movements as proxy forces against the West, the CPSU also founded in 1960 the Peoples' Friendship University (renamed Patrice Lumumba University in 1961) to train "freedom fighters" from the Third World who were not Communist Party members. Once the indoctrination was completed at Patrice Lumumba University, the recruits would receive more specialized training in terror tactics at one of several locations in Baku in Azerbaijan, Odessa and Simferopol in the Ukraine, and Tashkent in Uzbekistan.[23]

The International Department was also in charge of setting up front groups and nongovernmental organizations (NGOs) that could advocate by proxy for Soviet aims at the United Nations (UN) and other international governments. According to a U.S. House of Representatives Subcommittee on Oversight report of February 6, 1980, Soviet subsidies to international front organizations exceeded $63 million in 1979 alone.[24]

A May 1985 report by the Senate Select Committee on Intelligence stated that "the Soviets use the U.N. imprimatur and funds to lend credibility and prestige to Soviet front organizations involved in Moscow's peace offensive in the Third World and Western Europe." The report noted that the KGB and the Central Committee "actively promote" the UN imprimatur of the NGO front groups.[25] The International Department controlled the NGOs and held coordinating meetings twice a year, and an official of the Soviet journal *Problems of Peace and Socialism* (also known as *World Marxist Review*) would always attend.[26]

The committee report also stated that "the front organizations participate in the meetings of major U.N. committees, subordinate organizations, regional commissions, and specialized agencies," and "they are in contact with the Secretary General and departments of the Secretariat." According to the report, Anatoly Mkrtchyan, the Soviet director of the External Relations Division in the Department of Public Information, was in charge of the NGO section. The Soviet undersecretary-general at the UN (until he defected in 1978), Arkady Shevchenko, told investigators that Mkrtchyan was a KGB agent and that the Soviet political officer in Geneva, Vladimir Soloviev, was in charge of seminars and relations with NGOs.[27]

The Soviet Embrace of the New Terrorism

In 1951 Joseph Stalin dismissively referred to Latin America as the "obedient army of the United States," as most of the hemisphere was staunchly anticommunist at the time. Up until the early 1960s, the Soviets had an "official" presence in only three Latin American countries: Argentina, Mexico, and Uruguay. The Kremlin's policy on the new "revolutionary" groups in Europe at the time was equally dismissive. It considered them unsophisticated upstarts and a haphazard movement of pampered leftists, untethered to the rigid orthodoxy of the world's established communist parties. But unofficial policy began to change around 1968, as Palestinian terrorist groups became popular among international radical groups after they successfully conducted a string of audacious hijackings and assassinations.

In 1992 investigative journalist Yevgenia Albats was appointed to a Russian commission to investigate KGB involvement in the August Putsch, a 1991 coup attempt by hard-line communists opposed to Gobachev's reform program. As a member of the commission, Albats had access to KGB files and was allowed to interview KGB officers. Her research provided an unobstructed look inside the workings of the Soviet Union's most infamous agency—until access to the archives was cut off soon afterward.

Although she only had access to a small portion of the archives and was only allowed to take notes without removing any files, Albats's information has confirmed much of the speculation on Soviet support of terrorism. In her 1994 book *The State within a State*, Albats tells of a top-secret meeting in Libya in 1974 between the KGB station chief and Wadi Haddad, a leader of the Popular Front for the Liberation of Palestine (PFLP), in which Haddad laid out the PFLP's terrorism plans.

This revelation was included in a top-secret memorandum sent from Yuri Andropov, then chairman of the KGB, to Leonid Brezhnev, the general secretary of the CPSU, on April 23, 1974. The memorandum demonstrates the Soviet Union's policy of supporting terrorist groups while publicly maintaining a rhetorical aversion to the practice.

According to the memorandum, the Soviets had had direct contact with Wadi Haddad (transliterated as Waddih in the memorandum) since 1968 and were eager to support him, as long as they could maintain plausible deniability. Albats's summary of the top-secret memorandum follows:

> Since 1968, the Committee for State Security [KGB] has maintained clandestine contact with Waddih Haddad, Politburo member of the Popular Front for the Liberation of Palestine (PFLP) and chief of the PFLP's foreign operations.
>
> The chief purpose of the PFLP's special actions is to increase the effectiveness of the struggle of the Palestinian resistance against Israel, Zionism, and American imperialism. . . . At the present time, the PFLP is preparing a number of special operations, including a strike against the major oil reserves in various regions (Saudi Arabia, the Persian Gulf, Hong Kong, and others), the destruction of tankers and supertankers, operations against American and Israeli representatives in Iran, Greece, Ethiopia, and Kenya, a raid on the diamond center building in Tel Aviv, and others.

W. Haddad appealed to us to help his organization obtain several types of special technical devices necessary to conduct subversive operations.

In appealing for assistance, W. Haddad clearly recognizes our aversion in principle to terrorism, and so is refraining from raising any matters related to this direction of the PFLP's activities.

The nature of relations with W. Haddad enables us to oversee to a certain extent the operation of the PFLP's department of foreign operations, to influence it in ways favorable to the Soviet Union, and to carry out active measures in our interests with the forces of his organization, while observing the necessary secrecy.

Taking the abovementioned into account, it would seem expedient at the next meeting to treat favorably Waddih Haddad's request to help the PFLP with special devices. As for the specifics of providing aid, it is intended that these matters be decided on an individual case basis, keeping in mind the interests of the Soviet Union and avoiding any possibility of damage to our national security.

We request your consent.[28]

The first page of the Andropov memorandum contains the signatures of most of the politburo members, according to Albats.

The request from the terrorist group was granted, which according to Albats, explicitly approved arms shipments to terrorist groups that the Soviet leaders knew had a strong potential to be used to murder Americans and their allies. And despite the Soviets' public claims of an aversion to terrorism, a summary of the minutes from a meeting on November 27, 1984, showed that the KGB kept the politburo fully informed on the details of its terrorism support. A KGB report, issued on May 16, 1975, told the politburo that Soviet intelligence had sent Wadi Haddad fifty-three automatic weapons, two silencers, and 34,000 rounds of ammunition, and explicitly detailed the illegal method with which it made the delivery: "The illegal transfer of weapons was made in neutral waters in the Bay of Aden at night without making contact and with strict observance of security, using a reconnaissance ship of the USSR navy. Haddad is the only foreigner to know that the weaponry in question was transferred by us." The Soviets had also perpetrated an operation to exchange $20 million worth of weapons to the Palestinian Liberation Democratic Front (PLDF) for $9 billion worth of art and treasures stolen by the terrorist group from a Lebanese bank.[29]

As the client states of the Soviet Union in the Middle East and elsewhere began to overtly support international terrorist groups, official Soviet policy and rhetoric began to change. After 1968 almost any group that claimed to be a "national liberation" or "anti-imperialist" movement could receive both financial support and training in any of a number of camps throughout the world. One document found by Albats demonstrates the range of requests that were thought to be worthy of Soviet support. A letter from an unnamed Latin American terrorist group reads:

> Dear Comrades,
> We are of course trying to obtain financial means through our own efforts, including a ransom from representatives of the local oligarchy, if we succeed in kidnapping them. However, the progress of the armed struggle has caused almost all of them to flee the country, and they now live abroad. . . .[30]

Albats commented, "What childlike candor—no one to kidnap!"[31]

Soviet support for the PLO was openly acknowledged by Soviet leaders. In October 1969 the defacto head of the KGB, Alexander Shelepin, stated, "We consider the struggle of the Palestinian patriots for the liquidation of the consequences of Israeli aggression a just anti-imperialist struggle of national liberation and we support it." Later that same year in the newspaper *Pravda*, the Soviets praised a Palestinian attack on an El Al airliner, stating that the attack was "carried out by patriots defending their legal right to return to their homeland."[32]

But in October 1970, after a Lithuanian father and son defected by hijacking a Soviet passenger plane, and twelve days later two Soviet students defected by flying a small plane into Turkey, the Soviets began referring to hijackings as "acts of desperation" and "regrettable incidents." A month later, the Soviets would support a resolution by the UN General Assembly to designate hijacking a serious crime.

This new policy was officially revealed in 1971 in an article in the journal *Komunist* by Boris Ponomarev. Ponomarev acknowledged that the "New Left" was "neither ideologically nor organizationally homogeneous," incorporating the "various types of adventuristic elements, including Maoists and Trotskyites." Conceding that this new movement's members were "easily affected by revolutionary phraseology" and "clearly contaminated by anti-Communist prejudices," Ponomarev praised these groups' "overall anti-imperialist struggle . . . and the prospects for a united front against monopolistic capitalism."[33]

Ponomarev, it turns out, may have been feigning the Kremlin's reluctant embrace of the new radicals. When Czechoslovakian general Jan Sejna defected to the United States during the Prague Spring of 1968, he brought a cache of Soviet documentation that revealed that the Kremlin had decided as early as 1964 to appropriate a 1,000 percent increase in financial support for worldwide terrorism. Sejna had served for over twenty years as a military counselor to the Central Committee of the Communist Party of Czechoslovakia.

Sejna's documents confirmed that not only were the Soviets supporting these groups financially, but also they were directly involved in setting up guerrilla training camps in Cuba, Czechoslovakia, East Germany, and elsewhere. Moreover, they had long ago executed plans to infiltrate and manipulate many of the nascent extremist groups to their own ends.[34] On October 26, 1979, a statement published in the newspaper *Izvestia* confirmed the Soviets' increasingly overt support for "liberation movements" in Central America:

In the past few years, the national liberation movement has been actively gaining strength in Central America. Together with the events in Nicaragua, the removal of the overtly terrorist regime in El Salvador, which took place under the impact of the galvanization of the masses' struggle, attests to the serious undermining of the very structure of police states which the United States created for the defense of its interests in Central America.[35]

Fidel Castro and International Terrorism

Although Fidel Castro had made vociferous denouncements of U.S. involvement in the affairs of other countries in the hemisphere, he was in power less than six months before he welcomed the Soviets into Cuba and also began sending Cuban agents into other countries to undermine their governments.

Castro's dalliances with Middle Eastern governments also began almost as soon as he came to power. He met Egypt's Gamal Abdel Nasser for the first time at the United Nations in New York in September 1960, when Soviet premier Nikita Khrushchev was leading the Soviet delegation. Soon thereafter, Cuba joined the Non-Aligned Movement, which was sponsored by Egypt, India, and Yugoslavia. At that time, Castro attempted to buy weapons from Egypt, to no avail. It would take until 1965 before Ernesto "Che" Guevara finally convinced Nasser to cooperate with Castro's guerrillas in the Congo. An attempt to purchase artillery and small arms from Israel at the time also failed, but Israel did offer civilian assistance to Cuba's citrus-growing industry for more than ten years. Cuba and Israel maintained normal diplomatic relations until 1973, when Castro was finally convinced to break them. In the summer of 1959, Raúl Castro and Che Guevara flew to Cairo to make contact with the African liberation movements affiliated with Egypt. Both men made a visit to Gaza at the time and issued statements in support of the Palestinians.

Communist Cuba's first contact with Iraq was with Abd al-Karim Qasim, an Iraqi general who had taken power in a military coup in 1958 and ruled the country until he was overthrown and killed in 1963. Castro tried to negotiate an arms deal with Qasim to buy tanks, artillery, and small arms but was unsuccessful. The two countries did however establish diplomatic relations.

Cuba established relations with Algeria's National Liberation Front (FLN) in the early 1960s and helped facilitate weapons shipments to the group. Cuban military personnel were dispatched to Algeria in 1963, and the Cubans began to assist in counterintelligence as well. They also trained the Algerian army for over a year.

When the PLO was founded in 1964, Cuba was one of the first to announce its support and made initial contact with the group in 1965 in Algiers, where Guevara would make his last public speech. Delivered at an Afro-Asian conference of "economic solidarity," Guevara's address was so radical that he not only denounced "imperialism" but also included the Soviet Union in his criticism, accusing it of "complicity with imperialist exploitation." It was Guevara, in this speech, who first called upon the Soviets to support the "popular revolutions" in the Third World instead of pursuing "a selfish foreign policy."[36]

After being scolded by Fidel Castro when he returned to Havana for attacking the Soviets, Guevara eventually would go to Bolivia in his final attempt to subvert a Latin American government and die at the hands of a Bolivian soldier after he was captured in 1967. Meanwhile, Castro would move Cuba into the Soviet orbit and host the Tricontinental Conference in 1966 in Havana, cementing Cuba's position on the side of the Soviets in the Sino-Soviet split. The Tricontinental Conference turned out to be a seminal event, and its location in Havana established Cuba among the worldwide "anti-imperialist" players.

The decision to hold the conference in Havana was because of Mehdi Ben Barka, a Moroccan radical politician called the "Moroccan Che Guevara," who was serving as the secretary of the Tricontinental Conference. King Hassan II had exiled Ben Barka from Morocco in 1963 after the latter publicly encouraged Moroccan soldiers not to fight against Algeria in the so-called Sand War that year. Ending up in Algiers, Ben Barka met up with Guevara, West African nationalist Amílcar Cabral, and even American activist Malcolm X, as Algiers at that time had become the world's center of radical anti-imperialist movements. Even Henri Curiel, the Egyptian who formed the Solidarité terrorist support network in Paris (aka Aide et Amitié), was there at the time, organizing "solidarity networks" to train African National Congress activists. The 1961 Bay of Pigs fiasco had moved Fidel Castro even further into the Soviet orbit, as did Cuba's expulsion from the Organization of American States (OAS) in February 1962. Castro had capitalized on these events and took advantage of the Sino-Soviet schism to ascend the worldwide anti-imperialist hierarchy.

Ben Barka became Cuba's ally in the endeavor, agreeing to include Latin America in the upcoming Tricontinental Conference. In May 1965 the Organization of Solidarity with the People of Asia and Africa (OSPAA) agreed to consider bringing Latin America into the organization and to hold the Tricontinental Congress in Havana. OSPAA soon became OSPAAAL after adding Latin America to its ranks.

In a speech in October 1965 touting the upcoming conference in Havana, Ben Barka declared that the "two currents of the world revolution would be represented there: the current born with the October Revolution and the national liberation revolutions' currents." Ben Barka would never make it to the conference, as he was assassinated in Paris in October 1965. Castro eulogized him in his final speech of the conference. Just after the Tricontinental Conference, on January 6, 1966, the state-run Cuban newspaper *Granma* summarized the spirit of the conference in what sounds eerily familiar almost five decades later:

The strategy of the revolutionary movements in their struggle against imperialism, colonialism, and neocolonialism and, especially against Yankee imperialism—principal enemy of the people—calls for closer military ties and solidarity between the peoples of Asia, Africa, and Latin America, the working class, the progressive forces of the capitalistic countries of Europe and the United States and the Socialist camp.[37]

The Tricontinental Conference approved a number of anti-Israel motions and expressed support for the Palestinians. Yasser Arafat, known as Abu Ammar at the time, was reported to be in attendance, pushing the motions. Then Cuba still maintained good relations with Israel, and its state-run press removed the anti-Israeli portions of the meeting minutes when sending publications to Mexico and other countries. Even during the 1967 Six-Day War, Cuba refrained from singling out Israel, instead blaming Israeli "aggression . . . instigated and supported by imperialism." The relationship would not outlast the Israeli victory. On June 23, 1967, Ricardo Alarcón, the Cuban ambassador to the United Nations, adopted the extreme rhetoric of Cuba's Middle Eastern allies in a speech at the UN, accusing Israel of "armed aggression against the Arab peoples . . . by a most treacherous . . . surprise attack, in the Nazi manner."[38] After that, Cuba became fully supportive of Israel's enemies. In 1967 and 1968, Castro assisted South Yemen's National Liberation Front with arms that were shipped via Cairo and sent military advisers to North and South Yemen. The Cubans also developed a relationship with Syria. In 1968 Castro sent military advisers and trainers to Palestinian guerrilla training camps in Jordan to train the Palestinian fedayeen (from the Arabic for "those who are prepared to die for their cause"), and the PLO and its faction Fatah sent its first delegation to Havana in 1970.

By this time the Soviets had been convinced to support guerrilla movements in the Third World and had also begun sending personnel to South Yemen. In December 1970 South Yemen was changed to the People's Democratic Republic of Yemen, and the Soviets soon got access to all naval bases there.

After Arafat started the First Intifada in 1987, both the Soviet Union and Cuba increased military and intelligence support to the Palestinians, and PLO leaders began traveling to Cuba to receive specialized military and counterintelligence training. Through Cuba's long-established international propaganda network, Castro provided much-needed international public relations support to the Palestinians, often portraying U.S. and Israeli actions in the Middle East as hegemonic aggression against unarmed Palestinian victims.

In 1990 Havana sent assistance to Iran following an earthquake, and Iran started buying biotechnology products from Cuba. In the late 1990s Castro made a number of bilateral agreements with Iran, and several high-level delegations from Iran made trips to Cuba. In 1998 Cuba's minister of public health visited Iran to sign a series of agreements for Cuban doctors and paramedics to be contracted to offer medical service in the country, as well as agreements to buy Cuban pharmaceuticals and more biotech products.

A 1999 agreement contracted Cuban officials to travel to Iran to develop social assistance networks in Iran. These networks, called "zakat committees" in the Mid-

dle East for the obligatory Islamic charitable contribution of that name, have proven
to be quite beneficial to a number of the region's autocratic regimes. They have been
utilized by Hamas, Hezbollah, and other groups, and have helped to establish these
groups' legitimacy among the populations that have become dependent upon them.
Hamas was able to capitalize on the popularity it derived from this tactic to win a
majority of seats in the Palestinian Legislative Council in 2006.[39]

Soviet Surrogates and Plausible Deniability
In 1962, the CPSU helped to establish the Paris-based Solidarité terrorist support
network that was masterminded by Henri Curiel. Curiel was an Egyptian communist born to an Italian Jewish family who ran a highly successful clandestine organization providing everything from arms to safe houses to actionable intelligence for
terrorist groups from Brazil to South Africa.[40]

In 1981 a U.S. National Intelligence Estimate stated that Curiel's Solidarité "has
provided support to a wide variety of Third World leftist revolutionary organizations," including "false documents, financial aid, and safehaven before and after operations, as well as some illegal training in France in weapons and explosives." The
report further noted that the network's "association with non-Communist and non-
violent leaders, including clergymen, has tended to cloak the nature and extent of
its operations."[41] In May 1978 Curiel was shot dead in his home in Paris by assassins
still unknown. An anonymous caller to a French news agency said, "The KGB agent,
Henri Curiel, a traitor to France, which adopted him, finally ceased activity today."[42]

The KGB was even more direct in its involvement with terrorism than the
CPSU, establishing a recruiting and training center for terrorists under its own roof.
One of the KGB's greatest recruits was Ilich Ramírez Sánchez—Carlos the Jackal—
who not only was trained at Patrice Lumumba University but also established the
initial contact with Dr. Wadi Haddad, the head of the armed wing of the PFLP who
also became a paid agent of the KGB.[43]

Besides the direct support and training of terrorists, the Soviets made ample
use of front groups that posed as religious organizations, academic institutions, or
human rights advocates. A 1980 CIA report titled *Soviet Covert Action and Propaganda* stated:

> At a meeting in February 1979 of World Peace Council (WPC) officials, a
> resolution was adopted to provide "uninterrupted support for the just struggle

of the people of Chile, Guatemala, Uruguay, Haiti, Paraguay, El Salvador, Argentina and Brazil." Without resort to classified information, from this one may logically conclude that the named countries are the targets for Soviet subversion and national liberation struggles on a continuing basis. One may interpret "uninterrupted support to the just struggle" to mean continuing financial and logistic support to insurrection movements.[44]

The report provided, in comprehensive detail, the breadth and depth of Soviet propaganda campaigns targeted at the United States and its allies, as well as its covert operations. The Soviets, according to the report, were spending $3.5 billion a year, a gargantuan sum for a country that would collapse just a decade later.

The CIA report also stated that "a leader of the Mexican peace movement affiliated with the World Peace Council met recently with leaders of the North American Peace Movement in Los Angeles [and] agreed [among other things] to denounce the U.S. and especially CIA attempts to impede the Sandinistas in Nicaragua."[45]

On October 26, 1979, the Soviet military newspaper *Red Star* celebrated the fall of longtime Nicaraguan dictator Anastasio Somoza and the "upsurge in the national liberation movement in other Central American states." And the state-controlled media offered overt support for "liberation movements" in Central America in a statement published in *Izvestia*:

> In the past few years, the national liberation movement has been actively gaining strength in Central America. Together with the events in Nicaragua, the removal of the overtly terrorist regime in El Salvador, which took place under the impact of the galvanization of the masses' struggle, attests to the serious undermining of the very structure of police states which the United States created for the defense of its interests in Central America.[46]

Walter Laqueur, one of the progenitors of modern terrorism studies, quoted Soviet state media promoting its support for Palestinian terrorism in an article in *Commentary* in 1974. Laqueur cited Lev Tolkunov, a member of the Central Committee of the CPSU, writing in *Izvestia* in July 1974 that Palestinian leaders "talk about the Soviet Union as the force without which the Palestinian resistance movement cannot exist."[47]

While Tolkunov's statement was typical of the exaggeration of Soviet propaganda, it contained a kernel of truth. The Soviets were already recruiting the foreigners, through Patrice Lumumba University and other institutes, who would lend credibility to the Palestinian cause through cooperative terrorist attacks and hijackings. (See the account of the September 1970 El Al hijacking and May 1972 Lod Airport attack in chapter 3.)

In his article Laqueur noted the necessity of support and matériel, as well as the logistical cooperation and support, that is required to conduct successful terror operations on an intercontinental scale:

> To launch and sustain a modern guerrilla campaign not only takes money—and more money than robbing banks can usually yield—but it also takes things (sophisticated weapons and wireless equipment, open supply lines, support by foreign embassies) which cannot be bought with money. There is a fair amount of international cooperation among terrorists: Irish, Japanese, Turkish, Arab, Latin American, North American, West German, Italian, and others are known to have cooperated on various occasions. But in the last resort, a guerrilla movement with any hope of lasting success needs a major sponsor such as Castro or Qaddafi, the Soviet Union or China. Even Mao himself was able to start the offensive which eventually led him to victory only after the Japanese Kwangtung army had been destroyed in Manchuria, and after the Soviets had turned over their equipment to him.[48]

To Laqueur and a similar ilk of analysts, the rationale for cooperation between the Soviets and international terrorist groups seemed somewhat fundamental. It provided the Soviet Union a method to attack its enemies through surrogates while allowing it to maintain plausible deniability—a fundamental tenet of the nuclearized Cold War. Where Jimmy Carter had talked of an "inordinate fear of communism" and had made human rights the focus of his administration's foreign policy, the Reagan administration came into office with an entirely different perspective.

Reagan's secretary of state, former general Alexander Haig, a near victim of a terrorist attack in Belgium in June 1979, openly blamed the Soviets for their "conscious policy" of "training, funding and equipping" international terrorists.[49] Haig's pronouncements on terrorism were often dismissed by those who covered the White House, but his accusations would be corroborated in the coming years. In 1982 Secretary Haig commented on an intelligence report about foreigners fighting with the Sandinistas. It provoked the following response from Yasser Arafat: "[Haig] said:

I can stomach that there might be Soviet pilots in Nicaragua and possibly Cuban, but Palestinian pilots? I tell him: There are Palestinian pilots in Nicaragua! There are Palestinian revolutionaries with the revolutionaries in El Salvador, Angola and everywhere in the world there are revolutionaries. [applause] The Palestinian revolution reflects the march of free and honest men in the world."[50]

Haig set the tone for the new administration's foreign policy when he declared that "international terrorism will take the place of human rights in our concern because it is the ultimate abuse of human rights."[51] Both Haig and CIA director William Casey were convinced that the Soviets were involved in international terrorism, but this was not a concept readily accepted by the Washington establishment at the time, though it had been previously covered by terrorism analysts.

The 1978 publication of *International Terrorism: The Communist Connection* by Stefan Possony was one of the first to note the Soviet Union's involvement in worldwide terrorist networks.[52] Possony, a heavyweight in policy circles, served as a director of international studies at the Hoover Institution and cofounded the International Strategic Studies Association. But his thesis—that the Soviets were materially, but indirectly, supporting international terror networks—was dismissed by much of the media and the foreign policy establishment. A CIA official at the time even called it "nonsense."[53]

In 1979 at a Tel Aviv conference on terrorism, Dr. Yonah Alexander, currently the director of the International Center for Terrorism Studies, spoke about the ongoing terror sponsorship by the Soviet Union. Alexander stated that "despite all efforts at control, the level of terrorist violence remains high. There are many reasons for this, but there is one dominant factor: the toleration, encouragement, and even support of terrorism by the Soviet Union."[54]

A former senior GRU officer confirmed this when he made the following statement:

Ideological sympathy with the Soviet Union is unnecessary: anyone who helps destabilize the west is our friend: no one is excluded, even if they are anti-Russian or anti-Soviet. There are no limits on policy or ideological grounds: they are all useful. An Irishman who is anti-British, an Arab who is anti-Jewish, or a Jew who is anti-Arab. The Quebecois wanted to split Canada—they were bourgeois capitalists who hated Russia . . . but we liked them. The decision to make support for national liberation movements more active, in particular to give military training to Palestinians, seems to date back to 1968. Such a decision would have to be taken absolutely at the top—that's how the power structure works. . . . The Soviet Union exerts very little influence on how those groups fight. You have to fight for yourself, for your land and your cause. But the Soviet Union blows the spark into the fire—or puts the germ of a disease into the body of the enemy. But when we train them, we also infiltrate, by recruiting members of a movement to work for us—to find out everything they are going to do. In the Tenth Chief Directorate there's a special department which controls liberation movements. . . .

If I give you millions of dollars' worth of weapons, or cash, I have a small right to expect you to help me. I won't tell you where to place the next bomb, but I do expect to have a little influence on your spheres of action. And if someone later arrests an Irishman, he can honestly say that he has never trained in the Soviet Union. And he still believes he is fighting for himself.[55]

A KGB defector, debriefing counterterrorism officials, confirmed what Possony and others had been saying:

If you say the Soviet Union supports small terrorist groups you can't prove it. It is so cleverly done, you won't see any connections. There may be an invisible relationship—there could be. But no direct contact. You can speculate endlessly but there is no proof. It could be that the Soviet Union orchestrates Palestinian training for terrorists, but I doubt that it would be expressed straightforwardly. There are no documents, no signatures, nothing on paper. They are not that stupid. The Palestinians provide a very good cover for the Soviet Union to be involved in training other groups. But they can't be seen: no one can prove anything about it.[56]

In 1981 Claire Sterling published *The Terror Network*, which documented the collaboration among worldwide terror networks.[57] Sterling's work documented not only the widespread Soviet support of terrorist groups but also the underreported nexus between far-right and far-left terrorist groups. Sterling's book caused a sensation in Washington, which was in a transition period between two competing visions of counterterrorism policy.

In a 1981 hearing before the Senate Judiciary Committee's subcommittee on terrorism and security, former CIA director William Colby testified alongside Sterling.

Colby stated that the Soviet Union materially supported worldwide terrorist groups, and Sterling, speaking after Colby, underscored that "there is no mastermind." Colby reiterated that there was not "some sort of central war room with flashing lights on the wall, a kind of central headquarters," in the Soviet Union guiding the actions of terrorists in other parts of the world.[58]

The media, though, buried the lead. Press reports repeated the obvious point—that the Soviets were not directly controlling terrorist groups—as the headline. The point that both Colby and Sterling were making was that the Soviets supported terrorist groups as proxy forces, specifically to retain the appearance of distance from their activities. The more important point was that international terrorist groups would have been far less prodigious, and far less deadly, without the support that they received from the Soviet Union and its satellite states. Neither was charging them with murder—but accessory to murder would certainly be the legal equivalent. Sterling also testified that her research uncovered illicit training of Italian, Spanish, West German, Irish, and Latin American terrorists in Libya, Yemen, and Cuba, all with Russian-made weapons. Those weapons included not only small arms but also sophisticated surface-to-air missiles. "None of these groups were created by the Soviet Union," Sterling told the subcommittee, but they were the homegrown products of political grievances—real or imagined. The Soviet aspect could be seen as giving these groups "a do-it-yourself kit for terrorist warfare."[59]

Sterling's thesis became a target of many establishment figures still clinging to the idea of détente with the Soviets. But President Reagan's new CIA director, Casey, took it very seriously and ordered an agency intelligence review to check the competence and validity of the CIA's analysis of the subject. The review caused much consternation within the CIA bureaucracy, where the worldview and culture within the Soviet analysis section fiercely resisted the notion that the Soviets were involved in international terrorism. Much like in recent years, there were press leaks from within the agency that called it a "politicization of intelligence."[60]

The effort to discredit the notion of Soviet support for terrorism continues today, and it is not limited to the United States. As more evidence has emerged from Soviet and Stasi archives, the effort to push the contrary view has increased correspondingly.

In 2004 the BBC aired a documentary entitled *The Power of Nightmares*, which purported that the perceived threat from international terrorism "is a fantasy that has been exaggerated and distorted by politicians. It is a dark illusion that has spread unquestioned through governments around the world, the security services, and the international media." The documentary's rationale for this thesis was that "in an age when all the grand ideas have lost credibility, fear of a phantom enemy is all the politicians have left to maintain their power."[61]

The documentary also mentioned Sterling's *The Terror Network* and claimed that Sterling had been duped by CIA black propaganda that had been placed in European newspapers to damage the image of the Soviets—which, if true, would have made Sterling's book a smashing success for CIA operations. Instead, many inside the CIA bureaucracy went to great lengths to discredit it.

The importance of analyzing how this debate affected decision making within the intelligence community should not be understated, as the results will ensure that cognitive biases and false premises are not entering the chain of decision making and analysis when formulating today's security policy.

Robert Gates, who last served as secretary of defense in the Barack Obama administration, was Casey's chief of staff in the CIA at the time of this debate. Gates wrote a book titled *From the Shadows: The Ultimate Insider's Story of Five Presidents and How They Won the Cold War* that provides an insider's view into the internal divisions within the CIA over the question of the Soviets' support of terrorism.[62]

According to Gates, within a few weeks of Casey's confirmation in March 1981, he had asked for a new intelligence estimate that focused on the "intangible threat" to U.S. interests internationally, "with special attention to the degree to which it may be organized, supported, directed and coordinated by forces hostile to us in the world." Secondly, Casey asked for an assessment of economic forces that could provide leverage for or against U.S. interests and "instabilities and the potential for developing instability in those areas of the world which are of geopolitical importance and other areas of special interest to us."[63]

Within the CIA, responsibility for producing the estimate fell on the Office of Soviet Assessment (SOVA). According to Gates, the draft produced by SOVA claimed that the Soviets "disapproved of terrorism, discouraged the killing of innocents by groups they trained and supported, did not support or help free-lance Third World terrorist groups like the Abu Nidal organization, and under no circumstances did Moscow support the nihilist terror groups of Western Europe—the Red Brigades, the Red Army Faction, and so on."[64]

The report cited public condemnations of terrorist groups by the Soviets and took pains to describe the distinctions the Soviets made between "national liberation groups" and clandestine terrorist groups—a distinction unwarranted for radical groups that had all targeted innocents and who had all done so under similar claims of a "revolutionary" impetus. But because of the lack of "smoking gun" evidence of direct Soviet involvement, the SOVA analysts defaulted to the position of taking the Soviets at their word. According to Gates, "What it boiled down to was the basic outlook of the observer toward Soviet behavior."[65] While there had always been a divided culture within the intelligence community, it is rare that this division is captured in writing. The following is excerpted from a declassified CIA document responding to the release of *The Terror Network*. The document shows the clear distinction between those two cultures within the intelligence community. Regarding Sterling's assertion that the Soviets were aiding international terrorist groups, the CIA analysts wrote:

> The Intelligence Community assigns more demanding criteria to the accuracy of sourcing and reporting on these questions of terrorism than do most journalists. The publication of *The Terror Network* by Claire Sterling and the selections in the press have created a great deal of interest inside and outside the Intelligence Community. Although well-written and extensively documented, amassing information in public sources, the book is uneven and the reliability of its sources varies widely. Significant portions are correct; others are incorrect or written without attending to important detail. Sterling's conclusion is that the Soviets are not coordinating world-wide terrorism from some central point, but that they are contributing to it in several ways. "It was never part of the Soviet design to create and watch over native terrorist movements, still less attempt to direct their day-to-day activities" (p. 291).[66]

In response, the dissenting group, which included nearly every intelligence-gathering entity other than the CIA, added the following note:

> Following is an alternative view of the Director, Defense Intelligence Agency; the Assistant Chief of Staff for Intelligence, Department of the Army, the Director of Intelligence, Headquarters, Marine Corps; and the Assistant Chief of Staff, Intelligence, Department of the Air Force. They believe it is inappropriate to single out one publication of many on this subject. The last sentence of footnote 7 is a selective quote. More appropriate quotes of Sterling's conclusions are found on other pages of her book:

"The whole point of the (Soviet) plan was to let the other fellow do it, contributing to continental terror by proxy." (page 292)

"In effect, the Soviet Union had simply laid a loaded gun on the table, leaving others to get on with it." (page 293)

Moreover, Soviet support for terrorism and revolutionary violence has moved beyond the passive or indirect stage, and has become more active, as is reflected in paragraph 42 of the Estimate, describing Moscow's nurturing of terrorist movements in Latin America.[67]

The "empathic view" of Soviet pronouncements within the CIA was shared by many journalists. Stephen Segaller, in his book *Invisible Armies: Terrorism into the 1990s* written just six years after *The Terror Network* declared, "It is America's absolute conviction in the moral superiority of its own political system that permits the US government to stand in judgment on the activities of those nations which it declares are responsible for 'state-sponsored terrorism.'"[68]

In the decades since these books were released, revelations from Soviet and Stasi archives have shown that not only were the Soviets and their surrogates supporting terror, the extent of that support had been wholly underestimated. According to Gates, "We would learn a decade later that [CIA analysis] had been too cautious. After the communist governments in Eastern Europe collapsed, we found out that the East Europeans (especially East Germans) indeed not only had provided sanctuary for West European 'nihilist' terrorists, but had trained, armed, and funded many of them." Gates added, "It was inconceivable that the Soviets, and especially the KGB, which had these governments thoroughly penetrated, did not know and allow (if not encourage) these activities to continue. As it turns out, Casey had been more right than others."[69]

3

THE WOLF AT THE DOOR

The analytical bias that led the CIA's SOVA analysts to make critical misjudgments during the Cold War has a long history. In the fall–winter 2001 issue of the CIA journal *Studies in Intelligence*, CIA operations officer P. K. Rose published an article about the flawed intelligence provided by the CIA in the autumn of 1950, after North Korea had begun hostilities that summer. Though China had conducted a military buildup on the China–North Korea border in early 1950, the CIA had continually declared that the Chinese would not intervene in the conflict.[1]

The CIA's Office of Records and Estimates *Paper 58-50* stated on October 12, 1950, that "while full-scale Chinese Communist intervention in Korea must be regarded as a continuing possibility, a consideration of all known factors leads to the conclusion that barring a Soviet decision for global war, such action is not probable in 1950." However, Rose observed that "numerous intelligence reports indicated Chinese preparations for military intervention."[2]

The stubbornness with which this error was maintained, despite overwhelming evidence to the contrary, is alarming for an agency whose mission would seem to require that it assume the worst of our enemies. On October 13 and 14, 1950, as Chinese forces began pouring across the North Korean border, the CIA still refused to change its position. A CIA "Daily Summary" issued on October 15, 1950, declared that "China had no intention of entering the war in any large-scale fashion." Within the agency, a number of analysts claimed that the incursion of troops was only "to protect the hydroelectric plants along the Yalu River that provide power to the Manchurian industrial area."[3]

Soon, a Chinese invasion force of nearly half a million regular army soldiers and 370,000 additional security troops was across the border, and still the CIA refused to acknowledge the invasion. According to Rose, military intelligence on location reported seeing twelve Chinese military divisions inside North Korea, but "on 24 November, however, National Intelligence Estimate 2/1 stated that China had the capability for large-scale offensive operations but that there were no indications such an offensive was in the offing." Rose continued, "That same day, the second Chinese offensive started, leaving the 8th Army fighting for its life and most of the 1st Marine Division surrounded and threatened with annihilation."[4]

In 2001, well before the attacks of September 11, a blue-ribbon panel was put together that consisted of Asia specialists from the CIA and outside academics who were critics of the agency. The Tilelli Commission was led by the former commander of U.S. forces in South Korea, Gen. John H. Tilelli, Jr., USA (Ret.), and included Stephen Rosen of Harvard, Aaron Friedberg of Princeton, Peter Rodman of the Pentagon, and former ambassador and CIA operative in Asia James R. Lilley. The commission reviewed the CIA's China analysis and issued a classified report. The report declared that the CIA's China analysts had an "institutional predisposition" to underestimate or downplay actions by China and to portray the Chinese leadership in a favorable light.[5] The technical term for this in structured analysis is a "type II error," or a "false negative"—when cognitive bias or analytical error causes an analyst not to see the "wolf at the door."

The United States' past relationship with the recently deceased dictator Col. Muammar el-Qaddafi offers a good example of that bias. Since Qaddafi approached the United States and offered to give up his weapons of mass destruction program in 2003, he lived a Janus-faced existence, denouncing the United States at every extremist conference that he attended while simultaneously accommodating arms inspectors within his own country. During the coverage of Qaddafi's last stand in Libya, the extent of his terrorist past was rarely mentioned in the media, even while he was killing his own citizens. His contributions to international terrorism over the last forty years were vast, and it should be noted that he got his start in international terrorism by funding far-right extremist groups before he made the transition to bankrolling terrorist groups of the far left. In the 1970s, after Qaddafi made the transition from supporting the waning movement of far-right radicals to being the principle donor to Palestinian terrorists, almost any extremist group that called itself "revolutionary" could get a substantial donation from the Libyan dictator.[6]

In November 1976, Libyan and Algerian agents formed a clandestine agreement to train the ETA terrorists (Euskadi Ta Askatasuna; Basque Homeland and Freedom) of Spain and the Bretons and Corsicans in France. By 1980 Qaddafi's largesse would almost exclusively fund left-wing groups. In April 1983, Brazilian authorities stopped a Libyan plane bound for Nicaragua that was carrying weapons said to be for the Colombian terrorist group M-19. Qaddafi also funneled millions of dollars to the Sandinistas in Nicaragua and the Farabundo Martí National Liberation Front (FMLN) in El Salvador. Other recipients of Qaddafi's oil revenues were the Red Brigades of Italy, the IRA in the United Kingdom and Ireland, and groups in Thailand, Turkey, and Japan.[7]

David Newsom, a former ambassador to Libya, reported in 1980, "Apart from helping Palestinian groups, the Libyans have provided money, training and in some cases arms for virtually every group in the world with revolutionary credentials."[8] Aside from the financial support, Qaddafi set up training camps in Libya for foreign terrorists. He also sent Libyan military trainers to aid the PLO in Lebanon in 1981, as well as antitank and surface-to-air missiles.[9]

Qaddafi's financial support had earlier smoothed the way for international cooperation among the world's left-wing terrorist groups by helping Latin American guerrillas travel to Lebanon to receive terror training and by helping Yasser Arafat and PLO members travel to Havana to meet with Castro in 1974. Around the same time, Cuba, along with the non-aligned countries, would break relations with Israel and sponsor a UN resolution calling Zionism a form of racial discrimination.

After that, Castro built a stronger relationship with Saddam Hussein, providing medical services, loans, and development projects until the beginning of the Iran-Iraq War. Even though he had a close relationship with Hussein and his regime, Castro praised the Iranian revolution and withdrew his military advisers from Iraq once Hussein attacked Iran—although Cuba would adopt an official position of impartiality.

In 1982 Castro collaborated with Qaddafi to form the Mathaba News Agency in Tripoli, also known as al-Mathaba or the Anti-Imperialism Center (AIC). Mathaba began as a propaganda outlet for "anti-imperialist" forces worldwide but later became a coordinating organization designed to directly aid those terror movements. Mathaba also served to facilitate payments and supplies through Libyan embassies worldwide and set up and coordinated clandestine operations through its consulates.[10] After President Ronald Reagan bombed Tripoli in 1986, Libyan support to

Latin American terrorist groups dropped significantly, and Mathaba held what was thought to be its last meeting in Tripoli in 1990.

In August 2000 Qaddafi convened a conference in Tripoli at the AIC to commemorate the thirtieth anniversary of his revolution. A who's who of radical left-wing leaders attended the celebration, many of whom were graduates of Qaddafi's terrorist training camps. The attendees from Africa included Sam Nujoma (Namibia), Robert Mugabe (Zimbabwe), Yoweri Kaguta Museveni (Uganda), Blaise Campaoré (Burkina Faso), Alpha Oumar Konaré (Mali), Yahya Jammeh (Gambia), Idriss Déby (Chad), Abdou Diouf (Senegal), and Kumba Yalá (Guinea-Bissau). Representatives from Latin America included Schafik Handal (FMLN, El Salvador); Tomás Borge and Daniel Ortega of Nicaragua's Sandinista National Liberation Front (Frente Sandinista de Liberación, or FSLN); Raúl Reyes (FARC, Colombia); a personal representative of Hugo Chávez (Venezuela); Luiz Inácio Lula da Silva (Brazil); Gladys Marín, general secretary of the Communist Party of Chile; Marina Arismendi, general secretary of the Communist Party of Uruguay; and members of the Communist Party of Cuba and the Guatemalan National Revolutionary Unity (Unidad Revolucionaria Nacional de Guatemala). Attendees from Europe included members of the Communist Refoundation Party of Italy, the United Left of Spain, and members of OSPAAAL.[11]

Qaddafi's AIC also had a secondary purpose: to select candidates for terrorist training. For this type of training, Qaddafi founded the World Revolutionary Center (WRC) near the eastern Libyan city of Benghazi. The WRC was called the "Harvard and Yale of a whole generation of African revolutionaries."[12] At the WRC, revolutionaries and radicals ranging from African warlords to the Nicaraguan Sandinistas received training in weapons and counterintelligence techniques, along with ideological training. *The Green Book*, Qaddafi's brief treatise laying out his political philosophy, served as their classroom text.

When Colombia's armed forces killed FARC leader Raúl Reyes in 2008, they found a letter dated September 4, 2000, written by the FARC high command to "Comrade Colonel Gaddafi, Great Leader of the World Mathaba," which thanked Qaddafi for bringing a group of senior FARC commanders to Libya. The letter included an official request for "a loan of $100 million, repayable in five years," and stated, "One of our primary needs is the purchase of surface-to-air missiles to repel and shoot down the combat aircraft." The aircraft to which the FARC letter was referring were American aircraft provided to the Colombian Air Force.[13]

The environment for Qaddafi's terror support was cooled by the events of September 11, 2001, and when Qaddafi failed to respond to the FARC's request for money, Reyes wrote a letter dated February 22, 2003, to Nicaragua's leftist president Daniel Ortega to ask for an update. Marked "Hand Delivery," the letter stated:

Dear compañero Daniel,

This is to send you my warm and effusive revolutionary greeting, and that of commander Manuel Marulanda. We also are writing to see if you have any information on the request we made to our Libyan comrades, which was made in writing in the name of the secretariat of the FARC, and which I signed. The Libyans said they would answer us, but we have not yet received any information. While we were in Libya they explained to us that the political responsibility for carrying out Libya's policies in the region were in the hands of Daniel Ortega. For that reason, we are approaching you, in hopes of obtaining an answer.

I also want to reaffirm to you that the primary priority of the FARC, in order to achieve greater success in its military operations against enemy troops, in order to take political power in Colombia, is acquiring antiaircraft capabilities, in order to counteract the efficiency of the Colombian and U.S. aircraft against our troops.[14]

For his part, Ortega defended Qaddafi even after he had gunned down hundreds of unarmed Libyans in the streets in February 2011 and called for "rivers of blood." Ortega told the press that he had called his "brother" Qaddafi several times to "express his solidarity" while the Libyan dictator was still clinging to power, because, according to Ortega, Qaddafi "is again waging a great battle" to defend the unity of his nation.[15] Qaddafi would also get a vote of confidence from Fidel Castro and Bolivian president Evo Morales, and Hugo Chávez would make an offer to negotiate a "peace treaty" for Libya. Chávez's offer was dismissed out of hand in Europe. The Europeans had dealt with Chávez's diplomatic overtures before. During diplomatic negotiations on an October 2001 trip to France, Chávez had signed an agreement with the French government outlining the repatriation of detainees. Many speculated that Chávez was attempting to secure the release of Carlos the Jackal, but the French government, upon realizing his intentions, advised him that the agreement did not allow the repatriation of terrorists.[16]

From Carlos the Jackal to Osama bin Laden

One of the progenitors of Middle Eastern–Latin American collaboration, Carlos wrote a book in 2003 while serving a life sentence in a Paris prison. *Revolutionary Islam*[17] is a manifesto for the current ideological syncretism between Middle Eastern and Latin American autocrats and terrorist groups. In the book, Carlos praises Osama Bin Laden, calling him a shining example of "revolutionary Islam," which, according to the incarcerated author, offers a "new, post-Communist answer to . . . U.S. 'totalitarianism.'"[18]

This "post-Communist answer" is an apt description of the Middle Eastern–Latin American relationship today—a reconstitution of the old radical network that was forced underground after the fall of Soviet communism. The origins of this relationship go back to the post–World War II Sino-Soviet rift, when the itinerant Carlos the Jackal and Che Guevara were globe trotting to extremist strongholds throughout the Middle East.

In 1968 Carlos's father, a radical communist lawyer, placed him in Patrice Lumumba University. There Carlos would often ask his Palestinian classmates about the man he would later call his "master," Wadi Haddad, a Palestinian Christian and terrorist.

Haddad, like Guevara and a large number of terrorists, was born to upper-middle-class parents, who sent him to medical school to be a doctor. Along with a fellow medical student and future terrorist, Dr. George Habash, he started a medical clinic to treat warring Palestinians in Jordan. The pair founded the Arab Nationalist Movement and later moved into terrorism with the PFLP.

After fedayeen attacks on the Israeli military proved futile, Haddad decided that terrorism was the way to revolutionary victory. He believed that eliminating Israel and creating a revolutionary Palestinian state were the primary goals and declared, "After that we will overthrow the feudal Arab thrones and then we will spread our revolution to the whole world."[19]

It was Haddad who planned and executed the first Palestinian airline hijacking in 1968. The event garnered headlines worldwide, and Haddad's proclamations of world revolution sparked a fire in the mind of the young Carlos, who had been raised on Marxist doctrine. This was around the same time that the Soviets decided to make contact with Haddad and to utilize him as best they could to foment revolution throughout the Soviet Union's client states.[20]

According to Carlos, his first PFLP contact in Moscow was Rifaat Abul Anoun, a Palestinian who took him and his Latin American friends at Patrice Lumumba

University under his wing and invited them to go to a terrorist training camp for foreigners in Jordan. Carlos was the only one of the Latin Americans who ended up going to Jordan, where he met "the public face or terrorism," Bassam Abu-Sharif, so called for his role as spokesman for the PFLP.

Abu-Sharif was the de facto recruiter for numerous foreign revolutionaries, including Andreas Baader and Ulrike Meinhof of the West German terrorist group the Baader-Meinhof Gang. Abu-Sharif would later say of his young recruits:

> Haddad's spectaculars proved that a relatively small number of committed and well-organized people could kick the West up the backside and get away with it. This was like a magnet to these fledgling Che Guevaras. Many of them really hated the machinery of capitalism; the power of big business and big government, which crushed the spirit of the individual. They wanted freedom and power. And they hung their revolutionary aspirations on the peg of Palestine.[21]

It was Abu-Sharif who gave Ilich Ramírez Sánchez his nom de guerre, suggesting it because "Carlos" is the Spanish derivation of the Arabic name Khalil, which was introduced into Spain by the Moors.[22]

Knowing that the KGB would not allow him to return to Moscow, Carlos planned to take one or two training courses in Jordan and then return to Venezuela to offer his services to Douglas Bravo, a Venezuelan guerrilla leader who was so radical that he had been expelled from the Communist Party of Venezuela.[23]

While Carlos was receiving terrorist training in Jordan, Bravo formed a more militant party, the Party of Venezuelan Revolution (Partido de la Revolución Venezolana, or PRV), and was now heading its terrorist wing, the Armed Forces of National Liberation (Fuerzas Armadas de Liberación Nacional, or FALN) in an insurgency that would last until the mid-1970s. Besides having had several contacts with Guevara, Bravo would go on to recruit Venezuelan army officers sympathetic to militant communism in order to foment revolution in Venezuela. One of the officers he recruited in 1980 was a young Hugo Chávez.[24]

Carlos would never make it to Venezuela to fight alongside Bravo. Instead he became battle tested in Jordan during the Black September attacks of 1970, when King Hussein was forced to expel the amalgam of leftist terrorists that had been using his country as a training camp. At the time, a census by the Jordanian government found fifty-two different Palestinian groups within its borders, with "leftists proselytizing not Islam but Marxism from the minarets of its mosques."[25] During Black September, King Hussein would drive all of the terrorist groups, along with Yasser Arafat, out of Jordan to Lebanon.

Around the same time as the terrorists' expulsion from Jordan, several incidents occurred that illustrate the cross-cultural nature and cooperation that international terrorist organizations are willing to abide. In 1970 Oscar Turcios, a leader of the Sandinistas in Nicaragua, contacted the Marxist Fourth International, a loosely defined Trotskyist organization, in Western Europe to try to facilitate a meeting with other guerrilla groups that could offer training to the Sandinistas' fledgling movement. The Sandinistas' first such contact was with Na'if Hawatmeh's Popular Democratic Front for the Liberation of Palestine (PDFLP).

Patrick Argüello, a Nicaraguan raised in Los Angeles after his family was exiled following the assassination of President Somoza, was enthralled by the Cuban revolution and Che Guevara. Argüello was said to be deeply affected by the deaths in August 1967 of several Sandinista friends, as well as Guevara's two months later. A Fulbright scholar sent to Chile to study medicine, Argüello offered his services to the Sandinistas but was suspected of being an infiltrator because he had grown up in the United States. However, he and several other Sandinistas eventually established contact with Habbash's PFLP and were sent to PDFLP camps near Amman, Jordan, for guerrilla training from April to June 1970.

On September 6, 1970, Argüello and Palestinian terrorist Leila Khaled, posing as a married couple with Honduran passports, boarded El Al flight 219 from Amsterdam to New York. While attempting to hijack the flight, Khaled was subdued by passengers, and Argüello was shot and killed by Israeli sky marshals. Khaled would eventually be released by UK authorities in a prisoner exchange and go on to be hailed as a hero of the international left. A number of years later, she was often giving speeches even in the United Kingdom. She has also been a regularly scheduled speaker at the World Social Forum and was elected to the Palestinian National Council.

On May 26, 1971, Khaled told the Turkish newspaper *Hurryet* that

the Popular Front for the Liberation of Palestine (PFLP) sends instructors to Turkey in order to train Turkish youth in urban guerrilla fighting, kidnappings, plane hijackings, and other matters. . . . In view of the fact that it is more difficult than in the past for Turks to go and train in PFLP camps, the PFLP

is instructing the Turks in the same way as it trains Ethiopians and revolutionaries from underdeveloped countries. The PFLP has trained most of the
detained Turkish underground members.[26]

Within ten years, terrorist attacks in Turkey would be killing an average of nine to
ten people per day.[27]

John Follain, commenting in his book on Carlos the Jackal on the use of foreign
terrorists in PFLP missions, stated that "there was little reason to discourage such
volunteers. For Haddad, foreign blood was a precious asset because it demonstrated
that the Palestinian cause had universal appeal, and he liked to pool talent from different nations when selecting teams for his missions."[28]

The major advantage of the use of adventurist foreigners in the ranks of European and Middle Eastern terrorist groups was that it denied counterterrorism officials the ability to profile potential terrorists. For example, the Japanese Red Army,
a Marxist-Leninist terrorist group founded in Lebanon and based in Japan, was
originally funded and equipped by the PFLP.

On May 30, 1972, the Japanese Red Army surprised Israeli counterterrorism
officials, who were on the lookout for Arab terrorists, when three members dressed
in suits and carrying violin cases walked off an Air France flight from Rome into
Tel Aviv's Lod Airport (now Ben Gurion International Airport). Once inside the
airport, they threw open the violin cases, pulled out Czech-made vz. 58 assault rifles
and hand grenades, and began firing into the crowds.

They managed to kill twenty-six innocent people and wound eighty before security officers shot and killed one of the them. Another ran outside and shot at
passengers who were exiting another airplane. He then blew himself up with a gre-
nade. The third member, Kozo Okamoto, was captured and later told police that he
had nothing against Israelis but that he had engaged in the terrorist act because "it
was my duty as a soldier of the revolution."[29] The PFLP, in its communiqué taking
credit for the attack, called the terrorists who carried it out "the Squad of the Martyr
Patrick Argüello."

Once they came to power in Nicaragua, the Sandinistas would also attract a
large, eclectic group of fellow travelers to the country. A March 3, 1985, article in the
Miami Herald reported that a large number of Argentine and Uruguayan guerrillas
had been gathering at the Yerba Buena, a coffee shop and bookstore in downtown
Managua, and that the favorite hangout in Managua for Salvadoran guerrillas was

Los Gauchos restaurant.[30]

The article provided a list of terrorist groups living in Nicaragua at the time, protected by the Sandinistas: "Italians from the Red Brigades and Unità Comunista Combattente; West Germans linked to the Baader-Meinhof Gang; members of Spain's Basque ETA separatist guerrillas; leaders of Honduras's Cinchonero guerrillas; militants from Peru's Shining Path; Montoneros from Argentina; Tupamaros from Uruguay; and a hodgepodge of Salvadorans, Costa Ricans, Colombians, Chileans, Guatemalans, Paraguayans and Bolivians."[31] On February 8, 1985, Italian authorities presented the Sandinista government with a list of twenty-two left-wing Italian terrorists believed to be living in Nicaragua, many of whom had been convicted in absentia in their home country.

The Argentine Cauldron

Around the same time, Argentina had become a cauldron of disparate terrorist groups and ideologies and may be the most emblematic example of the melding of terrorist ideologies. By the 1970s, the Montoneros were becoming well known in international terrorist circles. In his 1996 book *We Were Soldiers: The Secret History of the Montonero Counteroffensive*, former Montonero Marcelo Larraquy gives details of the terrorist group's activities in the Middle East.

The Montoneros' first contact with the PLO took place in 1971, when Montonero leader Rodolfo Galimberti made an agreement with Saad Chedid, president of the Center for Arabic Studies (Centro de Estudios Arabes), to look for support for the Palestinian cause within Buenos Aires's Peronist movement. (The Peronist movement, named for Argentine president Juan Perón, looked like many of today's radical terrorist amalgams, combining far-left and far-right radical groups into a combined political movement.) A year later, on August 20, 1972, Galimberti made his first trip to Lebanon and received a letter of recommendation from Juan Perón himself, delivered by the PLO representative of Madrid. By the end of 1972, the first group of Montoneros would be receiving terrorist training in Lebanon. At first they served as political contacts with a group of Palestinians in Europe. Later they signed an agreement to handle logistics, falsify documents, and traffic arms.

The cooperation between the Montoneros and the PLO was made public in 1977 when Montonero *comandantes* Mario Firmenich and Fernando Vaca Narvaja flew to Beirut to meet and be photographed with Yasser Arafat. At that time, Arafat and the PLO were receiving financial and political support from far-left political parties worldwide. To capture some of that popularity, the Montoneros published the photo with Arafat as a symbol of political victory.

The agreement between the Montoneros and the PLO had a clandestine aspect. When the PLO split and Fatah was formed, the new militant wing offered the Montoneros training camps in Lebanon, military instructors, and heavy weaponry in exchange for the installation in southern Lebanon of a plastic explosives laboratory that had been developed by a Montonero with a PhD in chemical engineering. In Madrid in June 1978, Montonero comandante Horacio Mendizabal confirmed to reporters that a portable Montonero explosives unit had been set up in Lebanon for Fatah. And according to France's intelligence service Deuxième Bureau, the 1983 bombing in Beirut that killed 299 U.S. and French servicemen was carried out with the explosives technology developed by the Montoneros.[32]

Baath Party Terrorism

As the world watched Syrian dictator Bashar al-Assad crack down on dissidents and kill hundreds of civilians in the streets in 2011 and 2012, the only support coming from the West was from a delegation of foreign ministers of the ALBA countries of Venezuela, Bolivia, Ecuador, Nicaragua, and Cuba.[33] However, a review of the history of the Baath Party, for which Assad is the figurehead in Syria, provides some understanding of how far back the relationship goes.

Baath means "renaissance" or "resurrection" in Arabic, depending on the translation. Though the Baath Party founders rejected communism, they adopted its tenets of a "vanguard elite" but modeled it more along the lines of fascist parties. Former CIA director James Woolsey called it "a despotic organization modeled after the fascist regimes of Hitler's Germany and Mussolini's Italy."[34]

The Baath Party's founders were educated at the Sorbonne in Paris, where, incidentally, an inordinate number of the world's former dictators were schooled.[35] Commenting on this phenomenon, Egyptian journalist Issandr Elamsani said that Arab intellectuals still see the world through a 1960s lens: "They are all ex-Sorbonne, old Marxists, who look at everything through a postcolonial prism."[36]

The Sorbonne in the 1960s was one of the intellectual centers of radical political science. In the tradition of the Jacobins, it offered a pseudo-intellectual foundation for end-justifies-means terrorism, which many of its graduates—among them Cambodian dictator Pol Pot, Peruvian terrorist leader Abimael Guzmán, intellectual arbiter of the Iranian revolution Ali Shariati, and Syrian Baathist Michel

Aflaq—would utilize to justify mass murder.

Aflaq was a Syrian intellectual and political organizer who cofounded the Baath Party with Salah ad-Din al-Bitar in the 1940s. The Greek Orthodox Aflaq was its main ideologist, and Bitar, a Muslim from Damascus, was its more pragmatic politician. It was Aflaq who promoted Saddam Hussein to the Iraqi Baath Party's regional command in 1963, leading to his eventual rise as the country's dictator. The Baath Party platform touted Arab unity, socialist economics, and liberation from Western colonialism.

Having been founded in the tumultuous 1930s in France, Baathist ideology was infused with fascist elements, which included a fervent anti-Marxism but with a mercantilist economic policy that rejected Western capitalism. After World War II, the Baath Party rose to prominence largely because it was the only extant political entity with a coherent ideology and a ready political platform. It had also built a sturdy internal organization, while other party structures were loosely constructed and seen as corrupt.

The Baath Party built itself along the lines of the rigid hierarchy systems of fascist and communist parties. Similarly they built strong youth organizations that would be effective and militant recruiting forces. In 1947 the Baath Party was reorganized as a single party encompassing all Arab countries. The hierarchy consisted of a pan-Arab national body, with regional commands in each Arab nation.

Syria and Iran were the two countries where Baathism took root, although Iraq's Baathists vacillated among coups and changes of leadership in the 1960s. Both later accepted Soviet subsidies to remain viable, which simultaneously changed the anticommunist nature of the party's founding ideology.[37] The Syrian Baathists, more stable in the 1960s than their Iraqi counterparts were, began participating in more international alliances, even attending the Congreso de Chillán in Chile in 1967, a meeting that included most of the socialist and communist parties of Latin America.[38]

Building the Iranian Terrorist Infrastructure

Just as the Soviet Union had set up Patrice Lumumba University in 1960 to indoctrinate the children of Third World communists, Iran set up a similar institution in the 1980s at the former Melli University (or National Univerity) in Tehran. Renamed the Shahid Beheshti University, it has been utilized since the Iranian revolution as a highly specialized training site for foreign collaborators in international terrorist networks.[39]

According to a 1995 report by the Congressional Task Force on Terrorism and Unconventional Warfare, Shahid Beheshti University trained approximately a thousand terrorist operatives at a time, including members of allied terrorist organizations such as the IRA, the Armenian Secret Army for the Liberation of Armenia, and Spain's Basque terrorist group ETA, as well as terrorists from Sri Lanka, Senegal, Argentina, Brazil, Mexico, and Paraguay.[40]

According to the report, graduates of Shahid Beheshti were expected to set up terrorist networks in their countries of origin, and those designated as especially capable were given specialized training, headed by North Korean intelligence agents, to run clandestine operations in the West. Many were trained specifically for infiltrating the United States (mostly via the porous southern border) in order to establish operational and deniable networks. The Iranians set up additional, specialized guerrilla and sabotage training camps in Manzariyeh and Firuzkuh in the northeastern portion of Tehran Province. The report further stated:

> Emphasis is being put on clandestine operations in Westernized urban centers, on disruption of normal life through diversified methods, including access and sabotage of computerized networks, as well as interacting with and exploiting politicians, journalists and the clergy. Several Europeans, both West European terrorists and East European intelligence experts, serve as senior faculty as well as guest speakers in highly specialized sessions.[41]

The congressional report listed numerous examples of the use of non-Muslim foreign terrorists for operations in the West. Their diversity of nationality, ideology, and even religion showed their intention to utilize Haddad's tactic of diversifying the terrorist teams for maximum propaganda effect:

- The Lebanese Armed Revolutionary Faction (LARF), which consisted of Lebanese Christians, conducted many operations in Western Europe in the 1980s on behalf of international terrorists, including the assassination of American and Israeli diplomats and Foreign Service personnel. The LARF was also involved in a failed plot to smuggle explosives into the United States in 1981.
- The IRA ran a sophisticated arms smuggling operation for many years in

Western Europe and was involved in an attack on the prime minister's residence in London.

- Spain's Basque terrorist group ETA ran operations all over Latin America, including terrorist training and arms and drug smuggling.

- Japanese Red Army member Yu Kikumura was caught in a rest stop on the New Jersey Turnpike in April 1988 with three large pipe bombs and roofing nails. He intended to bomb a navy recruitment center in Midtown Manhattan. The bombing was set for April 14, the anniversary of the U.S. raid on Qaddafi's Libya. Kikumura had been stopped in Amsterdam two years earlier with a bomb in his luggage and was deported to Japan, where he was released on a technicality.

- North Korean and Vietnamese operatives provided support and intelligence to terrorist operations in the Middle East, Latin America, and the United States.

- Neo-Nazis provided both training and support services in the Tri-Border Area of Argentina, Brazil, and Paraguay for both the 1992 bombing of the Israeli Embassy and the 1994 bombing of the Argentine Israelite Mutual Association (Asociación Mutual Israelita Argentina, or AMIA), the largest terrorist attack in Argentina's history.[42]

After the Soviet Union fell, there was a short-lived dip in terrorist activity as former Soviet surrogates worked to regain their footing by finding other funding sources and developing new partnerships. Those partnerships would bring together the opposite ends of the ideological spectrum.

PART II
Joining the Two Extremes

4

REVOLUTION MAKES
STRANGE BEDFELLOWS

For millennia, wars were fought over whose prophet was the true vessel through which God spoke to his earthly followers. This liturgical distinction is no longer the principal motivation for men to take up arms and go to war. Today Mohammed and Jesus are just as likely to be on the same side, so long as they are both invoked by combatants joined in the amorphous movement known as the anti-imperialist revolution.

While the Islamist leaders of Iran and Syria may worship a different deity than the Catholic leaders of Venezuela and Nicaragua do, they have found a shared struggle under the flag of this common revolution. But, as this chapter will show, what brings these distinct cultures together is militancy itself, rather than the edifying tenets of the particular religion or ideology that motivates them to embrace terrorism.

Twin Revolutions

In 1979 two simultaneous revolutions took place on opposite sides of the globe: one by the Sandinistas in Nicaragua led by Daniel Ortega, and another in Iran led by the Ayatollah Khomeini. During his first presidency in the 1980s, Ortega donned the uniform, the ideology, and the atheism of the communists before being voted out in 1990 in Nicaragua's first free election under the Sandinistas. But in his most recent election in 2011, Ortega ran as a devout Christian, with campaign posters that touted: "Christian, Socialist, Solidarity!"[1]

In June 2007, Ortega made an official visit to Tehran and spoke to students of Tehran University at an event called the "World Resistance Front Rally," where he declared that the "revolutions of Iran and Nicaragua are almost twin revolutions . . . since both revolutions are about justice, liberty, self-determination, and the struggle against imperialism." He added, "We have begun a struggle for our independence and this is exactly what the Iranians, Palestinians and African nations are doing." Denouncing what he termed "bullying imperialism," Ortega said, "We are of the view that we should unite and become closer than ever to attain victory in view of such determination."[2] During the rally, an Associated Press stringer photographed a throng of cheering Iranian students holding up large placards that included the faces of Castro, Chávez, and Guevara.[3]

Aleida Guevara, the daughter of Che, made a trip to Lebanon in 2010 to lay a wreath on the tomb of former Hezbollah leader Abbas al-Musawi. At the ceremony, she echoed Ortega's sentiments, saying, "I think that as long as [the martyrs'] memory remains within us, we will have more strength, and that strength will grow and develop, until we make great achievements and complete our journey to certain victory." Guevara later told supporters while visiting Baalbek, "If we do not conduct resistance, we will disappear from the face of the earth." To make sure that the international press understood the subtext, Hezbollah's official in the Bekaa Valley said, "We are conducting resistance for the sake of liberty and justice, and to liberate our land and people from the Zionist occupation, which receives all the aid it needs from the U.S. administration."[4]

Though Guevara was parroting what has become standard rhetoric among revolutionaries in all parts of the world, her visit had the potential to become controversial. Just three years earlier, in 2007, she and her brother Camilo had visited Tehran for a conference that was intended to emphasize "the common goals" of Marxism and Islamist radicalism.

Titled "Che Like Chamran," the conference was a memorial to the fortieth anniversary of Che Guevara's death, which happened to coincide with the twenty-sixth anniversary of the death of Mostafa Chamran. Chamran, a radical Khomeinist who founded the Amal terrorist group in Lebanon, went to Iran in 1979 to help the mullahs take over and died in 1981 in the Iran-Iraq War (or, according to some, in a car accident).[5]

The Che Like Chamran conference, designed to showcase the new solidarity between Middle Eastern Islamists and Latin American Marxists, ended in farce. The first speaker at the conference, Hajj Saeed Qassemi, the "coordinator of the Association of Volunteers for Suicide-Martyrdom," offended the Guevaras when he claimed

that Che had been "a truly religious man who believed in God and hated communism and the Soviet Union." Aleida Guevara, indignant at the comment, retorted,
"My father never met God."[6]

It was the only disagreement the two groups would have. Everyone agreed on
the joint mission to destroy capitalism and the Western way of life by any means
necessary. Speaker Mortaza Firuzabadi, a Khomeinist radical, told the crowd that the
mission of both leftist and Islamist revolutionaries was to fight America "everywhere
and all the time," adding, "Our duty is to the whole of humanity. We seek unity with
revolutionary movements everywhere. This is why we have invited the children of
Che Guevara."[7]

Firuzabadi assured the crowd that the coalition of Islamist and far-left revolutionaries would defeat the United States because they do not fear death, while
"Americans are scared of dying." He ended his speech with an entreaty to all anti-
American revolutionaries in the world to accept the leadership of Iran's Mahmoud
Ahmadinejad and his revolutionary regime. Qassemi returned once again to the po-
dium to reinforce his point. "The Soviet Union is gone," Qassemi declared. "The
leadership of the downtrodden has passed to our Islamic Republic. Those who wish
to destroy America must understand the reality."[8]

Though it has been treated as a rarity by much of the Western media, collaboration between radical groups that might appear to have little in common have included joint operations of far-right, fascist, and neo-Nazi groups with far-left, Marxist,
and Islamist groups. These collaborations go back well before World War II.

The widespread misconception that a philosophical or religious wall of separation exists between the extremist ideological movements of the world is not only
demonstrably false, it is highly detrimental to a proper analysis of the terrorist threat
and to the public's understanding of counterterrorism efforts. This myth has served
well the forces of subversion.

The small subset of the population that is drawn to extremist movements is
not limited to those who profess the same or a similar ideology but instead includes
those who tend to seek personal fulfillment from extremism itself. Ideology can be
quite malleable when militants see an opportunity to take advantage of the popularity of a more militant group, regardless of any ideological differences between them.
In fact, these groups have often found common cause soon after seeing a a rival
group begin to dominate international headlines.

Rabbi Abraham Cooper of the Simon Wiesenthal Center told reporters in
2002 that "extremists manage to find ways to put aside their differences and find

common cause." Cooper was commenting on what has been termed the "Third Position," the name given to the alliance of Marxists and Islamists with neo-Nazis and far-right militants.[9]

Although political expediency often attempts to conjoin both fascist and neo-Nazi groups with the political right, throughout history these groups have tended to share far more in common with radical leftist groups both ideologically and tactically. Indeed, the motivating tenets of ideological and political violence—anti-Semitism, anti-Americanism, and anticapitalism—are universally distributed among groups with extreme leftist, extreme rightist, and extreme Islamist ideologies.

Today's neo-Nazi groups have mixed a portion of Hitlerian anti-Semitism with a modicum of Christian Identity racialism, and a growing number of neo-Nazis today are finding common ground with the antiglobalization and anti-Americanism that finds its home in international leftist movements. Moreover, radical Islamists are openly expressing support for the most extreme of the neo-Nazi groups. The *Washington Times* reported on June 3, 2009, about a Kuwaiti al-Qaeda recruiter, Abdullah al-Nafisi, who spoke to a group of supporters in Bahrain, where he expressed support for a neo-Nazi attack that was allegedly planned on a nuclear site in the United States:

In the U.S. there are 300,000 white militia members who are calling to attack the federal government and to banish the Arabs, the Jews, and the Negroes from the U.S. These are racist people, they are called "rednecks." The Ku Klux Klan, they are racists. These militias even think about bombing nuclear plants within the U.S. May Allah grant them success, even though we are not white, or even close to it, right? They have plans to bomb the nuclear plant at Lake Michigan. This plant is very important. It supplies electricity to all of North Africa [*sic*]. May Allah grant success to one of these militia members who is thinking about bombing this plant. I believe that we should devote part of our prayers to him. We should pray that Allah grants him success so he can complete this mission and we will be able to visit him and congratulate him, Allah willing.[10]

This expression of support was not nearly the first between these seemingly antithetical groups. As a brief reading of the history of extremist collaboration will show, it is an error of analysis to assume that extremist groups that claim separate sections of the political spectrum also eschew cooperation with groups at the other end of that spectrum.

The entire decade of the 1970s saw a near monopoly of terrorism by left-wing terrorist groups. Europe's Marxist-Leninist terror groups—the Baader-Meinhof Gang in West Germany, the Red Brigades in Italy, and Direct Action in France, among others—terrorized European citizens and even inspired American terrorist groups. Extreme right-wing radicals at the time were mostly dismissed as rebellious punk rockers or antisocial malcontents who posed no threat to the social order other than providing a bad example for the upcoming generation. A May 1980 report by the West German Ministry of the Interior noted that the potential for violence by neo-Nazi groups was negligible and that their adherents were "mostly armed with self-made bats and chains and knives."[11]

Der Spiegel reported in September 1980 that most of the population and most of the authorities in Germany believed that far-right extremists were "more or less content with calling attention to themselves by wearing uniforms, hoarding weapons, and using Nazi slogans. Most of the time, it all amounted to nothing more than brawls, vulgarities, and smeared slogans."[12] Just four months after the report was released, three bombings by far-right extremists underscored the report's deadly misjudgment. The bombings—one at a Bologna rail station that killed eighty-four people, one in Munich that killed eleven people at an Oktoberfest celebration, and one in Paris in front of a Jewish synagogue that killed four bystanders—would signal the rise of a new far-right terror contingent.

Police statistics had shown an escalation of violent acts as well as confiscated small arms and even hand grenades from extreme-right groups prior to 1980, but German authorities were not prepared for the leap in violence to come. Just two months before the Oktoberfest bombing, Germany's Federal Office for the Protection of the Constitution (Bundesamt für Verfassungsschutz) reported that their analysts had noticed "a clear falling-off of activities" of neo-Nazi groups and commented that they expected the trend to continue.[13] But the report left out any mention of three previous bombings that had been perpetrated by the German Action Group (Deutsche Aktionsgruppe).

These extreme right-wing groups didn't appear out of nowhere. The neo-fascist Armed Revolutionary Nuclei (Nuclei Armati Rivoluzionari) began attacking left-wing groups in Italy as far back as 1977 and even murdered a judge. Several other extreme right-wing groups were known by authorities to be active at that time as well, including the Mussolini Action Squadron (Squadre d'Azione Mussolini), Third Position (Terza Posizione), Black Order (Ordine Nero), and its successor organization New Order (Ordine Nuovo).

Many of these groups would become the midwives of what came to be called the "Years of Lead" (*Anni di Piombo*) in Italy, named for the large amount of bullets fired from the late 1970s until the early 1980s. One wealthy publisher, Giangiacomo Feltrinelli, would come to represent both the violent futility of these movements as well as the melding of ideologies between the violent factions of the far left and the far right.

In his 1968 tome *Italy 1968: Political Guerrilla Warfare*, Feltrinelli laid out an oft-forgotten objective of radical violence. While terrorist acts are usually explained by journalists and security analysts as a way to draw attention to the terrorist group's perceived grievances or to induce fear and uncertainty in a target population, a more fundamental and doctrinaire reason is often ignored. Feltrinelli offered the textbook reason for organized terrorism, citing the "imperious need" for more than just organized terrorism and calling on his fellow radicals to undertake "intensive provocation" to "reveal the reactionary essence of the state."[14]

Feltrinelli's call to fellow terrorists was to "violate the law openly . . . challenging and outraging institutions and public order in every way. Then, *when the state intervenes as a result* [emphasis added], with police and the courts, it will be easy to denounce its harshness and repressive dictatorial tendencies."[15] What Feltrinelli was describing, in terrorist parlance, is "propaganda of the deed."

The provenance of this concept goes back to another Italian radical, the famous anarcho-socialist Errico Malatesta, who coined the term, referring to the use of violence in order to catalyze the masses to revolution. Malatesta believed that "the insurrectional fact, destined to affirm socialist principles by deed, is the most efficacious means of propaganda."[16] One of the principal objectives of a terrorist attack that is often overlooked is the expected overreaction of the state in response to the threat.

In a taped interview shortly after the 9/11 attacks, Osama bin Laden indicated his belief in this concept, saying, "I tell you, freedom and human rights in America are doomed. The U.S. government will lead the American people in—and the West in general—into an unbearable hell and a choking life."[17] The theories of Che Guevara's "foco" method of using small, fast-moving rural guerrilla fighters who could garner rural support and Carlos Marighella's urban terrorism, espoused in his *Mini-Manual of the Urban Guerrilla* (which Feltrinelli published in Italy), which limited operations to heavily populated urban areas to blend in with the large population, both predicted the same reaction. With few exceptions, the concept of propaganda of the deed has failed. But that has yet to dissuade its use by terrorist groups.

Feltrinelli, like bin Laden and a significant percentage of terrorists in general, was born into a wealthy family and worked hard to compensate and establish his bona fides among international extremists. He called on radicals of all ideologies and races to join in the provocation of the state, all using the same methods, which included "striking indiscriminately at passengers on a train, etc." Feltrinelli's thesis, like those of many terrorism theorists before and after, was that this would bring "an advanced phase of the struggle" by forcing "an authoritarian turn to the right."[18]

Feltrinelli is emblematic of the ideologically itinerant radicals who wreaked havoc in the 1960s and 1970s in Europe, Latin America, and the Middle East. He was a close friend of Fidel Castro's, attended the Tricontinental Conference in 1966, and published its official magazine, *Tricontinental,* in Europe after the event. He also traveled to Montevideo in 1971 to support the Tupamaros and began wearing a Tupamaro uniform on his return to Italy. There Feltrinelli built his own publishing empire, flying to Moscow to secure the publishing rights to Boris Pasternak's *Dr. Zhivago* and publishing Giuseppe Tomasi di Lampedusa's bestseller *The Leopard,* after two publishing houses had turned it down. The profit from these blockbusters allowed him to fill bookstores throughout Italy with radical manifestos and terrorist literature. Alberto Korda, the photographer responsible for the iconic image of Che Guevara, gave a copy of the photograph to Feltrinelli, who sold copies throughout Italy in his bookstores.

According to Luigi Barzini Jr., an Italian journalist and author who was married to Feltrinelli's mother during his youth, Feltrinelli started out as a fanatic supporter of fascism who would have denounced his stepfather if he had caught him listening to foreign radio broadcasts "when he wore his black shirt [of the fascists]." Barzini wrote that it was a gardener who converted Feltrinelli to left-wing ideology—not the doctrinaire Marxism-Leninism that he would later embrace but "a utopian socialist enthusiasm which, when the revolutionary situation ripened, was to prepare for the great bloodletting." Barzini lamented, "It was hard for me, who believed in reason, to cope with this kind of romantic apocalypse."[19]

On March 15, 1972, the police found Feltrinelli's body in pieces at the foot of a high-voltage power line pylon. He had been placing explosives on the pylon with a group of fellow terrorists when one of his own explosives detonated accidentally.

For the first week after his death, left-wing radicals in Italy and throughout the rest of the world claimed that he had been set up and killed by the Italian secret services, and some even said that the United States was responsible. But evidence collected by police at his home led to a number of safe houses and weapon caches and even an underground "people's prison," where Feltrinelli and his terrorist comrades were planning to hold those that it kidnapped for ransom.[20]

Soon after Feltrinelli's death, his fellow terrorists not only would admit that Feltrinelli was a terrorist but would also claim that he had "fallen in combat." Though Feltrinelli had always stayed quiet about his early affinity for fascism while he was financing the far left, it was later revealed that he had met with Italian neofascist Prince Junio Valerio Borghese to discuss how Italian far-left and far-right groups could work together to fight "imperialism."[21]

5

THE TRANSFORMATION OF NEO-NAZI IDEOLOGY

Just as the Maoist- and Marxist-based ideology of terrorism in the 1960s and 1970s was supplanted by the ideology of Islamist-based terrorism in the decades since, neo-Nazi ideology has also evolved to fit into the more internationally acceptable ideology of the radical class. Although the far right and far left were often at odds and had physical confrontations in many parts of the world in the decades before, both groups have adapted their doctrines to be more aligned with Islamist radicals in recent years.

While far-left groups have shown support for the Islamists' socialism and anti-imperialism, neo-Nazi ideology has evolved over the last several decades to a more "racialist" view that eschews white supremacism for "racial determinism," the notion that each race has its own particular mores and destinies and should be allowed to develop its own enclave in which to pursue them. This more subtle approach has arisen for two reasons: it is a slightly more palatable worldview to the general public, and it also accommodates the worldview of Islamist extremists.

In 2003 German law enforcement authorities banned the Islamic Liberation Party (Hizb ut-Tahrir), an Islamist group that had been around for fifty years and had developed a large constituency within the Islamic enclaves in Germany. The group's prohibition came about because it had allegedly been collaborating with neo-Nazi groups and putting out propaganda calling for the destruction of Israel and for killing all Jews.[1]

In 2001 the Italian newspaper *Corriere della Sera* reported that German intelligence services claimed that Osama bin Laden had financed European neo-Nazi groups to persuade them to help carry out terrorist attacks at the G-8 summit in

Genoa earlier that year, though no attack took place after American and European intelligence captured several ring leaders before the summit.[2] In 2002 at the request of President George W. Bush, Switzerland began an investigation into collaboration between neo-Nazis in Europe and Islamic extremists. It was alleged that such an alliance had been funding al-Qaeda.[3] While collaboration among these groups received little coverage in the United States, it was more commonly known in Europe both before and after the 9/11 attacks.

Before it was shut down, the website of the U.S.-based Aryan Nations had a section called the "Ministry of Islamic Liaison," which was set up to do outreach in "solidarity, to the bona-fide adherents of Islam in the Arabic world and abroad."[4] The following are some of the selections taken from the site (with errors left in to reflect content and lack of erudition):

There never was a holocaust I wish there were but unfortunately it's nothing but another jewish fable, a holohoax as we call it, used to extort money out of countries, companies and anyone who will listen to the poor crying jews! . . .

we are NOT adherents of the christian cult and we do not call ourselves christians! . . .

When speaking of Aryan Islam, I'm referring to the spiritual and intellectual movement of those idealistic Aryan youth who embrace the TRUE Islam of the Qur'an and Sunnah. They include those who join or support the honorable warriors of Islam, the Mujahideen. We are an increasing number and can't be dismissed as "race-traitors" or any other labels attached to us by those who don't practice the TRUE National Socialism of honor and nobility. . . .

"A link is created between Islam and National-Socialism on an open, honest basis. It will be directed in terms of blood and race from the North, and in the ideological-spiritual sphere from the East."—Obergruppenführer Gottlob Berger; 1942

There is much information on the respect and cooperation that Adolf Hitler and others of the Third Reich had for Islam. This would be a good read for all those that claim to be National Socialists. . . .

The jew is a parasite, an enemy of our Western Civilization. . . .

Islam is our ally, and the 1500 cults all claiming to be "Christian" are our opposition. . . .

The site also sought to recruit "Phineas priests," a concept that was first promulgated by a Christian Identity minister from Virginia named Richard Kelly Hoskins in his 1990 book *Vigilantes of Christendom*. According to Hoskins's thesis, Christians should utilize vigilante violence to make sure that "God's laws" were followed. Much like the sleeper agents of al-Qaeda, they would act as lone-wolf terrorists—on their own accord, without any top-down direction.

According to terrorism analyst Jessica Stern, some al-Qaeda operatives have adopted the Aryan Nations' tactic of utilizing "cellular networks" in order to better operate in places like the United States, where there are effective law enforcement operations. This has long been a concept touted by neo-Nazis operating where government agents were conducting infiltration and disruption operations. According to researcher Michael Reynolds, the tactic was developed by Louis Beam, an Aryan Nations strategist whose essay on "leaderless resistance" has been translated into seven languages and has been promoted by jihadist websites to "homegrown" terrorists who can blend in with local populations.[5]

Beam correctly theorized that an organization with a hierarchical structure would be too easily detected, infiltrated, and defeated, especially in "technologically advanced societies where electronic surveillance can often penetrate the structure, revealing its chain of command." In leaderless organizations, said Beam, the individual actors and cells operate independently of one another, without ever reporting to a central headquarters or even to an individual leader.

In the American media, neo-Nazi affinity for Arab radical groups has generally been given scant coverage. For instance, David Duke, the former "grand wizard" of the Ku Klux Klan who ran for office in Louisiana in the 1990s as a Republican (much to the consternation of the Republican Party) was given frequent press interviews to embarrass Republicans nationwide. But Duke has received far less coverage about his recent endorsements of Democrats, or his pronouncements on the commonalities between the Christian Identity movement and Islamist radicalism.

Duke has become an advocate of the "racial determinist" position and describes himself as a "racial realist," claiming that "all people have a basic human right to preserve their own heritage."[6] And claiming that many Arabs living in the Holy Land are actually Christians, Duke attacked Jerry Falwell and Pat Robertson for favoring Jewish Israelis over supposedly Christian Palestinians. Duke has postulated often on religion, accentuating the differences between Christianity and Judaism, and on the closeness of his brand of Christianity with Islam:

The truth is there is no such thing as Judeo-Christianity. That would be saying Satanic-Christianity. The religion now called Judaism did not even come
formally into existence until six hundred years after Jesus Christ. It began
with the codification of the Babylon Talmud. . . .

Interesting enough, Islam is much closer to Christianity than Judaism.
For instance, Judaism condemns the Virgin Mary as a prostitute and viciously
condemns Jesus as an evil sorcerer and a bastard. . . . In stark contrast, although
Islam certainly does not share all the Christian views of Jesus Christ, it views
Christ as the true prophet of God, virgin-born, and that God resurrected Jesus
from the dead. Ironically, the chief religious book of Islam, the Qur'an, actu-
ally defends Jesus Christ from the obscene slanders made against Him in the
Jewish Talmud.[7]

Most media reports that have delved into this unconventional relationship have
tended to focus on personalites within the American neo-Nazi movement. In one
interview, a CNN reporter asked if non-white al-Qaeda members were considered
"mud people," as nonwhites had been called in earlier neo-Nazi literature. The in-
terviewee, August Kreis, a leader of the Aryan Nations, offered a glimpse into the
changing rhetorical dynamic of modern neo-Nazi movements. "That's old-school
racism, white supremacy, this is something new," he said. "We have to be realists and
realize what didn't work [previously] isn't going to work in the future."[8]

One of the regularly featured writers on the Aryan Nations' Islamic liaison website was David Myatt. A British iconoclast who has lived a somewhat itinerant life
and has undertaken an equally desultory intellectual quest, Myatt is emblematic of
the modern syncretism of radical ideologies. Myatt's father worked abroad for the
British government, which took the family to the Far East where the son became
engrossed in the study of martial arts. Upon his return to the United Kingdom in the
late 1960s, Myatt studied physics at Hull University. He later studied both Taoism
and Buddhism, spending time in a Buddhist monastery and then a Christian one.
He later delved deeply into the occult and pagan secret societies and even dabbled in
Satanic ritualism. Myatt later affiliated with two neo-Nazi groups, Column 88 and
Combat 18, and wrote a manual for neo-Nazis titled *Practical Guide to Aryan Revolution*. After his promiscuous sampling of a range of ideologies, Myatt ultimately
converted to Islam and adopted the Arabic name Abdul Aziz.

Myatt admitted that the militancy of Islam was what attracted him to it, and he described his agreement with Islamists about the "influence of international finance with its materialistic, culture-destroying, capitalist-consumer ethos." Describing in his online autobiography his discovery of Islamic extremist groups, Myatt said:

> The more I discovered about these groups, the more I came to admire them, for I still retained the wish, the hope, that this ignoble System would be destroyed within my own lifetime. Was it possible for such groups to bring about the breakdown of the System, somewhere, and if so, what kind of State would they create? Would or could such a State be an ally to a group struggling for freedom against the capitalist enemy? Would, or could, such a State create a new Empire founded on spiritual values? Would these groups be interested in co-operating with another anti-capitalist movement? . . . Since many of these militant religious groups also regarded the capitalist-consumer West, and international finance, as enemies, there was a certain common ground: a common enemy. Would it be possible for there to be co-operation between these militant, Islamic, groups and National-Socialists? Maybe just a tactical co-operation in the future? We both, it seemed, wanted to overthrow the existing power-structure of the West.[9]

Myatt recounts the history of Muslim and Nazi collaboration, recalling, "I knew that over sixty thousand Muslims had joined the SS, and that many National-Socialists—Hitler, Himmler and Leon Degrelle included—had a great respect for Islam. I also knew that Major General Otto Ernst Remer—one of my National-Socialist heroes since the early days of my political involvement—had lived for several years in exile in Egypt and Syria and had made many Muslim friends in those countries."[10]

According to the Aryan Nations' website, the premise that could bridge the ideological gap between these ostensibly disparate worldviews was that Muslims are of the same "Aryan" lineage. This view was not hard to concoct. Adolf Hitler's minister of economics, Hjalmar Schacht, had professed a similar theory, which was once promoted by King Darius the Great: the Persian bloodline was of Aryan lineage. This, Schacht argued it made the Persians—and therefore, somehow, all Muslims—the natural allies of Hitler's vision of a superior Aryan race that should rule the world.

The idea was given greater import in 1935 when Reza Shah Pahlavi, a supporter of Hitler's racial policies, issued a decree that Persia should now be referred to in official correspondence as Iran, its native name that meant "Land of the Aryans."[11] Soon afterward, the rise of the Third Reich became a rallying point for many Muslim leaders, who fostered a bit of Muslim mythmaking by claiming that both Hitler and Mussolini were closet Muslims. One rumor had it that Hitler had secretly converted to Islam and that his Muslim name was Hayder, translated as "the brave one." Mussolini, the rumors told, was really an Egyptian Muslim named Musa Nili, which translated into "Moses of the Nile."[12]

It was Hitler's relationship with Haj Amin al-Husseini, the grand mufti of Jerusalem, that did the most to cement early ties between the Islamists and the Nazis. Husseini is said to have created the first fedayeen in modern times. These would-be martyrs attacked moderate Arabs who were not sufficiently supportive of his cause.[13] And as far back as 1933, Arab nationalists in Syria and Iraq were supporting Nazism. Young Egypt, an early Egyptian fascist group also known as the Green Shirts, was said to have been helped in its formation by Husseini.[14]

Husseini first traveled to Berlin to meet Hitler in November 1941, where he offered his full support. This meeting, it is said, was the genesis of Nazi-influenced anti-Semitism as a mass movement in the Arab world. Husseini stayed in Berlin throughout World War II and was treated as if he was a foreign dignitary. Hitler even offered to make him the "Arab führer" after the war.[15]

Husseini would eventually help Hitler by traveling to Bosnia in 1943 to set up the Waffen-SS Handschar Division, a unit of Bosnian Muslims, and by making radio broadcasts transmitted throughout the Arab world to encourage Muslims to take up the Nazi cause. In return, Husseini was rewarded by being named the supreme religious leader of the Muslim troops fighting for the Axis powers.[16]

Many other smaller Muslim units were also established, such as in Chechnya and Uzbekistan. A number of other extreme-right luminaries would visit the grand mufti after World War II, including the infamous Otto Ernst Remer. Remer also got to know Yasser Arafat, a cousin of the grand mufti. Arafat often stayed with the grand mufti while he was studying engineering at the University of Cairo. From this initial contact, Remer formed an enduring alliance in the coming years with Arafat, who helped bridge the gap between the far right and the far left.[17]

Arab support for Hitler was widespread by the time he rose to power. And when the Nazis announced the Nuremberg Laws in 1935 to legalize the confiscation of Jewish property, "telegrams of congratulation were sent to the führer from all over the Arab and Islamic world."[18]

Heinrich Himmler, Hitler's overseer of both the Gestapo and the concentration camps, planned a great alliance between the Nazis and the Islamic world. Himmler's aide, Obergruppenführer Gottlob Berger, once stated that "a link is created between Islam and National-Socialism on an open, honest basis. It will be directed in terms of blood and race from the North, and in the ideological-spiritual sphere from the East."[19]

Hitler's Nazi Party inspired the formation of many similar parties in the Middle East. The Syrian Social Nationalist Party was formed in 1932 by Anton Sa'ada, who gave himself the name "Führer of Syria." Sa'ada would also put a swastika on a black-and-white background for the party's flag.[20] Sami al-Joundi, a founder of the Syrian Baath Party, was quoted as saying, "We were racists. We admired the Nazis. We were immersed in reading Nazi literature and books that were the source of the Nazi spirit. We were the first who thought of a translation of *Mein Kampf*. Anyone who lived in Damascus at that time was witness to the Arab inclination toward Nazism."[21]

But it was Germany's war against the British Empire that motivated much of the early support for the Nazi regime. Hitler was, after all, fighting the three shared enemies of Germany and the Arab world at the time: Zionism, communism, and the British Empire. But that inchoate collaboration has continued long past any original motives.

After World War II, many German officers and Nazi Party officials were given asylum in the Middle East, mostly in Syria and Egypt, where they were utilized to help set up clandestine services throughout the region—this time in support of many of the anticolonialist forces fighting the British and French. Many others fled to South America via one of several "ratlines," the underground escape routes operated by Nazi or fascist sympathizers.

Throughout World War II, Argentina was considered by the United States and the Allies as the regional hub of Nazi spying. There was also an active attempt to win over neighboring countries to the Nazi cause, most notably Brazil, Chile, and Paraguay. Sicherheitsdienst (SD), the intelligence apparatus of the German state as well as of the Nazi Party under Heinrich Himmler, ran agents out of Argentina throughout Latin America for the entire duration of the war. Despite a specialized Argentine federal police unit dedicated to root out spies, SD operatives moved about the area seemingly at will. And when they were actually captured at the cessation of the war, most were released immediately.[22]

Postwar Argentina has always been reputed to have been a refuge for escaped Nazis. However, the leading theory for some time, promoted most notably by Ronald Newton, a Canadian academic who wrote *The "Nazi Menace" in Argentina, 1931–47*, has been that the rumors of collaboration are greatly exaggerated.[23] Newton's thesis was that the tales of Nazi-fascist settlement in Argentina was the result of British disinformation, designed to thwart postwar market capture of Argentina by the United States. This theory was refuted in 1998 after Argentine president Carlos Menem put together a commission to study the issue. The commission uncovered the fact that much of the postwar collaboration was done according to the instructions of then president Juan Perón. While dictating his memoirs in Madrid, he was quoted as saying in reference to the Nuremberg Trials:

> In Nuremberg at that time something was taking place that I personally considered a disgrace and an unfortunate lesson for the future of humanity. I became certain that the Argentine people also considered the Nuremberg process a disgrace, unworthy of the victors, who behaved as if they hadn't been victorious. Now we realize that they [the Allies] deserved to lose the war.[24]

But according to Menem commission member Uki Goñi in his book *Peron and the Germans*, the Rámon Castillo administration had filled the Argentine Foreign Ministry with Nazi sympathizers as early as 1942.[25] If anything, the reports of unrepentant Nazis and former fascist refugees in Perón's Argentina were vastly understated. Argentina not only took in top-level Nazis but supported their escape and even employed many in the Perón administration under assumed names.[26] Perón also hid numerous escaped Nazis in the Argentine armed forces as "technicians."[27]

The architect of the Nazis' "Final Solution," Adolf Eichmann, was perhaps the most notorious of the lot. Eichmann took up residence in Palermo Chico, a small suburb of Buenos Aires. There the Peronists helped him build considerable wealth while he worked under a pseudonym until 1960, when the Mossad captured and exfiltrated him to Israel, where he was tried for war crimes and hanged.[28] Among his last words were "Long live Argentina!"[29] Eichmann and the other Nazis who prospered under Perón were but a few of the refugees received with open arms by Argentina.

Uki Goñi followed up his first book on the subject with *The Real Odessa* in 2002, utilizing newly allowed access to Argentina's government archives to reconstruct the elaborate network that stretched from South America to Europe to the Middle East and that rolled out the red carpet for Nazi and fascist war criminals. Goñi uncovered that not only had the Argentines fully collaborated with the ratline set up by Croatian Roman Catholic priest Krunoslav Stjepan Draganović, they had also gone so far as to set up their own called the "Nordic Route," which ran through Scandinavia, Switzerland, and Belgium.[30] Draganović had also been a collaborator of the Ustashe, the Croatian movement whose ideology was a mixture of Nazism and fascism.

Beginning in January 1946, a pair of Argentine priests—Bishop of Rosario Antonio Caggiano and Tucumán bishop Agustín Barrére—traveled to Rome, where they met with French cardinal Eugène Tisserant. The pair delivered the message that "the Government of the Argentine Republic was willing to receive French persons, whose political attitude during the recent war would expose them, should they return to France, to harsh measures and private revenge." The message was later found in Argentina's diplomatic archives.[31]

In 1946 the priests were able to smuggle to Argentina a large number of French war criminals, Vichy officials, and escaping fascists. Most of these fugitives were given passports by the Red Cross in Rome that were then stamped with Argentine tourist visas. Upon Caggiano's suggestion, the Red Cross eschewed the normally required health certificates and return tickets. Goñi further reported on the culpability of the Red Cross in the operation: "The Red Cross proved extremely accommodating to Nazi fugitives in northern Europe, its ambulances reportedly transporting Germans clandestinely across Scandinavian borders after the war."[32]

Perón's Information Bureau, the operation set up to facilitate the human smuggling, formed its own ratline in 1947, partially in order to smuggle Nazi jet designers into Denmark and Sweden, where they were given false documentation to go to Argentina and work on his plans to develop a military aeronautics program. A simultaneous operation carried out by Carlos Schulz and German-Argentine businessman Friedrich Schlorrmann sought to smuggle as many fugitive Nazis as possible so that they might escape justice after the war.

Once the Argentine ratline was up and running, Perón appointed Santiago Peralta, a well-known anti-Semite, to the position of immigration commissioner and placed Ludwig Freude, a former agent of German foreign minister Joachim von Ribbentrop, as his head of intelligence. Peralta and Freude, according to Goñi, set up a "rescue team" that consisted of secret service agents and so-called immigration advisers, most of whom were fugitive war criminals from Europe who had been given Argentine citizenship and jobs in the Perón government or with government-friendly businessmen.

Peralta gave Schulz a thousand landing permits and a stack of recommendation letters. Armed with the documentation and claiming to be a representative of an evangelical church in Argentina, Schulz conned officials in Oslo into releasing Nazi prisoners into his custody and flew them to Argentina.[33] It is believed that between 150 and 300 Nazi war criminals escaped to Latin America, mostly to Argentina and the other countries of the Southern Cone. However, according to author Paul Manning, "eventually, over 10,000 former German military made it to South America."[34] Both the Italian and the Argentine ratlines were only confirmed somewhat recently, owing to the declassification of Argentine government archives and the investigative work of Uki Goñi and others.

Argentina's Ideological Admixture

As far back as the 1880s, Argentina had served as a repository for wayward radicals expelled from their European homelands. Errico Malatesta moved to Buenos Aires in 1885 to escape a jail sentence in Naples. There, he resumed publishing the radical newspaper *La Questione Sociale* (The Social Question) and helped radicalize the Bakers Union, which would retain its radicalism for decades after Malatesta's influential stay.[35]

At the beginning of the twentieth century, Argentina was the engine of growth and commerce in Latin America, dwarfing its neighbors in the region in trade and economic growth. Yet, once it abandoned its laissez-faire attitude toward commerce and trade, it sank into the "eternal recurrence" that has bedeviled the rest of Latin America for the breadth of its existence.

Of all the countries in Latin America (excluding Cuba, where polling is impractical), Argentina has been shown to have the lowest opinion of the United States, according to polling done in 2007. While that may be attributable to Argentina's financial meltdown in 2001, which many blamed on the peso's peg to the dollar and on U.S.-based institutions such as the International Monetary Fund (IMF), much of the attitude is a remnant of Juan Perón's anti-Yanqui rhetoric, which still permeates much of the culture.[36]

A substantial number of political candidates in Argentina today must still claim to be Peronists to be politically viable, a result of the Peróns' personality cult (both Juan and Evita), much of which was created while Juan manipulated Argentine politics from exile in Madrid from 1955 to 1973. It was during this period, after a military coup drove him from power, that Perón began a close collaboration with Jean-François Thiriart and Otto "Scarface" Skorzeny.

THE TRANSFORMATION OF NEO-NAZI IDEOLOGY

Jean-François Thiriart was a Belgian who cut an ideological swath from far left in his early years to the far right in his more prolific adulthood. Thiriart served in the United Socialist Young Guard and the Socialist Antifascist Union as a young man and was quoted as enthusiastically supporting the Molotov-Ribbentrop Pact: "The most beautiful, the most exciting part of my life, I admit, was the German-Soviet pact. . . . National Socialism was not an enemy of Communism, but a competitor."[37]

Walter Laqueur has classified Thiriart's ideology as a form of "fascist Maoism," and Edouard Rix has written that Thiriart's group, Young Europe, professed an original ideology, "National European Communitarianism," which Thiriart called "European and elitist socialism" that was "de-bureaucratized and given a spine by European nationalism."[38] Professor George Michael, author of *The Enemy of My Enemy*, reported that Thiriart served as an adviser to the PLO's Fatah in 1969.[39]

Enthralled by the fascist tendencies of Romanian communist Nicolae Ceaușescu, Thiriart traveled to Romania in 1966 and introduced himself to the budding dictator. Ceaușescu arranged for Thiriart to meet Zhou Enlai in Bucharest, where he tried to convince the Chinese foreign minister that Europe could form part of an anti-American alliance. To that end, Thiriart asked Zhou for funding to build a revolutionary guerrilla force to attack American targets in Europe, but his request was never granted.[40]

Perón expressed support for Thiriart's politics and tactics in an interview with the Paris-based journal *La Nation Européenne* in February 1969.[41] In his autobiography, *Peron as He Is*, he declared that in Latin America, Soviet influence was not a problem, but economic, political, and cultural domination by the Yankee menace was.[42] But it was Perón's collaboration with Skorzeny and Thiriart in Madrid, and the ideological admixture of these three oddly positioned politicians, that resulted in Perón's eclectic ideology, which incorporated the elements of fascism and socialism that characterized his second tenure as president.

Thiriart would say of his time with Perón during his exile in Madrid, "I was a close friend of Perón during his exile in Madrid. By this time Skorzeny had made a new life for himself in Spain as a civilian. . . . We formed a friendly threesome, meeting together frequently. . . . Early on, Peron got into contact with me when he learned of my anti-American stance through Skorzeny. When it came to discussing the United States, we were definitely on the same wavelength."[43]

It was Skorzeny who had arranged for the exiled Juan Perón to live in Madrid after a military coup ousted him in September 1955.[44] The notorious Skorzeny, the Nazi commando leader who had masterminded Mussolini's escape from captivity, was called by the Office of Strategic Services "the most dangerous man in Europe." After Germany's defeat, Skorzeny served under Nasser in Egypt. Skorzeny would be declared "denazified" in absentia in 1952, allowing him to travel freely between Francoist Spain and Argentina, where his stated goal was to set up with Perón a "Fourth Reich" centered in Latin America.[45]

In the 1960s Skorzeny founded the Paladin Group, which specialized in arming and training guerrilla groups. Skorzeny called it "an international directorship of strategic assault personnel [who would] straddle the watershed between paramilitary operations carried out by troops in uniforms and the political warfare which is conducted by civilian agents." One of the Paladin Group's first clients was Muammar el-Qaddafi.[46]

As many who ride the ideological waves and seem to be the most committed ideologue while that particular movement is cresting, Perón often followed the movement of the moment. In 1968, not long after the international success of the Tricontinental Conference, he wrote a book called *La Hora de los Pueblos* (The Time of the People), in which he summarized the basis of what he came to call his new "Tricontinental ideology." He declared, "Mao is at the head of Asia, Nasser of Africa, De Gaulle of the old Europe and Castro of Latin America."[47]

The Tacuara

Perón's ideology spawned a number of radical offspring, one of which was the Tacuara, known as Argentina's first urban guerrilla group. Named for the makeshift weapons used when the gaucho militia would tie knives to the end of sugarcane stalks during Argentina's war of independence (1810–1818), the Tacuara started out as a radical nationalist and fascist group. In 1962 *Time* magazine published an article about the group titled "Argentina: Resurrecting the Swastika," which began with the following paragraph:

> Behind the bolted doors of a headquarters in downtown Buenos Aires, 150 youths snapped to attention, clicked their heels and gave a Nazi-style straight-arm salute. At a command, three high school boys entered the room. The neophytes chorused an oath, swearing to defend with their lives "the permanent values of Christianity and country." Then they swelled their chests as a blue and white Maltese Cross was pinned to their lapels. Cried the leader of the meeting, Alberto Ezcurra Uriburu, 26: "We must fight with one hand against capitalism and Zionism, and with the other against Communism!"[48]

Even after they were officially outlawed in 1965, the Tacuara held public meetings where they were able to make such pronouncements unmolested by police. One Tacuara announcement stated:

[We] defend Catholic values against Marxist-Jewish-liberal-Masonic-capitalist imperialism. We are not anti-Semites with racialist aims, but we are enemies of Jewry. In Argentina the Jews are the servants of Israeli imperialism [who violated] our national sovereignty when they arrested Adolf Eichmann. In this struggle we have much in common with Nasser.[49]

When the Mossad team captured Eichmann in Argentina, the Tacuara went on an anti-Semitic rampage, firing machine guns into Jewish businesses and homes, throwing Molotov cocktails into synagogues, and painting "Jews to the gas chambers!" on city walls.[50]

Two years later, after Adolf Eichmann was hanged in Israel, Eichmann's son, Horst Adolf Eichmann, still felt comfortable enough in Buenos Aires to hang a swastika flag on his front porch and hold a press conference, where he told reporters that he had joined the local neo-Nazi National Socialist Party. Horst would defend his father, who at the time of his death was known to have played a major role in killing six million Jews, by blaming those Jews who were still living: "The Zionists . . . through their trusts and monopolies are carrying out their program for world exploitation. My father fought [for] those who are suffering from the international Zionist conspiracy. . . . On this anniversary, I want to remember that he did not die in vain."[51]

Argentine Jews had already suffered for years under the thuggery of the Tacuara. The Tacuara had supporters among the exiled Nazis who were serving in the Argentine bureaucracy and security forces. They gave the Tacuara access to weapons and a bit of impunity for petty crimes. Because of this, the Tacuara ran rackets in Buenos Aires, charging a "revolutionary tax" to Jewish business owners in the Once district until Jewish groups were able to organize and stop the practice.

In the 1960s, the Tacuara experienced several schisms within its ranks owing to power struggles and the ideological pull of the Cuban and Algerian revolutions. In 1963 José "Joe" Baxter, a radical Yugoslav-born Argentine student in his early twenties, split a portion of the Tacuara to the left to fight a "war on imperialism." Along with José Luis Nell, he created the Revolutionary Nationalist Tacuara Movement (Movimiento Nacionalista Revolucionario Tacuara, or MNRT), which would eschew earlier Tacuara affiliations with the Catholic Church and anti-Semitism. Martin Lee, in his book *The Beast Reawakens*, notes that the political shift of Baxter and his MNRT paralleled that of Jean Thiriart, whose leftward transformation would occur at the same time.[52]

Both Baxter and Thiriart were in close contact with Juan Perón in Madrid. It was after getting the personal imprimatur of Perón that Baxter would turn the MNRT into an organized urban terrorist group. Baxter and several other members of the MNRT flew to Havana to train in one of Fidel Castro's guerrilla camps. Baxter also visited communist China in 1965, and after returning to Argentina, he moved further and further left, eventually losing many of his group's more radical and violent members to the country's two main terrorist groups: the People's Revolutionary Army (Ejército Revolucionario del Pueblo, or ERP) and the Montoneros.

During the worst part of Argentina's left-wing terror in the 1960s and 1970s, Fidel Castro utilized the Cuban Embassy in Buenos Aires to coordinate operations with the ERP and the Montoneros. In 1973 Castro convinced the Montoneros to join forces with the Castroite Revolutionary Armed Forces (Fuerzas Armadas Revolucionarias, or FAR), and at a February 1974 meeting in Mendoza, Argentina, the Revolutionary Coordinating Junta (Junta de Coordinacion Revolucionaria, or JCR) was formed. The JCR was supposed to be a continent-wide guerrilla force and consisted of the National Liberation Army (Ejército de Liberación Nacional, or ELN) of Bolivia, the Revolutionary Left Movement (Movimiento de Izquierda Revolucionaria, or MIR) of Chile, the Tupamaros of Uruguay, and the ERP of Argentina.

The ERP had provided a terrorist training school in Argentina, but it was discovered and closed by the military junta in 1975. After that, all training was done in two locations in Cuba—a training camp at Guanabo and another at Pinar del Rio. These locations typically trained guerrillas from all over Latin America as well as from "anti-imperialist" countries in Europe and the Middle East. ERP and Montonero members were also sent to training camps in Libya and Iraq.

There had been plans to bring the other members of the JCR to fight alongside the ERP and the Montoneros in terrorist operations in Argentina, but the plan was abandoned after a military coup. Castro invited the top cadre of the Montoneros to move the group's headquarters to Havana. Members of these Cuba-domiciled Montoneros were then sent to the Middle East to receive terrorist training as part of a joint effort among the Cubans, the PLO, and the exiled Montoneros. Once the Montoneros were trained in the Middle East, the plan was for them to return to Argentina to undertake urban terrorism operations.[53]

The decline of the Montoneros began—and the boiling cauldron of Peronism's contradictory ideologies finally exploded—on June 20, 1973, the day when Perón arrived back in Buenos Aires from exile. While waiting for Perón to speak at Ezeiza Airport, the Montoneros, who long believed that they would be the vanguard of a Peronist social revolution, were fired upon by neo-fascist snipers organized by one of Perón's chief advisers, José López Rega. The Montoneros had reason to believe that they would be Perón's chosen allies, as he had talked glowingly of "the glorious youth" who had done his bidding while he was in exile. All of these revolutionary delusions were smashed as the "Ezeiza massacre," as it came to be known, left at least thirteen dead and nearly four hundred wounded.[54]

Perón had used the Montoneros as shock troops to clear the path for his return, but once he was back in power he quickly denounced any talk of a "socialist fatherland." Perón would be overthrown shortly after his return by a military coup, which ended up casting Argentina into seven years of the Dirty War, in which, according to Martin Lee, "several European neofascists specializing in torture and murder assisted the Argentine military regime."[55]

The Quebracho

A still existing Argentine group reminiscent of the Peronist past is called the Patriotic Revolutionary Movement (Movimiento Patriótico Revolucionario) and is also known as the Quebracho. The Quebracho began from an accord reached on August 31, 1996, between several "popular organizations" that were the offspring of such terrorist organizations as the Montoneros, the PRT-ERP (a fusion of the Workers' Revolutionary Party [Partido Revolucionario de los Trabajadores] and the ERP), and the Mothers of Plaza de Mayo. The Quebracho claims to be fighting for a "socially just, economically independent and politically sovereign country" for the "National Anti-imperialist Revolution."

Like members of other syncretic radical groups, Quebracho adherents do not define themselves as being on the left or right ideologically. They call themselves "revolutionary patriots" whose enemies are "imperialism and the great capital: the big financial monopolies, the IMF, the World Bank, the Inter-American Development Bank, the U.S., the E.U., Japan and Israel, among others." Hezbollah Argentina proclaimed on its website in September 2006 that a demonstration by the Quebracho had prevented a protest by Argentine Jews in front of the Iranian Embassy. The group has touted its cooperation with the Argentine Arab Home (Hogar Árabe Argentino) and the Argentine-Islamic Association (Asociación Argentino Islámica, or

ASAI) and has expressed "solidarity" with Hezbollah in Lebanon and with the Palestinians for what they term "terrorist attacks of Israel and the genocide of thousands of their people."[56]

The Palestinians as Terrorist Rallying Point

This affinity for the Palestinians has a long pedigree and became somewhat of a litmus test for radical groups in the late 1960s and early 1970s. The audacious acts of terrorism committed by Palestinian terrorists in the 1970s quickly drew the attention of neo-Nazis in Europe, but there had already been extreme-right collaborationists fighting alongside the Palestinians prior to that.

The earliest known neo-Nazi to join the Palestinians' fight was Karl von Kyna of West Germany, who died in combat in the Suez in 1967, and Belgian SS veteran Robert Courdroy, a friend and collaborator of Jean Thiriart's, was killed fighting for the Palestinians in June 1968.[57]

The early ties between the PLO and neo-Nazis began shortly after the Six-Day War, when the Association of Young People Loyal to the Homeland (Bund Helmattreuer Jugend) formed the Arabic Reserve Corps (Hilfskorp Arabien) and attempted to form a coalition with Arafat's Fatah movement, to no avail.[58]

More than two dozen members of either the PLO itself or its affiliate groups have taken a nom de guerre that includes the name "Hitler." Abu Hitler was the pseudonym of Fawzi Salim el-Mahdi, a senior member of Force 17, Yasser Arafat's personal bodyguards and hit squad.[59]

Another Force 17 member, a British citizen named Ian Michael Davison, participated in the assassination of three Israeli citizens on a yacht in Cyprus in 1985. In the Cypriot courtroom where he was tried and convicted, police read a statement quoting him as saying that he was "totally happy" to have done something for the Palestinian struggle.[60] Davison was also said to be one of Arafat's closest bodyguards. Prior to traveling to the Middle East to work for Arafat, he was an ardent neo-Nazi in the United Kingdom.[61]

Arafat's Fatah trained members of the Military Sports Group Hoffman (Wehrsportsgruppe-Hoffman), a German neo-Nazi group, during the 1980s. The leader of the group, Karl Heinz Hoffman, had made contact with the PLO in Damascus in 1980 while on a mission to develop contacts between the PLO leadership and East German intelligence. Hoffman traded used vehicles to the PLO in exchange for guerrilla training.[62]

On July 13, 1981, *Der Spiegel* published an interview with Salah Mesbah Khalaf, a deputy chief and head of intelligence for the PLO, whose nom de guerre was Abu Iyad. Abu Iyad would eventually become the second most senior official of Fatah and was assassinated in 1991 by Abu Nidal terrorists. *Der Spiegel* questioned Abu Iyad in July 1981 about the relationship between the PLO and Hoffman, as well as other neo-Nazi groups:

Spiegel: Do you know a Karl-Heinz Hoffman?

Abu Iyad: I have never met him. He has constantly tried to meet me, though.

Sp: The PLO is being accused of having accommodated and protected members of his "Military Sports Groups." Do you concede that?

AI: Yes.

Sp: Why is that? While considering yourselves a leftist liberation movement, you shelter neo-Nazis?

AI: Let me explain something: there is an enormous distance between us and the fascist ideologies of the Nazis. I will tell you one thing; even if the Nazis were to tell us today, "We are going to liberate Palestine for you," we would say, "We would then give that Palestine to the Russians."

Sp: All the more reason to ask why you have cooperated with such people.

AI: He told us he was no such thing as a neofascist. While his group was a national movement that wanted to reunite Germany, it was more of a sports association, a kind of scouts organization. If we should have any fascist ideas, he said, we stand ready to be convinced by you. . . . We told him about other European groupings that also were patriots, progressive forces cooperating with us here. . . .

Sp: From what countries?

AI: From Norway, Sweden, Denmark and so on and so forth, a kind of association of Palestinians and forces supporting us. On that level, we explained to Hoffman, we could also cooperate, if he was interested.

Sp: How did you get in touch with him?

AI: Last May we arrested some West Germans who admitted having been trained with the Falangists. They refused to make any further statements, saying, "We have a boss who will talk to you about this, his name is Hoffman." After a month, he actually came to see us, accompanied by another four men. He said we should release his men. . . .

Sp: How many Hoffman people were there in fact?

AI: Altogether 12 at one time.

Sp: Are the Germans still in this country?

AI: No, they are gone—we don't care where. After the Munich bomb attack I
      said, "No matter whether they are supporters or not, they have to leave."

Sp: But that was 9 months ago, and in mid-June some were still with you.

AI: First of all, we wanted to part peaceably. But Hoffman shamelessly took
      advantage of that. He constantly embarrassed us. "I must first look for a
      new hiding place," he said. And then again: "You must help me; let them
      stay till I have found something." He constantly asked for a respite—for
      example in January, when he said: "I must find an asylum for them; they
      are being persecuted in Germany." And then he was gone again for a
      month. We didn't know just what would happen with that fellow.[63]

Members of Wehrsportsgruppe-Hoffman actually received training in PLO
camps in Jordan and even fought in combat with the Palestinians there in 1970. The
collaboration between the groups ended when German law enforcement began prosecuting members of the neo-Nazi group.[64] In 1986 Hoffman was arrested on charges
of planning the 1980 murders of Shlomo Levin, a Jewish German publisher, and his
wife. Hoffman accused one of his subordinates of the murder and managed to elude
a conviction but was sent to jail on other charges. The subordinate escaped to Lebanon. Another subordinate of Hoffman's, Michael Kühnen, would go on to create
several more neo-Nazi groups.

Another German neo-Nazi Udo Albrecht founded Adolf Hitler Free Corps
(Freikorps Adolf Hitler), a German neo-Nazi group that would end up fighting
alongside the PLO in Jordan against King Hussein. Albrecht's group would also
work with Black September, the terrorist group behind the 1972 Munich massacre.

Albrecht was captured in 1976 in West Germany while carrying PLO credentials and spent two years in prison. While incarcerated, he enlisted the help of Manfred Roeder and his far-right German Action Group to maintain ties with the PLO.
Roeder traveled to Lebanon in those two years to meet with Abu Jihad, Arafat's
deputy. In a 1976 trial in Berlin, four German neo-Nazis testified that Albrecht recruited them to go to Lebanon, where the PLO trained them in terrorist operations.
It was reported that Abu Jihad became distrustful of Roeder and the relationship
soured. But when Albrecht escaped from prison in 1978, he rebuilt the relationship
between the neo-Nazis and the PLO.[65]

6

THE THIRD POSITION

German terrorist Manfred Roeder was one of the pioneers of what became known as the Third Position, which melded radical elements of both far-left and far-right ideologies. Roeder told reporters in Germany that the objective of the German Action Group was "the establishment of the first radical-democratic and anti-imperialist state on German soil."[1] Roeder said that this would be accomplished by borrowing the revolutionary tactics of the left and adhering to the left's "code of conduct" of "public relations–oriented" terrorism.[2]

For its part, the PLO began in the mid-1970s to seek out British and French neo-Nazi groups, and in 1977 Fatah made a deal with the French Work (L'Oeuvre Française), a neo-Nazi group, to train its members in terrorist operations. L'Oeuvre Française agreed to conduct terrorist operations on behalf of Fatah.[3]

The stated aim of right-wing extremist groups had always been to bring down the leftist democratic state model and bring about a national socialist or fascist state. But that ideology began to devolve in the 1980s as neo-Nazi groups started to see the fame and legitimacy that was afforded to left-wing terrorist groups that were committing far more violent acts and seemed to be rewarded proportionately.

Two years after Palestinian terrorists killed eleven Israeli team members at the Munich Olympics in 1972, PLO chairman Yasser Arafat was invited by the United Nations to address its General Assembly, and the PLO was awarded UN observer status shortly after that. Moreover, by the mid-1980s the PLO had been accorded diplomatic relations with more countries than Israel had.

As more left-wing groups were afforded greater legitimacy on the world stage, far-right extremist groups began to co-opt more of the left's ideological tenets. Michael Kühnen stated in 1983, "We have always said we are socialists," and his group joined the German left in the 1980s to oppose the deployment of U.S. missiles on German soil.[4]

Kühnen is an interesting example of the confluence of far-left and far-right extremism, as well as the attraction to militancy itself, that drives the bent toward terrorism. Kühnen was one of the first Germans after World War II to openly call for a return to Nazism, even advocating for the formation of a Fourth Reich. Raised in a strict Roman Catholic family, Kühnen announced that he was gay in 1986, making him somewhat of an iconoclast within neo-Nazi circles, and he eventually died of complications from AIDS in 1991. He cut his political teeth as a Maoist, then later joined the far-right National Democratic Party of Germany but found it too mainstream for his radical tastes.

During the Gulf War, Kühnen had negotiated an agreement to provide Saddam Hussein with a hundred neo-Nazi troops—an "Anti-Zionist League"—to fight against Coalition forces. Kühnen died before he could fulfill that contract, but French neo-Nazi leader Michel Faci stepped in to recruit an unknown number of "storm troopers" to fight with the Iraqis against what Faci called the "present aggression of Zionist and US imperialist forces." The war ended before Faci could mobilize the troops for Hussein.[5]

Kühnen's handpicked successor was Christian Worch, who has continued to lead numerous neo-Nazi groups in Germany. Worch and a number of his neo-Nazi followers have been photographed sporting the kaffiyeh, the traditional checked scarf worn by Arafat. A number of other neo-Nazis in Germany have also been photographed wearing T-shirts bearing Che Guevara's image. Both the kaffiyeh and Che are nearly universal symbols of the militant left. But a 2008 *Der Spiegel* article reported on "an alarming uptick in [neo-Nazi] youth participation in what's become a 'trendy culture'":

> "They are getting harder to spot," [Esther Lehnert] said, taking a picture out of a folder showing far-right and far-left activists facing off at a march. Both groups wore Che Guevara T-shirts and checked scarves—long a leftist symbol of solidarity with Palestinians. But the far right co-opted both symbols, she explained, just as neo-Nazis have taken to wearing all black, which used to be an anarchist fashion statement.[6]

Both the development of al-Qaeda as a militant force and the rise of neo-Nazi groups in Europe came about in the political vacuum that was created after the fall of the Soviet Union. As these movements began to look for logistical cooperation and moral support among other extremist groups, an even rarer mixture of ideologies began to take shape. German neo-Nazi leader Gottfried Küssel developed close ties to Louis Farrakhan's Nation of Islam, for example, and French neo-Nazi leader Robert Faurisson developed close ties with Ahmed Rami, a former voice of Radio Islam, a now defunct anti-Semitic radio station in Stockholm. Rami's bodyguards had always consisted of skinheads from Swedish neo-Nazi groups.[7]

Another of the influential ideologues who once made an impact on Arab radicals as well as Third World socialists was Martin Heidegger, a German philosopher and and a leading supporter of the Nazis. In Heidegger's convoluted social theory, the Nazi embrace of terror and violence to "push behind the modern present" was where the origin of the term "postmodernism" was derived.

Heidegger made a big impression on the post–World War II left in France and influenced the writing of Jean-Paul Sartre and of his protégé the Algerian writer Frantz Fanon, who would condense postmodernist theory in 1961's *The Wretched of the Earth*. Fanon's book made an impact in the Middle East as well, and many of the Shiite revolutionaries who led the Iranian revolution in 1979 had ingested Fanon's brand of Marxist ideology. Ali Shariati, the "intellectual father of the Shiite revolution," was the first to translate Fanon's book and Sartre's *Being and Nothingness* into Persian.[8]

One of Heideggers's intellectual heirs was Sayyid Qutb, whose *Signposts on the Road* in 1964 influenced the writings of numerous Islamic radical groups. Qutb was the philosophical mentor of Osama bin Laden. Incidentally, Qutb's brother, Muhammad Qutb, became a university professor of Islamic studies in Saudi Arabia, where he actually taught Osama bin Laden. His philosophy consisted not just of a hatred of "international Jewry," as the Nazis called it, but of the "Zionist-crusader alliance" and, in the end, all "infidels."

Egypt under Nasser was one of the earliest places where collaboration between the far left and Islamists occurred, as both groups joined him to fight their common enemy, King Farouk. Nasser, a socialist, personally sought the support of Qutb, who had become the head of the Muslim Brotherhood after the death of Hassan al-Banna.

In Egypt in 1952, Nasser, along with the "Free Officers," overthrew the monarchy in a coup that would see the alliance between Egypt and the West destroyed.

Despite adopting a "positive neutralist" position toward the Soviets during the Cold War, Nasser moved closer to the Soviets to acquire military equipment to boost his stature in the region. After the defeat of Egypt in the Six-Day War, Nasserism was severely discredited. This led the PFLP, started by George Habash in 1953 as a spin-off of the Arab Nationalist Movement, to break up into a number of smaller groups. These splinter groups soon dropped pan-Arabism for the newly popularized revolutionary Marxism.[9]

Another exemplar of those who moved freely about the far ends of the ideological spectrum was Swiss journalist Ahmed Huber. Born Albert Friedrich Armand Huber, he was once kicked out of the leftist Social Democratic Party of Switzerland for his far-right political beliefs. Huber worked as a journalist until 1989, when he was fired from a Swiss news service for openly supporting the Ayatollah Khomeini's fatwa to kill author Salman Rushdie for his book *The Satanic Verses*. Huber had become a Sunni Muslim in 1962 and was soon after invited to Egypt. There he met Nasser, who expressed great support for Nazism and endeared himself to Huber.[10]

Back in Switzerland in 1965, Huber met with the former grand mufti of Jerusalem, Haj Amin al-Husseini, who encouraged his Nazi sympathies. Huber also talked later with Johann von Leers, a Nazi propagandist who had sought refuge after World War II in Egypt, where he continued his propaganda activities for Nasser (mostly anti-Semitic tropes). Von Leers also converted to Islam, taking the Arabic name Omar Amin. Additionally Huber was a friend of François Genoud, a Swiss financier who protected Nazis fleeing Germany after the war, as well as of the PLO and Islamist groups.

Huber's case also demonstrates how even the deep schism between Sunni and Shiite Muslims can be overcome in order to fight a common enemy. Although a Sunni, Huber traveled to Shiite Iran in 1983 to speak to the Iranian parliament and continued to make trips after that. The Iranians were hoping that Huber would use his contacts to build support for Iran among the European extremist right. Though rare for a Sunni, Huber openly advocated that the Shiite revolution in Iran be an inspiration for all Muslims.[11]

Of the noncooperation myths that cloud our understanding of the enemy, this overemphasized rift between Shiite and Sunni Muslims is one of the most persistent. The Sunni-Shiite split stems from a medieval dispute among Arabs over the true lineage of the Prophet Muhammed. According to author Thomas Joscelyn, the rift is greatly exaggerated:

It is frequently argued that ideological differences preclude sustained cooperation between the Shiites of Iran and the Sunnis of al-Qaeda. The fundamental split between their competing versions of Islam, caused by a medieval disagreement over the proper line of succession from the Prophet Mohammed, is thought to be insurmountable. This belief stems not from an in-depth knowledge of Islam's history, but from a deep ignorance of our terrorist enemies. In fact, Iran has consistently allied itself with ideologically diverse players throughout the Middle East and the world, including prominent Sunni Muslim terrorist organizations. When it comes to confronting the West, the leading Sunni terrorists have also proven to be remarkably tolerant of their Shiite brethren.[12]

There has certainly been a historical animosity between Sunnis and Shiites, where Sunni tradition claims that Shiites suffer "because the Jews invented the Shi'a" and that the latter's religion "is pervaded by [the Jews'] beliefs."[13] But there is one historical common denominator that is a sufficient motivator to overcome centuries of tribal and religious feuds: the more immediate necessity of tyrannical Muslim regimes to prolong their longevity in power. Ahmed Huber provided the Iranians a bridge to both the militant Sunni community as well as far-right militants.

In the 1980s Huber began to attend Islamic conferences and far-right meetings worldwide, always promoting greater cooperation between the two groups. Huber espoused the ideology that became known as the European New Right, which he hoped would provide a vehicle for an alliance between Islamists and neo-Nazi groups.

Though there is a dearth of information on Ahmed Huber, George Michael conducted an interview with him in 2003. The following is excerpted from Michael's book, *The Enemy of My Enemy*:

Well, it was a very simple thing. I was then a member of the Social Democratic Party of Switzerland. I had been a member of the party for forty-two years, but I was kicked out in 1994 because of Khomeinism, right-wing extremist contacts, revisionism, and so on. That's another story. In 1959, the Social Democratic Party of Switzerland had asked me—I was a young socialist journalist— to hide a few Algerians. At that time, there was a war between Algeria and France—the liberation war. Some Algerians had brought weapons and arms into Switzerland. They were being arrested by the police, so they had to hide.

. . . So I took in these young people, and they were brilliant people. We had long discussions. It was, for me, the first real [encounter with] Islam. I asked them precise questions and I got precise answers.

I was myself a Protestant Christian, very tolerant, liberal, and not practicing. I didn't go to church. I was religious, but not too much. And here I found something very interesting especially two things. I found a concept of God which was fascinating because it was antitheology. The notion of Allah is a declaration of war against all theology. Allah Akbar means Allah, not god, Allah is always greater and greatest and completely different. It is beyond all human reason. . . . And then the idea that there was no church; the only authority of the message and of the messenger. In Islam, the religious, the political, the social are [all] one, are together, which does not include the separation of the state and the mosque or the church or the synagogue. . . .

This always fascinated me. And it took me two years to slowly come to Islam. Then I became a Muslim by saying the *Shahadah* [declaration of faith] in 1962 in an Islamic center in Switzerland. The Egyptian embassy knew about it, though it had to be kept secret in a certain way. I said, "I don't want it to become public"; only my superiors in the Socialist Party knew about it at the time. They said, "Religion is a private matter. We don't care, as long as you don't make Islamic propaganda as a journalist." I said, "Of course. I will not then.". . .

Then I was received by Gamal Abdel Nasser. For me it was a tremendous thing, and thus I entered into Islam.

Nasser explained to me some things about the Third Reich and about the Second World War, and about Adolf Hitler and some things that I have never known. It was for me a complete cultural shock.

The grand mufti of Jerusalem, Haj Amin al-Husseini, also played a part in Huber's transition from far-right extremist to Islamist extremist. Iran's Ayatollah Khomeini mentored Huber as well. Huber is supposedly the only European Muslim to have given a speech at Khomeini's tomb.[14] In his interview with Michael, Huber also said that he believed that the 9/11 attacks were a joint operation by Islamists and U.S.-based far-right extremists. He claimed that before 2001, he had spoken to both Islamists and to neo-Nazis who had told him of a "Pearl Harbor type plan" that was going to wake up the American people to the Zionists controlling them.

Huber claimed that far-right extremists in the United States had taken responsibility for 9/11 in phone conversations with him and that their aim had been to weaken the country to the point that would bring about a far-right revolution. Huber often stated that the "Zionist Israel lobby controls the U.S. government and mass media and shapes U.S. policy."[15]

Another exemplar of terrorist collaboration that made the transition from extreme right to left was that of Libya's Col. Muammar el-Qaddafi and his supporters. After taking over Libya in a coup against King Idris in 1969, Qaddafi became the chief financier of terrorism of every stripe throughout the world. And though he became known as the principal donor to worldwide leftist groups, he began his terrorist franchise with those of the extreme right.

In the early 1970s, Qaddafi, flush with oil money, was the biggest financier of extreme-right groups. The head of Qaddafi's Italy-Libya Association, Claudio Mutti, was a well-known "Nazi-Maoist" terrorist who was jailed in 1980 for a railroad station bombing in Bologna. Mutti was considered so radical that he was expelled from the neofascist Italian Social Movement (MSI) for being too extreme. He would be the first to translate *The Green Book* into Italian and would write a hagiography titled *Qaddafi: Templar of Islam*. Mutti told reporters that he was inspired by Qaddafi's idea of "Islamic socialism."[16] Mutti would show his solidarity with the Palestinians by forming the group Struggle of the People (Lotta di Popolo). The added advantage of the name was that it didn't arouse suspicion of its extreme-right ideology, thus allowing Mutti to recruit among campus leftists. Mutti got the funding from Colonel Qaddafi.

Mutti would also provide an example of the preference for militancy over ideology. His collaboration with a pro-China student organization provided the vehicle for what became known in Italy as Nazi-Maoism. Based on the philosophy of Jean-François Thiriart, the new group of Italian radicals began to idolize Mao, Hitler, and Qaddafi and even added Gen. Juan Perón to their pantheon of heroes as well. The group's slogans were illustrative: "Hitler and Mao united in struggle!" and "Long live the fascist dictatorship!"[17]

After Mutti was kicked out of the MSI in 1964, he published a number of books in Italian, ranging from Indo-European shamanism to a book of quotes by the Ayatollah Khomeini. Mutti was the most prodigious with books touting Holocaust denial and claimed, "The submission of Europe is based on the culpability of Germany. If revisionism can demonstrate that Germany is no more culpable than other nations that waged World War II, then the basis for the subjugation of Europe is demolished."[18]

More recently, Mutti has worked alongside Marco Battara, a neofascist-turned–National Communist who edited a journal in Milan called *Orion*. *Orion* mostly endorsed candidates of the Communist Refoundation Party, a far-left splinter party that split with the Communist Party of Italy when the latter became more moderate. *Orion* would also publish a number of paeans to Joseph Stalin. Battara described his journal's support for Communist Refoundation candidates thus: "They were the only candidates who seriously opposed U.S. imperialism." Moreover, Battara explained, "We have the same position as the Communist Refoundation on many issues, including the defense of Cuba." The April 1992 edition of *Orion* praised Fidel Castro for standing up to the "U.S.-dominated New World Order."[19]

In 1975 one of Mutti's associates, Mario Tuti, received a payoff from the Libyan Embassy in Rome just before murdering two policemen. Tuti claimed to have been inspired by Qaddafi, Mussolini, Hitler, and Mao. In those days, Qaddafi was also bankrolling National Vanguard (Avanguardia Nazionale), a fascist group started in 1960 by the Italian government to disrupt the activities of leftist groups.

Avanguardia Nazionale rejected electoral politics, instead wanting to subvert the system clandestinely to bring about a return to fascism in Italy. Its posters were almost prescient of today's anti-Semitic rhetoric: "We are with you, heroic Arab-Palestinian People, and not with the Dirty, Fat Jews!" read a typical one.[20] It was this early fascist sentimentality for the Palestinians that eventually led Qaddafi to become the biggest supporter of the radical left. As left-wing terrorists grabbed the headlines in the 1970s, he began to transfer his financial support from the Italian extremists to the Arab terrorists. Qaddafi had stated his desire to "spearhead an Arab-Islamic revolution in which he saw himself not only as the chief ideologist (by virtue of *The Green Book*) but also as a chief strategist."[21]

Qaddafi started his financing of the left by providing the money, arms, equipment, and training to the Black September terrorist group that carried out the 1972 Munich massacre. But his ideological conversion would move more slowly than his monetary support. In 1973, as the international left began to embrace the Palestinians, Qaddafi cut off their $40 million a year payroll "until the movement modified its leftist stance."[22]

After an intense week-long meeting between Qaddafi and Palestinian leaders in Libya in 1973, he resumed payments. Qaddafi's funding of the PLO would help to launch it into the top realm of international terrorist fame. Soon afterward, Qaddafi began to fund the mélange of ideological groups that made up the Paris terrorist network supporting him, including the Marxist terrorist Carlos the Jackal.

Another connection that bridges this historical cooperation between the far right and far left into the modern age of terrorism is that between Carlos the Jackal and the Swiss Nazi François Genoud. Genoud's life, in fact, spans the history of this collaboration.

François Genoud was an early admirer and proponent of Adolf Hitler's, and a founder of the National Front, a Swiss Nazi party. Genoud met and befriended Haj Amin al-Husseini and worked with him to recruit Arabs into the service of the Nazis. He also set up the Banque Commerciale Arabe in Geneva with Syrian money and ran the Banque Populaire Arabe in newly independent Algeria. In the early 1960s Genoud helped fund Eichmann's legal defense and in the 1980s that of Nazi war criminal Klaus Barbie in France. When three PFLP terrorists were arrested after an attack on an El Al plane in Zurich in 1969, Genoud helped pay for their legal defense as well. Genoud was close to both Wadi Haddad of the PFLP and the murderous "Red Prince," Ali Hassan Salameh, who masterminded the Munich massacre and founded Force 17. Genoud would say, even in his later life, that Hitler's actions were "proper and in support of peace."[23] Evidence has come out since Genoud's death that he was also the financial manager for the Swiss assets of the Nazis after World War II.[24] In May 1996 it was announced that bankers in Switzerland had agreed to cooperate with Jewish leaders to delve into the normally secretive Swiss banking system and government files to search for assets of Holocaust victims. Less than a month later, on May 30, Genoud drank a poison cocktail and committed suicide.

Though he had been a committed Nazi, Genoud spent his life helping to finance and facilitate the terrorist actions of many left-wing groups and individuals. He also paid for the defense of Carlos the Jackal after he was arrested in France in 1994. Genoud described the left-wing Carlos as being accepting of his extreme-right past: "He knew my past. I never hid it. I was always accepted." Carlos would write to Genoud from prison in France, "In this period of revolutionary ebb, men of your vision and faith in Victory are more necessary than ever."[25]

Like Genoud's trail of money, Carlos the Jackal's trail of blood runs throughout the history of terrorism over the last forty years, and his collaborations with fellow terrorists also ran the ideological gamut. In his book *Revolutionary Islam*, Carlos tried to join the two strongest currents of revolutionary terror, declaring that "only a coalition of Marxists and Islamists can destroy the United States." The book, written in French, announced Carlos's conversion to Islam and promoted his strategy for "the destruction of the United States through an orchestrated and persistent campaign of terror." The book calls on "all revolutionaries, including those of the left, even atheists," to follow the leadership of Islamist terrorists such as Osama bin Laden to turn Afghanistan and Iraq into "graveyards of American imperialism."[26]

Carlos's book would be little noticed until Hugo Chávez, speaking to a gathering of worldwide socialist politicians in November 2009, called him an important revolutionary fighter who supported the Palestinian cause. Chávez said during his televised speech that Carlos had been unfairly convicted and added, "They accuse him of being a terrorist, but Carlos really was a revolutionary fighter." Chávez punctuated the point by calling Mahmoud Ahmadinejad and Zibabwean dictator Robert Mugabe his "brothers" and stated that the late Ugandan dictator Idi Amin wasn't that bad either.[27]

Two years later, as Colonel Qaddafi was swept from power and went into hiding during the "Arab Spring" of 2011, one of the few world leaders to publicly maintain support for the dictator—even while his loyalists were killing civilians in the streets—was Hugo Chávez.[28] What Chávez learned from Qaddafi's fall—and from his own short-lived ouster in 2002—was that the most important factor for a revolution is to have a plan in place to prevent a rebellion from occurring before you can bring your own revolution to fruition.

PART III
Step-by-Step Subversion

7

SLOW-MOTION REVOLUTION

"There is a revolution going on in Venezuela, a revolution of an unusual kind—it is a slow motion revolution." Thus declared Richard Gott in an interview with *Socialist Worker* on February 12, 2005.[1] Gott, a British author and ubiquitous spokesman for all things Chávez and Castro, is not the first to note the nineteenth-century pedigree of Chávez's 21st Century Socialism. A January 17, 2011, editorial in the Caracas daily *El Universal* titled "Protosocialism" also made note of Chávez's "Fabian," or incremental, approach to implementing socialism in Venezuela and throughout the Americas.[2]

The incremental implementation of socialism was the dream of the Fabian Society, a small but highly influential political organization founded in London in 1884 and made famous by Sidney and Beatrice Webb and George Bernard Shaw. The logo of the Fabian Society, a tortoise, represented the group's predilection for a slow, imperceptible transition to socialism, while its coat of arms, a "wolf in sheep's clothing," represented its preferred methodology for achieving its goal.

The Fabian Society was named for Quintus Fabius Maximus Verrucosus Cunctator, known to modernity simply as Fabius, who served as a Roman general during the second century BC. Fabius is remembered for the indirect, delaying tactic that he advocated and utilized successfully against Hannibal's forces in the Second Punic War. His unorthodox method was considered cowardly at the time, but several upstart rivals lost disastrous battles and many lives trying to upstage him by directly confronting the Carthaginians.

Fabianism has been adapted in many iterations of warfare since its success against Rome's enemies. Wellington is said to have utilized it to defeat Napoleon, as well as Sam Houston against Santa Anna. And George Washington was called the "American Fabius" for using similar tactics to defeat the British during the Revolutionary War. Fabianism picked up momentum in the United States when Arthur Schlesinger Jr. became a leading proponent of "a theory of piecemeal socialism through the democratic process" among the American progressive movement. In a 1947 article in Partisan Review, Schlesinger stated, "There seems to be no inherent obstacle to the gradual advance of socialism in the United States through a series of New Deals."[3]

Gradualism has always been considered "anti-revolutionary" in communist and socialist circles. But pragmatism has taken the place of idealism after the events of 9/11 increased international scrutiny on radical groups, forcing revolutionists like Chávez and Ahmadinejad to use the Fabian strategy as a "soft subversion" tactic with which to undermine their enemies. In the past decade, Chávez and his allies in Latin America have all embraced Ahmadinejad's Iranian regime, and all have developed their strategic relationship based on mutual support for this incremental subversion.

Potemkin Democracy

It was Che Guevara, the icon of subversives worldwide, who said over forty years ago, "Wherever a government has come to power through consulting the people, even through fraudulent means, and maintains at least a semblance of legality, there the guerrilla seed will not germinate because the possibilities of legal struggle have not yet been exhausted."[4] It was perhaps the truest—though inadvertently so—piece of advice in Guevara's "foco" theory of guerrilla warfare. Guevara understood that "legitimacy," even if illegitimately gained, was essential to acquiring power. Since Guevara's death in 1967, his revolutionary theories have been field-tested and have failed throughout the world. But his disciples have since adapted and have learned to become the establishment rather than continually attack it, enabling them to subsume the system from within. In January 2011, The Economist magazine wrote about Chávez and his regional allies: "Today, the biggest threat to democracy in the region comes from leaders who, once elected, set about undermining it from within."[5] In Latin America the emerging autocrats allied with Chávez have all come to power democratically. And once in positions of power, they have learned to maintain that power by utilizing the facade of a Potemkin democracy, at least until a point is reached that threatens their hold on power.

The step-by-step subversion process has been led by Chávez. In 1992, Chávez tried the direct method in a military coup and failed. But his televised speech after the failed coup taught him the value of political warfare. He would soon after adopt the incremental approach. And though he was a political neophyte when he was first elected, he has had a seasoned mentor in Fidel Castro, who has filled the Chávez administration with Cuban security personnel whose mission is to keep him in power and to keep the subsidized oil flowing to Havana.

Long before advising Chávez, Castro had adapted, refined, and exported the incremental subversion strategy throughout the Americas. And now, with Venezuelan oil proceeds serving as a replacement for Soviet subsidies, Castro is able to make one last attempt to install the Cuban model throughout the hemisphere and to try to humble the United States in the process.

Castro has had a lot of practice in the art of subversion. Within a short time after he came to power in Cuba, he began trying to subvert other governments in Latin America and the Caribbean. On May 10, 1967, Castro sent an invasion force to Machurucuto, Venezuela, to link up with Venezuelan guerrillas to try to overthrow the democratic and generally popular government of President Raúl Leoni.[6]

Led by Arnaldo Ochoa Sánchez, the invasion force was quickly vanquished, and the Venezuelan armed forces, with the help of peasant farmers leery of the guerrillas, pacified the remaining guerrilla elements before the end of the year. Then the Venezuelan government issued a general amnesty to try to quell any violence from the remaining guerrilla holdouts. But the PRV, Red Flag, and the Socialist League continued to operate clandestinely. Douglas Bravo, the Venezuelan terrorist who inspired Carlos the Jackal, remained the intransigent leader of the PRV. One of Bravo's lieutenants was Adán Chávez, Hugo's older brother, who would serve as Hugo's liaison to the radical elements throughout the hemisphere for years to come.

After suffering calamitous defeats at the hand of the Venezuelan armed forces, the PRV decided that the best way to continue the revolution would be to infiltrate the "system" and subvert it from within. In 1970, they would first make a move to infiltrate the armed forces.[7] Bravo first contacted Lt. William Izarra (now a Chávez ideologist) in 1970. A year later, Chávez entered military school and started to recruit leftist military members to what became a clandestine fifth-column group, the Revolutionary Bolivarian Movement (Movimiento Bolivariano Revolucionario, or MBR). The failed 1992 coup that launched Hugo Chávez's political career would be planned and executed jointly by the MBR, PRV, the Socialist League, and Red Flag.

After making his famous speech to TV cameras in which he first used what would become his catchphrase, *por ahora* (for now), he went to prison with his coconspirators. While there, he received financial support from Colombian guerrillas. After his release in 1994, Chávez spent six months in Colombia receiving guerrilla training, establishing contacts with both the FARC and the ELN of Colombia, and even adopting a nom de guerre, Comandante Centeno.[8]

Chávez would suggest to his guerrilla comrades that they establish a combined guerrilla force similar to the Unified Revolutionary Directorate (Dirección Revolucionaria Unificada, or DRU) in El Salvador, in order to fight a "true independence war"—the dream of his idol Simón Bolívar. After establishing his guerrilla "street cred" in Colombia, Chávez made a pilgrimage to Havana to pay homage to, and get the imprimatur of, Fidel Castro. Once he was elected president four years later, he would repay the Colombian guerrillas with a $300 million "donation" and thank Castro with the subsidized oil deal.

Ironically the information about the FARC payment would come to light by the fault of Chávez himself—when a call that he made to the satellite phone of FARC commander Raúl Reyes allowed the Colombian military to pinpoint Reyes's location and deliver a fatal strike. The soldiers recovered the dead guerrilla's hard drives, which revealed the money transfers from Chávez.[9]

In his 1992 televised speech, Chávez stated that "people went into the streets and this so-called democratic government answered with guns and rifles—we had two alternatives as soldiers: continue massacring our people on the order of the tyrant dressed as a democrat, or aim the rifles against him."[10] Chávez was referring to Plan Ávila, a civil disturbance plan that the president could invoke that would authorize the military to use lethal force against civilians. Plan Ávila had been in place since the 1960s, and Chávez's nemesis, President Carlos Andrés Pérez, had invoked it in the "Caracazo," the 1992 wave of protests and riots that resulted in hundreds of civilian deaths. Though Chávez would denounce Plan Ávila often, it would be his own decision to order its activation in 2002 that would provoke his own military to remove him from power.[11]

In a televised address in 2002 once he was returned to power after a forty-eight-hour ouster, Chávez struck a conciliatory tone toward those in the opposition. But his conciliation would prove to be short lived. Soon, Chávez seemed to take the near death experience as a sign from divine providence of his right to rule and began a purge of the military and the government of anyone who might later threaten his power. Chávez then began radicalizing the remainder of the Venezuelan military by replacing its historical training regimen with a doctrine of asymmetric warfare that involved all sectors of society. He would call his new military doctrine *la guerra de todo el pueblo*—"the war of all the people."

Subversion by the Numbers

In October 2010, *El Nuevo Diario*, a daily newspaper in Managua, published the contents of a recovered document said to outline the revolutionary plan for Venezuela and Nicaragua, as well as the plan for Honduras, Ecuador, Bolivia, and El Salvador. The undated document, titled "Revolutionary Brotherhood," laid out the steps of Chávez's plan to convert Latin America into a socialist stronghold. Joel Hirst, Human Freedom Fellow at the George W. Bush Center and former acting country representative of the U.S. Agency for International Development (USAID) in Venezuela, classified the document as follows:

> Specifically, the document lays out, in as concise a fashion as I've ever seen, the fundamental building blocks used to construct 21st Century Socialism. These tenets include extending presidential mandates, changing political constitutions, co-opting the branches of government under the party's revolutionary tutelage, fomenting social conflict between different strata of society, limiting basic rights such as property, speech and assembly, and using the resources of the government for partisan political purposes.[12]

Shortly after the document was discovered, on the thirtieth anniversary of the Sandinista revolution Daniel Ortega announced that he would seek a constitutional referendum allowing him to run for reelection.[13] President Manuel "Mel" Zelaya of Honduras had already called for a similar referendum in Honduras, but his haste provided the impetus for his ouster in June 2009. Zelaya's removal from the presidency would make Honduras the first ALBA ally to fall out of the plan set forth in the Revolutionary Brotherhood document. The other ALBA countries have taken the lesson and have continued to follow a more incremental plan.

According to Hirst, the Revolutionary Brotherhood plan laid out the following steps, among others:

- Create conflicts, both external (with the United States and Latin American neighbors) and internal (between the poor and the rich)
- Rewrite constitutions and remove presidential term limits
- Create citizen power organizations, and do away with other institutions
- Co-opt institutions of the state under the banner of the party
- Transform armed forces to defend the "Bolivarian revolution"
- Infiltrate and divide the opposition

- Ally with key sectors of business
- Rebuild revolutionary spirit
- Dominate all forms of media
- Expand control in the hemisphere[14]

This was not the first document of its type discovered in Nicaragua. Nor was it the first to lay out the desire to spread Marxism throughout the hemisphere. In September 1979, while the Jimmy Carter administration was still sending aid to the Sandinista government after it had been discovered that it was sending weapons to Salvadoran terrorists, the Sandinista leadership produced the infamous "72-Hour Document." This internal party document declared that "the real enemy that we would have to confront was the imperialist power of the United States, the treachery and demagoguery of the reactionary local bourgeoisie being less important."[15] The "72-Hour Document," actually titled "Analysis of the Situation and Tasks of the Sandinista People's Revolution," also called the United States "the rabid enemy of all peoples who are struggling to achieve their definitive liberation" and declared that the Sandinistas were a Marxist-Leninist "vanguard party" that "would lead the class struggle not merely in Nicaragua but across borders in Central America" in an alliance with Cuba and the Soviet Union.[16]

These plans to expand the socialist franchise throughout the rest of Latin America are entirely consistent with more recent plans outlined by members of Chávez's security apparatus. On July 18, 2007, a six-phase plan was laid out in a speech by Gen. Gustavo Reyes Rangel Briceño as he accepted his appointment as Chávez's new minister of defense for the national reserve and national mobilization. Max Manwaring, the architect of the "Manwaring Paradigm" that served as the basis for Gen. David Petraeus's counterinsurgency strategy in Iraq and Afghanistan,[17] analyzed the plan set out in Rangel Briceño's speech. Dr. Manwaring's translation and analysis are as follows:

- Organize to propagate Latin American nationalism, train a cadre of professionals (propagandists and agitators) for leadership duties and political-military combat, and create selected environments of chaos.
- Create a Popular (political) Front out of the "debourgeoised" middle classes and other like-minded individual who will work together to disestablish opposed societies and defend the new social democracy.

- Foment regional conflicts. This would involve covert, gradual, and preparatory political-psychological-military activities in developing and nurturing
popular support. As the number of recruits grows and the number of activities increases, the fomentation of regional conflicts would also involve the
establishment and defense of "liberated zones."
- Plan overt and direct intimidation activities, including popular actions
(such as demonstrations, strikes, civic violence, personal violence, maiming,
and murder) against feudal, capitalistic, militaristic opponents and against
Yanqui imperialism. The intent is to debilitate target states and weaken enemy military command and control facilities.
- Increase covert and overt political-psychological-economic-military actions directed at developing local popular militias to fight in their own
zones, provincial or district militias to fight in their particular areas, and a
larger military organization to fight in all parts of the targeted country with
the cooperation of local and district militias.
- Directly, but gradually, confront a demoralized enemy military force and
bring about its desired collapse—or, simply, invade a targeted country with
the objective of imposing appropriate New Socialist governance.[18]

Rangel Briceño's plan is also consistent with what military and Latin America
analysts have predicted. Manwaring described the current phase of Chávez's "Bolivarian Revolution" as "preparatory work" that is designed not to provoke the United
States or his other enemies past the "threshold of concern," or the point at which they
might react militarily or with sanctions. According to Manwaring, "Chávez expects
to put his enemies to sleep—to later wake up dead."[19]

Manwaring has opined that Chávez is only in the initial phase of his "Organi-
zational Stage of the Program for the Liberation of Latin America" and that stages
two and three are "several years down the revolutionary path." On a strategic level,
according to Manwaring, Chávez is waiting for the proper time to expand his revolution to a "supra-national Latin America scale," while he works to consolidate his base
at home. On the future of Chávez's slow-motion revolution, Manwaring predicts:

He will likely continue to focus his primary attack on the legitimacy of the
U.S. economic and political domination of the Americas and on any other
possible rival. And he will likely continue to conduct various rhetorical and

political-military attacks on adversaries; continue to cultivate diverse allies in Latin America, the Middle East, and Asia; and to engage his allies and his popular militias in propaganda and agitation "seeding operations" for the creation of a receptive political climate in selected parts of the Western Hemisphere. In the meantime, Chávez supporters are organizing and preparing for the future.[20]

While Chávez calls his hemispheric governing plan "21st Century Socialism," his critics have given it another name—*democradura*.

Democradura: Dismantling Democracy from Within

Democradura is a Spanish neologism that has come to define the budding autocracies in Latin America that have incrementally concentrated power in the executive branch under the guise of constitutional reform. The term is a portmanteau of the Spanish words for "democracy" and "dictatorship," and it denotes those governments that creep toward dictatorship under the guise of democratic reform. When Chávez launched his presidential campaign while visiting Mexico in 1997, one of the objectives that he mentioned was to scrap Venezuela's constitution and rewrite it. On the day he was inaugurated, he told the crowd, "The constitution and with it the ill-fated political system to which it gave birth 40 years ago has to die: it is going to die, sirs, accept it. There will be no backtracking in the political revolution upon which we are embarking."[21] Though constitutions in Latin America tend to be expressions of the political zeitgeist at the time they are written rather than long-term governing documents, Chávez's constitution would lay the groundwork for an organized plan to implement "Bolivarian socialism" in Venezuela that would be repeated in several neighboring countries.

A socialist think tank in Spain, the CEPS Foundation, part of the Center for Political and Social Studies (CEPS), was founded in Valencia in 1993 by left-wing academics supporting Spain's Socialist Party as well as the FARC and ELN terrorist groups in Colombia. It put together a team of Marxist constitutional scholars to write the new constitutions of Venezuela, Bolivia, and Ecuador, turning them into "socialist constitutions" but with variations applicable to each particular country. Bolivia's constitution would exploit ethnic resentments between its highland indigenous populations and the lowland minority descended from Europeans.

Ecuador's new constitution, approved six months earlier, was also written by the same Spanish socialists. During a radio interview, President Rafael Correa admitted that "advisers" from the CEPS Foundation were paid $18,000 a month. But Correa attempted to downplay the importance, stating that "$18,000 was paid by the Attorney General's office, which has financed many advisors."[22] (The CEPS Foundation has also defended Chávez's decision to suspend the broadcast licenses of unfriendly radio and TV stations.[23])

President Correa also brought in a U.S.-based environmental NGO called the Community Environmental Legal Defense Fund (CELDF), a far-left group that seeks to "change the status of ecosystems from being regarded as property under the law to being recognized as rights-bearing entities."[24]

Where Bolivia's indigenous president Evo Morales had utilized race to marginalize his opposition, Correa used the rhetoric of environmental radicalism to demonize the mining, oil, and gas sectors in Ecuador. Anyone who opposed the anthropomorphic environmental language in the constitution was called a "lackey" of multinational corporations and oligarchs. This stance also allowed Correa to eventually break the contracts with these companies in order to demand higher government revenues from their operations, which was then used to support government-funded projects in government-friendly provinces.

According to Roberto Viciano, a law professor of Spain's Valencia University and one of the CEPS Foundation lawyers responsible for the socialist constitutions, the process of Marxist constitution making first caught the attention of the revolutionary left during Colombia's constitutional change in 1991.[25] The Colombian constitution had been in place since 1886, a long time for regional constitutions, and was only able to be changed with some political machinations and legal subterfuge.

While these types of constitutions do little to check the consolidation of power, they do serve to provide the veneer of legitimacy to the power grabs that inevitably follow their implementation. And though the structure of the new Colombian constitution would not serve as a legal model for its neighbors, one of its provisions would—the provision to legitimize former terrorist groups by transforming them into political parties in exchange for their disarming and renouncing violence.

As M-19 guerrillas began demobilization talks with a weak Colombian government in the late 1980s, the group took advantage of its position to transition from an armed insurgency to a political party. By 1991 M-19 was able to get one of its leaders, Antonio Navarro, included as one of the three copresidents of the constituent assembly that drew up the new constitution.

Navarro was able to negotiate a prohibition against any attempts by the state to organize the population against the armed guerrilla groups. Not only would this

provision end up escalating the violence in Colombia, but it would inspire other terrorist groups throughout the Americas to seek both an armed and a "political wing,"
which would be utilized skillfully to prolong their longevity as insurgents.[26]

After witnessing the ease with which the Colombian constitution was changed,
"constitutional subversion" became standard operating procedure for those countries headed by Chávez's allies. Morales admitted to reporters that in a meeting with
Castro in 2003, the Cuban dictator advised him not to take the armed route to power.
Castro urged, "Don't do what I did, don't have an armed uprising. Lead a democratic
revolution, like Chávez's, with a constitutional assembly."[27]

Chávez had been in office for only a few months before he began calling for
a constituent assembly to rewrite Venezuela's constitution. But most Venezuelans
knew it was coming long before. On July 25, 1999, the BBC had offered this prescient outlook on Venezuela's future under Chávez: "Depending on who you talk
to, the Venezuela election will either lead to an unprecedented era of prosperity and
good government, or straight to Latin America's newest dictatorship." Under the
headline "Fear of too much power," the article quoted a political analyst who was
afraid to give his name: "Its a frightening situation. Because there would be no mod-
erating set of rules, whoever controls the assembly can shape the country in whatever
form they want. And if the president gets a clear majority I'm really worried that he'll
assume dictatorial powers."[28] The anonymous analyst, who at the time still harbored
a somewhat sanguine outlook for his country, continued, "I'm convinced [Chávez's]
intentions are good now, but he has already demonstrated a willingness to bulldoze
his way through any obstacle that stands in the way of reform. And if he decides that
he knows best, that makes it dangerous for anyone who disagrees." But the former
Venezuelan ambassador to the United Kingdom, Jorge Olavarria, assessed the situation with a bit more apprehension and foresight: "The constituent assembly is nothing more than a camouflage to make the world think that the coming dictatorship is
the product of a democratic process."[29]

Where most Latin American constitutions contained between 100 and 200 articles, the new Venezuelan constitution had 350, or 98 more than its predecessor.
According to Professor Carlos Sabino of Francisco Marroquín University in Guatemala, the essence of the new constitution was "too many rules, no system to enforce
them." Sabino further noted that the new constitution would give Chávez the op-
tion of reelection, which had never been the case in Venezuela's democratic history,
and "would consolidate an authoritarian government with a legal disguise, necessary

in today's new globalized world where the respect for democratic values is the key to good international relations."[30] The "Bolivarian constitution" would be only the first step in Chávez's imcremental revolution. Like subsequent referenda and elections, the purpose of these measures was to consolidate power in the office of the presidency. And once the 1999 constitution was ratified, every action of the government would be for one of two purposes: the further consolidation of power—incrementally and always with the patina of legal and democratic legitimacy—and the extension of the time that the regime could hold on to that power.

Many luminaries and heads of state in the region have sounded the alarm about this constitutional subversion. In February 2010, Nobel Peace Prize–winner and ex-president of Costa Rica Óscar Arias, in his farewell speech at the Rio Group–Caribbean Community Unity Summit, summed up this constitutional crisis in the region by declaring the need for "strengthening our systems of checks and balances, which are profoundly threatened by the presence of tentacular governments that have erased the boundaries between governor, party and state." Without mentioning Chávez, Arias made his point:

> We should not confuse the democratic origins of a regime with the democratic governance of a state. In our region there are governments that use electoral results to justify their desire to restrict individual liberties and to pursue their adversaries. They use democratic mechanisms to subvert the bases of their democracy.[31]

As predicted, just eight years after the ratification of his Bolivarian constitution, Chávez held a vote to modify sixty-nine articles of the original constitution, taking him one step closer to democradura, or a constitutional autocracy. Even when he was thwarted in his attempts to subvert the rule of law, Chávez has turned defeat into strategic victory. When Chávez first attempted to change the law to allow his own reelection, the measure was defeated. He told reporters that "Venezuelan democracy is maturing," and he took the opportunity to use the loss to claim the mantle of a democrat, stating, "There is no dictatorship here." In what many would come to see as faux humility, Chávez said, "I understand and accept that the proposal that I made was quite profound and intense."[32] Had Chávez won the referendum, it would have decimated Venezuela's already tenuous laws on private property and created a new type of "communal property." Further, it would have allowed Chávez to not only gerrymander the political map but also to handpick local political positions as well.

The vote would turn out to be unnecessary. Utilizing a lame-duck national assembly still stacked with his supporters in the last days of 2010, just two weeks before a new, less friendly assembly was to be sworn in, Chávez crossed the authoritarian line by pushing through a number of measures under the name of "organic laws." Citing recent flooding in the states of Miranda, Falcón, and Vargas, he used the emergency as an excuse to impose the laws by fiat. In congressional elections in September 2010, Chávez had been dealt a defeat by a somewhat unified opposition, which saw its candidates elected to 61 of the 165 seats in the national assembly. Those members would be sworn in on January 5, 2011. But during the week of Christmas 2010, the slowest week of news coverage, Chávez passed the new laws by decree.

The Defense of Political Sovereignty and National Self-Determination Law would prohibit organizations, as well as individuals, that advocate for the political rights of Venezuelans from accepting funds from any foreign entity. It also prohibited them from having any representation from foreigners and even sponsoring or hosting any foreigner who expresses opinions that "offend the institutions of the state." This law was included with the International Cooperation Law, which would force all NGOs to reregister with the government and include a declared action plan on their future activities, along with a list of any financing that they expected to receive. The law stipulated up front that these activities could only include those approved by the government and its "national development plan."[33]

Comments by Chávez-allied lawmakers at the time revealed the purpose of the law. Carlos Escarrá, vice chair of the Foreign Policy Commission, said: "These are the same organizations that backed the coup that did not denounce those deaths of peasants; definitely they are lackey organizations.... Of course we are going to control these organizations. This is what the people are asking for."[34] The vast majority of funding for these groups comes from outside the country, so the law is a de facto prohibition.

The law has many similarities with a January 2010 edict in Iran that forbade Iranian citizens from having contact with over sixty international organizations. Iran's intelligence ministry described its blacklist as proscribing contact with a number of think tanks, universities, and news organizations that it claimed were waging a "soft war" designed to topple the country's Islamic government. The list also included the U.S. government–funded Voice of America and Radio Farda, both of which broadcast in Farsi, as well as Wilton Park, a U.K. organization that organizes foreign policy conferences. Also included were Yale University, the Brookings Institution, and George Soros's Open Society Foundation.[35]

Both Iran and Venezuela have moved incrementally toward a full prohibition of independent NGOs. In Iran there have been previous cases of citizens being arrested or intimidated for being involved with foreign organizations. The formal list was a much bigger step in the regime's efforts to ban NGOs, which have been one of the few remaining checks on the regime's illegal activities.

The rhetoric that both Iran and Venezuela used to justify the law was very similar as well. Iran's state news agency, IRNA, quoted the deputy intelligence minister of foreign affairs as calling one of the organizations "counter-revolutionary." The minister also was quoted as saying that contact with the groups was "prohibited and considered as cooperation with foreign overthrowing organizations." The unnamed minister said that the contact ban was designed to combat the practice by the West of using "special groups" that included artists, academics, and scientific experts who were in Iran to undermine the regime under the guise of being part of scientific and cultural exchanges.[36] The minister continued, "Our revolution has become a target to be overthrown by the intelligence services of some countries, particularly America and Britain, and they have established soft invasion and overthrow strategies against the Islamic republic of Iran. . . . They have allocated extraordinary formal budgets to fulfill this aim." The ban also prohibited "irregular contact" with foreign embassies as well as foreigners in general.[37]

"Jadi," a twenty-seven-year-old Iranian, explained in an English-language posting in his blog how the Iranian government operated against NGOs and had started its own "gNGOs" to counter the effectiveness of the legitimate organizations: "At first [the Iranian regime] started [its] own 'NGOs' which are better called a gNGO; Governmental Non-governmental Orgs. One good example of these fake NGOs are the Organization For Defending Victims of Violence. . . . With all of their luxury magazines, seminars, buildings and money, they have never told anything about the brutal violence which is happening in Iran. They only condemn Lebanon, Israel, Russian School attacks and even on the case of Saddam." Jadi further described the Iranian harassment:

So at first the government tried to start many fake NGOs (i.e. gNGOs) and put pressure on the real ones not to participate at International events and not to publish anything or start any website. They did not success [sic] so they

changed their attitude by shutting down NGOs, arresting activists and sentencing them to long prisons and threaten others not to participate any event
[sic].[38]

In May 2006 Russia, which had been moving closer and closer to both Venezuela and Iran, had passed a similar diktat that gave the Ministry of Justice and the
Federal Registration Service power to oversee NGOs in the increasingly autocratic
country. The law, passed under Vladimir Putin, sought to severely curtail the operations of foreign NGOs and their representatives in Russia and required them to
register as Russian public policy associations. They would also be required to file
copious financial and activity reports that would be scrutinized by a bureaucracy that
had added five thousand new agents just for this purpose.[39]

The Sandinista government in Nicaragua has been even more aggressive against
civil society groups, raiding the offices of long-established NGOs and launching
what it called Operation No More Lies, a crackdown against those that it accuses of
money laundering, embezzlement, and subversion. The Interior Ministry called the
NGOs "modern-day trojan horses" and a "rightwing plot to destabilise the administration." The Interior Ministry also opened an inquiry into seventeen groups, including Oxfam GB, one of the biggest and longest-established NGOs in the country.[40]

In August 2011, President Rafael Correa shut down sixteen NGOs in Ecuador
for failing to meet a government deadline to provide detailed reports about their
work in the country. These details included up-to-date information about partner
organizations, annual budget numbers, and the objectives of the organization, and
they were the result of a set of controversial laws passed shortly before that closely
resembled those passed by Chávez and others in the region. Correa said on state
television that foreign NGOs working in Ecuador were "extreme right-wing NGOs
that seek to replace governments to impose their policies, and if they cannot, they
destabilize government." He added, "The party is over."[41]

This was not the first time that Correa had shut down NGOs in his country,
and he even targeted those normally considered friendly to leftist governments.
In 2009, despite his inclusion of radical environmental tenets in the constitution,
he attempted to close the environmental NGO Ecological Action, after it spoke
out against his administration's environmental policies and showed support for
protests by indigenous groups against mining operations in the country.[42]

In June 2010, as the U.S. State Department was working on a rapprochement
with Bolivia and the return of the two country's ambassadors, President Evo Mo-

rales accused USAID of financing NGOs and foundations that actively opposed his government. At the inauguration of a congress of coca farmers in Cochabamba, Morales said, "If USAID continues working in this way, I will not hesitate to expel them because we have dignity and sovereignty, and we are not going to allow any interference."[43]

At the end of March 2011, former president Jimmy Carter made a trip to Cuba to meet with members of the regime. About the time he arrived, Cuban state television aired a series in which it portrayed independent NGOs as subversive organizations that sought to "erode the order of civil society" in Cuba. The report claimed that "via the visits to the country of some of its representatives and behind the backs of Cuban authorities, these NGOs have the mission of carrying out evaluations of the Cuban political situation and instructing, organizing and supplying the counter-revolution." It accused the organizations of hiding "their subversive essence [behind] alleged humanitarian aid."[44] The series featured Dr. José Manuel Collera, who was revealed as "Agent Gerardo," a Cuban spy who had infiltrated the NGOs in the United States "to monitor their work and representatives."

Along with thwarting the oversight power of NGOs in Venezuela, Chávez also included a number of "economic" laws designed to put the stamp of legitimacy on his new "communal" economic system that had caused shortages throughout the country. The economics-related laws in the new package included names such as People's Power, Planning and People's Power, Social Control, and Support of the Communal Economy. These laws made communes the basis of the Venezuelan economy and established "People's Power" as the basis of local governance. It is codified as being responsible to the "Revolutionary Leadership," which is Chávez himself. This effectively supplanted the municipalities and regional governments.

To give these laws the patina of constitutionality, the Chávez-controlled National Assembly passed them under the "System for Transferring the Responsibilities of the States and Municipalities to the People's Power." And it also modified the Law of the Treasury and National Fiscal Control in order to be able to show that it utilized existing constitutional law to lock the new laws into place. The Banking Law turned the financial sector into a public utility and mandated that a 5 percent tax go to a "social fund."[45]

The education law that was part of this raft of laws would have put the central government in charge of selecting university directors and boards of directors, and even more alarming it would give the government a say in the elections of student governments, where many of the radicals in the government had cut their political teeth. In language that has remained archaic since the fall of communism, the education law mandated that all curricula be focused on "revolutionary principles" and specified that students be taught the concept of "people's power."[46]

As a last measure to ensure that new communication technologies couldn't be utilized to bypass the clampdown on the traditional media, the assembly passed a law that banned for the first time any Internet content that could cause social unrest, that condones crime, or that "challenges legally established authorities." The law, an adjunct to a 2004 law that made antigovernment speech illegal on TV and radio and in print, claimed "to establish social responsibility in the diffusion and reception of messages, to promote democratic balance between the duties, rights and interests" of media producers and consumers.[47]

In 2008, after Chávez pushed through a series of laws by decree, he also invoked a "corruption law" that allowed him to blacklist hundreds of the most competitive opposition candidates from running for local and national offices. None of the candidates that Chávez blacklisted had been convicted of any crime.

In July 2008, Dr. Norman Bailey, former special assistant to President Reagan for national security affairs, testified before the Western Hemisphere Subcommittee of the House Foreign Affairs Committee about the blacklists and the similarities between these types of electoral machinations in Iran and Venezuela: "The most recent outrage, however, is the disqualification of about 200 opposition candidates for governorships, mayoralties and legislatures. This is directly out of the Iranian playbook and the reasons given for the disqualifications range from the ludicrous to the absurd."[48]

Both in 2008 and in 2010, Chávez and a rubber-stamp National Assembly passed the decrees just ahead of the expiration of the special legislative powers, again allowing him to rule by decree for eighteen months. He reacted to criticism by saying, "This is a democracy. They call me a tyrant—tyrants govern without laws. We're making laws, and all those laws are for the benefit of the country."[49]

In Ecuador, Rafael Correa also made a ham-handed effort at constitutional subterfuge, initially announcing in December 2010 that he was going to introduce a referendum to stop bullfighting and casino gambling. A month later the referendum was expanded to include a provision to change the way judges are chosen, which opposition critics claimed would allow Correa to appoint his own judges without opposition.

Correa wanted to change the system so that judges would be chosen by an independent oversight group and by members appointed by the executive branch and the Ecuadorian congress. The underlying intent of the referendum was cast further in doubt when Correa added another provision that would limit the ability of bankers and media owners to own other businesses—a move that would strike a blow to independent media companies critical of Correa.

Correa downplayed the magnitude of the proposed changes, saying that the judicial change was needed to fight the escalating crime in Ecuador. But Ecuadorians became skeptical when members of Correa's political party issued a statement supporting the referendum as a way to "deepen the principles of the citizens' revolution." In February 2011 several members of the fragile alliance that Correa had put together in congress defected because of the referendum. He did little to quell their fears when he dismissed the defections by saying, "Every revolution has its traitors."[50]

Honduras's Constitutional Stand

In 2009, Honduras became a flashpoint that seemed to revive the policy battles of the 1980s on Cold War policy in Central America. President Zelaya, elected via a normally America-friendly political party and expected to maintain stability, soon fell into the Chávez orbit and began calling for constitutional change. Honduras's constitution, like many in Latin America, contained an article that strictly prohibited more than one term of office for its president—a remnant of the decades of military dictatorship that had bedeviled the continent for much of the twentieth century. But in the recent spurt of constitution making, these provisions were the first to go.

When Zelaya began making speeches about changing the constitution and mentioned the term limits provision, alarm bells began to sound both in Honduras and in Washington. Most had seen the result of these changes in Venezuela, Bolivia, and Ecuador and saw it for the disguised power grab that it was. Though, instead of relenting, Zelaya turned up the rhetoric and began to get help from Venezuela.

Honduras's constitution, adopted in 1982, contains a provision that establishes that some parts of the constitution are prohibited from any change or amendment. One of those "unamendable" tenets is the single term limit of the president. Article 239 states that a president who attempts to change the term limit provision not only gives up his presidency but his Honduran citizenship as well.[51]

In July 2008, Zelaya declared that he would move Honduras into the ALBA alliance with Chavez. And in November of that year, he announced a "Cuarta Urna," or a fourth ballot, that would include a nonbinding referendum on whether to hold a constituent assembly to draft a new constitution—the same first step that Chávez and the other ALBA presidents had taken to usurp power in their countries.[52]

After a corruption scandal about Zelaya using public funds to advertise the fourth ballot in newspapers, talk about it subsided for much of 2008. But at a public showcase of tractors donated to Honduras by Chávez on February 17, 2009, Zelaya once again announced that he was going ahead with the plan. In an attempt to skirt the constitutional prohibition, and to avoid more condemnation from the public, Zelaya declared that he would instead hold a preliminary poll to gauge public support for including the question on the ballot in the upcoming election in November 2009. Shortly after the announcement, an administrative court, the Supreme Court, and the National Assembly ruled the ballot question illegal, and Zelaya was officially admonished to correct his administrative conduct and drop any talk of the referendum or he would be considered in breach of his constitutional obligations.

But rather than back down, Zelaya became even more intransigent, defying virtually every other branch of government. The constitutional crisis reached a climax on June 24, 2009, when Zelaya fired Brig. Gen. Romeo Vásquez Velásquez, the head of armed forces, for refusing to carry out the illegal referendum. Immediately after, the defense minister, along with the heads of the army, navy, and air force, all tendered their resignations in protest. The following day, the Supreme Court ruled unanimously that Vásquez Velásquez be reinstated. Zelaya, even more defiant, issued executive decree PCM-20-2009 on June 25, which annulled two earlier illegal decrees, to attempt to legalize the referendum. Supreme Court president Vilma Morales declared that by then Zelaya was unquestionably in violation of Article 239 and was no longer president.[53]

He was removed from his home the next morning by the Honduran military and flown to Costa Rica and dropped off on the tarmac of San Jose's Juan Santamaría International Airport. The decision to take Zelaya out of the country was roundly criticized as the one extralegal measure taken during the crisis, though the military stated that it was necessary to prevent violence and potential bloodshed by Zelaya supporters. These supporters had previously marched to a military base the week before and stolen referendum ballot boxes that had been provided by Chávez and confiscated by the military.

The constitutional crisis that Zelaya set in motion, by lurching rather than tiptoeing toward autocracy, had drawn too much attention and had given the world a peek behind the curtain of continental Chavismo. By breaking the Fabian rule of baby-step subversion, Zelaya had revealed too much too soon and was deposed as a result.

Still, almost two years after he was removed from office and had become the head of a new political coalition known as the National Popular Resistance Front (Frente Nacional de Resistencia Popular or FNRP), Zelaya and his supporters were still angling for a constitutional change. On February 27, 2011, the FNRP held a general assembly where it elected Zelaya as its leader and decided that in lieu of forming an official political party to run in the next elections in 2013, it would push for a constituent assembly to rewrite the constitution.[54]

In June 2011, a diplomatic cable released by Wikileaks revealed that members of the group had attempted to buy arms from the Sandinista regime in Nicaragua in September 2009, and the Nicaraguan foreign minister Samuel Santos had notified U.S. assistant secretary for Western Hemisphere affairs Thomas A. Shannon about the plot. According to the cable, President Ortega also called Shannon shortly after the meeting with Santos to confirm the information. Later reports from inside the FNRP indicated that the group planned to use the arms to go "to the mountains to start a campaign of armed struggle" against the government.[55]

Ortega's outreach to the U.S. government about the threat of Zelaya supporters seeking arms is illustrative of his political acumen. After being voted out of office in mid-revolution in 1990, Ortega had spent the next decade and a half working his way back into power. Since returning to the presidency in January 2007, he has shown himself to be a much more shrewd politician and a far more skillful purveyor of constitutional subversion.

On August 5, 2010, *El Nuevo Diario*, a Nicaraguan daily, ran the headline "Dictatorship, Step by Step," which revealed a leaked Sandinista Party internal document that laid out the plan to "formalize our only candidate for the 2011 elections, the commander of the revolution, Comrade Daniel Ortega."[56] According to the document, the Sandinistas expected the "recalcitrant opposition" to rant that he was ineligible to be reelected, which he was. Nicaragua, like Honduras, had not one but two articles that prohibited running for successive terms as president. But this would prove to be an insufficient obstacle to a seasoned political practitioner like Ortega, whose implementation of the process was sufficiently slow so as not to cause an international backlash.

Professors Forrest Colburn and Alberto Trejos of the INCAE Business School in Nicaragua and Costa Rica described this process in the July 2010 edition of

Dissent: "Opportunistic political elites don't have to break the law when the rule of law is so weak—and public and private institutions are so pliable—that the constitution can simply be refashioned." Colburn and Trejos called this method of constitutional subversion "the latest and most fashionable incarnation of dictatorship."[57]

In October 2009, Ortega and his supporters used the occasion of the death of a non-Sandinista judge to call a session of the Nicaraguan Supreme Court in which a quorum of sympathetic judges met and declared that the constitutional article that limits presidential terms didn't apply to Ortega. This led the former Sandinista and current director of the Nicaraguan Center for the Defense of Human Rights, Vilma Núñez, to state, "This is the only country in the world where the court has declared the constitution unconstitutional."[58]

After Ortega was reelected, the former Sandinista guerrilla leader and revolutionary comandante Victor Tirado said, "Nicaragua is a country that has always abused its Constitution and government institutions. And Ortega is a continuation of that tradition." Tirado added, "This is a dictatorship. Nicaragua can't get out of this cycle; we are returning to where we started."[59]

8

MANAGING THE MEDIA

Speaking in September 2010 at a Washington event to celebrate the sixtieth anniversary of Radio Free Europe/Radio Liberty, the chairman of the Broadcasting Board of Governors, Walter Isaacson, warned, "We can't allow ourselves to be outcommunicated by our enemies. There's that Freedom House report that reveals that today's autocratic leaders are investing billions of dollars in media resources to influence the global opinion. . . . You've got Russia Today, Iran's Press TV, Venezuela's TeleSUR, and of course, China is launching an international broadcasting 24-hour news channel with correspondents around the world."[1]

Isaacson was referring to the state-controlled media outlets that have sprouted up recently from many of the declared and non-declared enemies of the United States. These satellite broadcasts, which can cheaply reach millions of viewers worldwide, are a modern innovation of the old propaganda techniques that were mostly confined to indoctrinating "captive" domestic audiences in the past.

Their techniques are similar: hire young, inexperienced correspondents who will toe the party line as TV reporters, and put strong sympathizers, especially Americans, as hosts of "debate" shows. These small press operations tend to show up at events that major media outlets have little interest in covering, such as hearings on Capitol Hill that condemn the actions of their home countries.

Where normal media outlets will film only the speakers at such an event, these state-sponsored media units will often turn the cameras toward the audience in order to capture on film those in the audience who may be government critics. Their purpose for this is twofold—to later screen the video to see who might be attending such a conference and to intimidate exiles from attending such events.[2]

The video reports produced by these state-run news operations are broadcast on state-run television and immediately posted online. The aim is to "flood the zone" with the regime's talking points so that anyone searching for information online about a particular person or event will be inundated with search results that reiterate the message.

TeleSUR was the first Latin America–based satellite TV channel and is funded primarily by Venezuela, along with contributions from several other ALBA countries. It covers news from a far-left perspective and features propaganda programs with sophisticated production values that are made to look like serious news shows and documentaries. TeleSUR's president, Andrés Izarra, is a professional journalist who formerly worked for CNN en Español. He also serves as Chávez's minister of communications and information. Izarra said of TeleSUR's launch, "TeleSUR is an initiative against cultural imperialism. We launch TeleSUR with a clear goal to break this communication regime." Izarra's father, William Izarra, is a retired air force officer who has served as Chávez's deputy foreign minister and ideologue of Bolivarian socialism. In a speech touting Chávez's media plan, William Izarra illustrated the importance of propaganda, declaring, "The media are more important than [military] divisions."[3]

In 2006 TeleSUR signed an agreement with Al Jazeera to share content. This move led U.S. congressman Connie Mack, a longtime foe of the autocratic regimes in Latin America, to issue a press release calling the network a "global television network for terrorists and other enemies of freedom."[4]

Another effective propaganda tactic undertaken by Chávez has been the formation of the Venezuelan News Agency (Agencia Venezolana de Noticias, or AVN). The AVN was created as an operation similar to the Associated Press or Reuters, though it is owned and funded by the Venezuelan government.

These Washington-based propaganda operations have long been a tactic of so-called revolutionary regimes in Latin America. Che Guevara wrote in his diaries that "a foreign reporter—preferably American—was much more valuable to us at that time (1957) than any military victory. Much more valuable than rural recruits for our guerrilla force, were American media recruits to export our propaganda." In a 1954 letter to a comrade, Fidel Castro wrote, "We cannot for a second abandon propaganda. Propaganda is vital—propaganda is the heart of our struggle."[5]

The importance of propaganda continued through the Central American wars of the 1980s. On February 16, 1982, the *New York Times* reported, "In recent months, with increasing sophistication, the leaders of the guerrilla movement in El Salvador have mounted a public relations campaign directed at world opinion in general, and at American opinion in particular. 'We have to win the war inside the United States,' said Hector Oqueli, one of the rebel leaders."[6] And after the Sandinistas first took power in Nicaragua in the 1980s, the late Tomás Borge, who served as the interior minister and head of state security for the Sandinista regime, told *Newsweek*, "The battle for Nicaragua is not being waged in Nicaragua. It is being fought in the United States."[7]

It has not been difficult for the revolutionary left in Latin America to find willing allies in the United States to help with its propaganda effort. An illustrative example is William Blum, the author of several anti-American books that have called U.S. foreign engagements "holocausts." Blum has described his life's mission as "slowing down the American Empire . . . injuring the beast."[8] Blum's treatment of U.S. involvement in Latin America is noteworthy, because it is emblematic of what often passes as scholarship on the subject and because it gets repeated in many universities across the country where he is often invited to speak to students. Blum's books have been endorsed by a coterie of left-wing celebrities and scholars, including Noam Chomsky, Gore Vidal, and Oliver Stone. Stone even entered into talks with Blum at one time to make one of his books into a movie. And in January 2006, Blum's *Rogue State* got an endorsement by Osama bin Laden, who recommended the book in an audiotape and agreed with Blum's idea that the way the United States could prevent terrorist attacks was to "apologize to the victims of American imperialism."[9]

In a chapter of his book *Killing Hope: U.S. Military and CIA Interventions since World War II*, Blum writes about U.S. involvement in Guatemala in the 1960s and 1970s. He quotes U.S. ambassador to Guatemala John Gordon Mein in a speech given in 1967 when delivering a shipment of military equipment to the Guatemalan armed forces. Immediately following Mein's quote, Blum quotes the last entry in the diary of a Michele "Kirk," who committed suicide when police came to her room to make "inquiries," as Blum puts it, suggesting that the innocent "young French woman" took her own life to avoid torture by corrupt Guatemalan police.[10] It is an amazing juxtaposition. What Blum fails to mention is that Michele Firk (not Kirk), a militant of the French Communist Party, had flown to Guatemala from Paris to assist the terrorist group Rebel Armed Forces (Fuerzas Armadas Rebeldes, or FAR) kidnap Ambassador Mein. When the ambassador tried to escape from his vehicle, they murdered him with submachine gun fire to his back.

It was Michele Firk who had rented the car that the terrorists used to assassinate Ambassador Mein—a more salient fact that doesn't get mentioned in Blum's book. Even more noteworthy for a historian who often lectures on Latin American history, Blum failed to include that Mein was murdered or that the person he mentions in a following paragraph as a fearful victim of oppressive authorities was directly involved in his murder. Another glaring omission is that Mein was the first U.S. ambassador ever to be assassinated while serving in office.

Blum's book is typical of a genre that has long eschewed scholarship for sensationalized anti-Americanism. At the Summit of the Americas in April 2009, Chávez handed President Obama a copy of *Open Veins of Latin America* by Eduardo Galeano, about which Michael Reid, the Americas editor at *The Economist*, wrote, "[Galeano's] history is that of the propagandist, a potent mix of selective truths, exaggeration and falsehood, caricature and conspiracy theory."[11] Called the "Idiot's Bible" by Latin American scholars, Galeano's 1971 tome was translated to English by Cedric Belfrage, a British journalist and expatriate to the United States who was also a Communist Party member and an agent for the KGB.[12]

Chávez's presentation of Galeano's book, delicately timed for the cameras, was an act of propaganda in itself. The copy that Chávez gave President Obama was in Spanish, so Chávez was well aware that it would not end up on the president's nightstand. But the Amazon ranking of Galeano's book skyrocketed as a result, introducing the genre of Latin American victimology to a whole new generation.

The Artillery of Ideas

Another Chávez propaganda effort designed to reach English-speaking audiences is the state-funded newspaper *Correo del Orinoco*, named for a newspaper started by Simón Bolívar in 1818. Editor in chief and state-funded author Eva Golinger explained:

This will be the first newspaper of its kind in Venezuela. We will produce news and information for an international audience, but from the Venezuelan perspective. Most of the news that's out there in English comes from international news agencies that report with a biased perspective and tend to ignore important human interest stories that paint a positive picture of the Chávez government.[13]

Golinger, a New York attorney turned Chávez amanuensis, continued, "Our most important mission is to combat the massive media manipulation and information blockade against Venezuela and to inform the international community about many incredible events taking place daily inside Venezuela that rarely receive attention from the corporate media." Golinger went on to cite Chávez's hero Bolívar as encouraging writing and reporting as the "Artillery of Ideas."[14] In what must be seen as "cross promotion" in the small world of state-funded news organizations, Eva Golinger was hired by Russia Today in early 2011 to host her own Spanish-language show.

In April 2010 Chávez held a celebration of the eighth anniversary of the coup that earlier had removed him from office for two days. He named the celebration the "Day of the Bolivarian Militias, the Armed People and the April Revolution" and held a swearing-in ceremony for 35,000 new members of his civilian militia. As part of the festivities, Chávez also had a swearing-in ceremony for a hundred young community media activists, calling them "communicational guerrillas." This was done, according to Chávez, to raise awareness among young people about the "media lies" and to "combat the anti-revolution campaign of the opposition-controlled private media."[15]

Chávez delivered speeches to Venezuelans almost daily, interrupting programming to make even the most mundane announcements about the Bolivarian revolution's latest endeavor. All TV and radio stations, public and private, are required to broadcast these *cadenas* (government broadcasts) live. He has utilized these cadenas to announce such things as his decision to change the country's clocks by a half hour after hearing a child's story about walking to school in the dark. Chávez told Venezuelans on his weekly TV show that the purpose of the time change was to achieve "a more fair distribution of the sunrise," which would help poor children who have to wake up before sunrise to go to school. To give the measure an appearance of seriousness, Chávez said, "Very rigorous scientific studies have determined that . . . the metabolic activity of living beings is synchronized with the sun's light." A Chávez aide added that additional measures would also be announced at a later date to "make more effective use of time."[16]

Chávez has also counseled Venezuelans during a water shortage on how to take a shower, stating that he was able to do so in less than three minutes, and so should they. "If you are going to lie back, in the bath, with the soap and you turn on the, what's it called, the Jacuzzi . . . imagine that, what kind of communism is that? We're not in times of Jacuzzi," Chávez told Venezuelans during his TV show.[17]

The Venezuelan regime's subsequent attempts at media censorship have grown even more peculiar. In January 2011, the Venezuelan Telecommunications Commission issued a statement telling the TV network Televen to stop airing a comedic soap opera filmed in Colombia called *Chepe Fortuna* because it was making fun of Venezuela and of Chávez. Two sisters on the show are named Colombia and Venezuela, and the latter—the bad sister—has a dog named Little Hugo.

A stern directive from Chávez's telecom agency about the show stated, "After careful analysis, it was found that these contents promoted political and racial intolerance, xenophobia and incitement of crime." The commission posted several video clips from the show on its website that featured the offending excerpts. In one of the videos, Venezuela is crying as she speaks to a friend on her cell phone while looking for Little Hugo. She asks the friend, "What will become of Venezuela without Little Hugo?" The friend answers, "Venezuela will be free. Lately, Little Hugo was defecating all over everything."[18] While these comical examples serve to illustrate the lengths to which Chávez's defenders will go to thwart criticism of their leader, other efforts have been far more serious. The most notorious propaganda and cover-up operation to date has been that of the Puente Llaguno shooting in 2002, in which nineteen people were killed and sixty injured as Chávez's henchmen were videotaped shooting into a crowd of marchers from a bridge overhead.

When Chávez came back to power after his forty-eight-hour ouster, Freddy Bernal—the Chávez-allied mayor of the district and leader of the Bolivarian Circles, a group of armed, motorcycle-riding thugs that serve as enforcers for the regime— ordered the cleaning and repair of Baralt Avenue, ground zero of the Puente Llaguno shootings. It was perhaps one of the very few times that the bureaucracy moved so efficiently, spackling bullet holes and repainting entire blocks. Within ten days, a street that had been the site of a massacre witnessed by millions on TV was wiped clean of any evidence of the crime. And any police investigator who opened a case about the shooting was quickly dismissed and replaced by a Chávez-appointed official. After the Baralt Avenue cleanup, the Chávez government began an effort to collect faux victims to counter the flood of actual victims who were showing up in hospitals and on newscasts.[19]

With their own victims, the government could claim that the Baralt Avenue shooting was simply "a confrontation between brothers," rather than Chavista gunmen shooting into a crowd. It also reported that the marchers were armed as well and had even fired on the Chavistas first. This was supplemented by the claim that many of the victims in the opposition march had been shot by friendly fire.

Parts of the propaganda effort were undermined by the sometimes uncontrolled loquaciousness of Chávez himself. Both he and his spokesmen made a full-throated effort to claim that the video footage of the shooting had been doctored. Chávez went so far as to say that Venevisión, the media company where the cameraman worked, had contacts in Hollywood who had fabricated the video in a special-effects studio.

Later, seemingly oblivious to the contradiction, Chávez said, "The truth is that these four [sic] compatriots with their short-range weapons had the courage to stand up to snipers and terrorists dressed as policemen firing with their military weapons upon thousands of defenseless compatriots. To them [I wish all] the honor they deserve and the acknowledgment of our people."[20]

Despite the self-contradictory storytelling, the massive propaganda campaign was effective. The three gunmen caught on camera were given medals and a monument on the very bridge from which they had fired on unarmed civilians. One of the three men, who had given a tearful confession to police when he was arrested the day after the shooting, was tapped by Chávez to lead an armed militia in Caracas. Another ran for public office.[21]

The Puente Llaguno footage of the three gunmen firing from the overpass ran constantly after it became public. Of all the evidence showing the culpability of the Chávez supporters, this was far and away the most damning. Cleaning up Baralt Avenue of any evidence would be easy with enough paint and plaster, but the video images were by then being seen worldwide.

Unable to effectively discredit the footage, Chávez went after the cameraman instead. The night that Chávez was returned to power, the Venevisión reporter who shot the footage, Luis Fernández, received a death threat in a phone call from someone representing M-28, a radical student group based out of the Central Univeristy.

After the call, the video footage must have seemed foreboding to the cameraman. On the wall, just in front of where the shooters were perched on the overpass, was a propaganda message in spray paint stating, "Peña es de la CIA ([Caracas mayor Alfredo] Peña is with the CIA)." The graffiti was signed "M-28." Peña was a onetime Chávez ally who had switched to the opposition after Chávez insisted that he appoint a military officer to head the Metropolitan Police, because Chávez thought that they could be a threat to his power.[22] As part of the cover-up of the Puente Llaguno shooting, eight officers of the Metropolitan Police were detained and accused of "conspiring with the opposition." Brian A. Nelson, the author of *The Silence and the Scorpion,* a highly detailed account of these events, interviewed the officers and stated that "they seemed to have been picked completely at random and most of them said they hadn't even been in *El Silencio* [where the shooting took place] on April 11." Nelson further noted that the officers "were eventually moved to a proper prison, where they sit today [in 2009]. Even though it has been more than seven years since they were arrested, they have never been tried." Three police commissioners were also arrested on frivolous charges and were kept in jail for more than four years without a court ruling.[23]

According to Nelson, the reason that Chávez felt the need to go after the Metropolitan Police was because they were the largest armed group in the country, aside from the army. This, feared Chávez, made them a potential threat for another coup against his regime. After he was briefly ousted from office in 2002, Chávez skillfully utilized the canard that the Metropolitan Police had fired the first shots at the Bolivarian Circles as an excuse to take away much of their firepower and equipment, leaving them with only their .38 caliber pistols. And once a Chávez loyalist took over as mayor of Caracas, the Metropolitan Police were completely purged. According to Nelson, loyalty to Chávez's political party became much more important than expertise or experience on the police force.[24] In short order, any threat to the regime from the police or the military was nullified, and the storyline from the damning video footage had been quieted.

Informational Hegemony

The only remaining challenge to Chávez's increasing accumulation of power was the independent media. Chávez has battled with the media from the day he was elected. But in the years since he returned to power, his loathing for independent media that published or broadcast any criticism of his governance became more pronounced, as did his regime's militancy against them. In January 2007, the president of TeleSUR, Andrés Izarra, revealed the thinking behind Chávez's campaign against the media: "We have to elaborate a new plan, and the one that we propose is the communicational and informational hegemony of the state."[25]

Just four months after Izarra's announcement, the Chávez government pulled the broadcasting license for Radio Caracas Televisión Internacional (RCTV), one of the last independent stations in Venezuela, as well as the most popular. Not only did the Chávez government refuse to renew the station's license, the Chávez-controlled Supreme Court ordered that its broadcast equipment be seized and given to Venezuelan Social Television (Televisoria Venezolana Social), a newly formed government-owned TV station, which was oddly scheduled to begin broadcasting the day after RCTV was raided and shut down.[26]

In the aftermath of RCTV's shutdown, as student protesters flooded Caracas, Chávez attacked the only remaining opposition all-news television station, Globovisión, and threatened to revoke its broadcast license. Chávez then called its employees "enemies of the fatherland, particularly those behind the scenes." On a state-controlled TV station, Chávez said, "I will give you a name: Globovisión. Greetings, gentlemen of Globovisión, you should watch where you are going." To maintain the facade of being a democratically elected leader with an active opposition, Chávez has so far not closed Globovisión. Instead, just three years later, he fabricated criminal charges against its owner and drove him into exile in the United States.[27] To bring the point home, Chávez urged "the people of the slums" to storm Caracas, adding that he wanted to lead the fight against the "counterrevolutionaries" himself. To punctuate the bravado, he stated that he hoped that the owners of Globovisión were as prepared to die as he was to defend the revolution.[28] On December 7, 2010, the *Wall Street Journal* reported that Venezuela's government had acquired a 20 percent stake in Globovisión, which it said was "the last local television station that offers news and views critical of President Hugo Chávez." The day before, Chávez's government released a statement announcing that it had officially become a 20 percent shareholder because it had completed its takeover of Banco Federal, whose president owned a minority position in Globovisión.

Chávez had ordered Banco Federal to be shut down in April 2010, and by July he had announced that he wanted to appoint a member of his government to Globovisión's board of directors, causing many to question the veracity of the charges during the original takeover of the bank. The doubt was compounded when Chávez's government officials were interviewed about the situation. Rodrigo Cabezas, who had served as finance minister during several currency devaluations, had long railed about "the fight against monopolistic private property, which produces distortions in the allocation of food and of prices." Cabezas denied that the Chávez government wanted to outlaw all private property but noted that it would create the conditions in which "social property, the property that emphasizes attending to necessities, can and should be hegemonic."[29]

Cabezas had earlier attacked critics of a previous currency devaluation, saying it was an "act of justice" that would only affect the "bourgeoisie" that had grown used to "asking for [cheap] dollars to travel, to import luxuries, top-of-the-range vehicles, and so on." Jesus Faría, a socialist economist and adviser to the Central Bank, also commented on the state-controlled TV channel: "This government has declared war on speculation, on large estate owners, and against anyone who attempts to harm the economic and political stability of the country. It is a just war."[30]

When the government took over Banco Federal, Faría revealed what many had speculated was the true purpose of the move: "This is a group of economic tycoons with a lot of money and a media outlet that they use to repeatedly bombard a democratic system, and they participated openly in a coup d'état." Faria was referring to the shareholder stake that the owner of Banco Federal had in Globovisión, which the Chávez government had blamed for the forty-eight-hour coup that had removed Chávez temporarily from power in 2002.[31] The takeover of Banco Federal would not only be a random act of revenge against one of the class of elites that Chávez blamed for his ouster, but it was also a subversive way to try to wrest control of one of the last opposition TV stations without overtly taking it over and drawing worldwide criticism.

Chávez's propaganda operation has not been limited to media operations. In the airport in Caracas, oversized posters were hung from the ceiling with the caption "LIVE! in Socialism," with dubious statistics of the vast improvement under 21st Century Socialism. One claims, "Corn production has increased 132 percent," and another says that "under socialism, our children are now growing faster."

But in a September 2010 *New York Times* story about extreme poverty in Venezuela, one sentence mentioned the ironic propaganda effort in Ciudad Guyana, where Warao Indians subsist on scavenging in a large landfill called Cambalache: "Some Warao wander the broad avenues here, begging for food. Others sell wares like bracelets at intersections. Others subsist at Cambalache, located minutes from boutiques selling luxury goods and the headquarters of government factories *adorned with huge photos of Mr. Chávez* [emphasis added]." Besides the oversized murals of Chávez throughout the town, the municipal trucks carry a message as well: "Entire families arrive at sunrise each day, chasing after trucks that unload fresh cargoes of trash. One truck that arrived at Cambalache this month had painted on its side the name José Ramon López, Ciudad Guayana's mayor, under the words 'Socialist Beautification Plan.'"[32]

Allies in the Struggle Against the Free Press

Chávez's ally to the south, Argentine president Cristina Fernández de Kirchner, has used a slightly more oblique approach to silence her critics. Her government conspired to take over Papel Prensa S.A., the largest supplier of paper to the two largest newspapers in the country. Kirchner claimed that the sale of Papel Prensa in the 1970s had been executed under duress by the military junta that was running the country at the time, a charge that came back to embarrass her when the seller told the press that the sale was open and the price was more than fair. While Kirchner sought creative ways to either punish or control those media outlets that criticized her, her ministers actually singled out two reporters and compared them to Nazis. Not to be outdone by her ministers, Kirchner has also called Grupo Clarín, the largest media company in Argentina—with newspaper, cable television, and Internet holdings—an "enemy of the state."[33] She also accused a political cartoonist of acting like a "quasi-gangster."[34]

Despite condemnation from international press freedom groups, Kirchner has grown more antagonistic over time with the independent media in Argentina. In December 2011, fifty police were sent to storm the offices of Cablevisión, a cable TV company that happened to be owned by the media conglomerate, and Kirchner nemesis, Grupo Clarín. The raid was conducted without a court order and was the second time the company had been raided; once before it was targeted for alleged tax discrepancies.[35] Kirchner has also attempted to create a government watchdog to monitor for racial and discriminatory media practices, a move that was called a "covert attempt to control the media" by the existing media freedom watchdog. And on March 13, 2012, Kirchner had a live broadcast of a highly popular political talk show taken off the air in mid-sentence when her late husband's chief of staff was criticizing her on a live broadcast.[36]

Bolivia's Evo Morales has been one of Chávez's closest allies in the project to implement 21st Century Socialism in the hemisphere. After winning the presidential race in 2005, Morales first traveled to Cuba to meet Fidel Castro, where the dictator advised him to follow the Chávez model of constitutional subversion. As soon as he took office, Morales heeded Castro's advice and started with the media. On January 22, 2009, three days before Bolivians were to vote on the country's new constitution, Morales announced the launch of *Cambio*, a state-run newspaper with the Orwellian slogan "The truth will set us free." Morales told reporters that the state-owned paper would counter the antigovernment slant of the local private media.[37]

Since assuming office, Morales has targeted Bolivia's independent media. In May 2007, at an event in Cochabamba called the "Fifth World Conference of Artists and Intellectuals in Defense of Humanity," he called the owners of the privately owned media in Bolivia "the principal enemy," stating that "the main adversaries of my presidency, of my government, are certain communications media."[38]

Morales told the audience that his government should be "drawing on the experience of our friends in Venezuela and Cuba" to more effectively control the independent press in Bolivia. Alongside the Bolivian president was Cuba's minister of culture, Abel Prieto, who punctuated Morales's statement by saying, "I wish that we could imprison the owner of a media outlet. With much pleasure we would give him a life sentence for lying, for confusing the people."[39] Prieto stated that it was imperative that they set up a tribunal that would "permit the evaluation and work of the media. Not only local and national but of all the great disinformation machinery in decisive media outlets with enormous world influence." A banner headline in *El Mundo*, a Santa Cruz newspaper, read "Morales Identifies His Enemies" and showed a newsroom behind the crosshairs of a rifle scope.[40]

A declaration issued by the conference stated, "We also denounce communication groups and institutions that in the name of a distorted idea of the freedom of expression are serving economic and imperialist structures, such as Reporters Without Borders and the Inter-American Press Association."[41] Under Morales, Bolivia passed a law similar to the one attempted by Kirchner in Argentina that gives the government the power to shut down media companies that publish or broadcast anything that the government deems racist.[42]

In Ecuador, President Rafael Correa has actually sued the authors of a book that uncovered corrupt state contracts given to his brother. He also sued the president of the editorial board of *La Hora*, an Ecuadorian daily, for criticizing him in an editorial. But the most emblematic case to date was Correa's lawsuit against the editorial page editor and three directors of *El Universo* for an editorial that called Correa a dictator and said that he could one day be subjected to the courts for ordering his military officers to fire on striking police officers.

At trial Correa barred any press from attending but showed up on the day of sentencing to sit in the gallery. Incredibly, the judge who had presided throughout the trial supposedly went on vacation the day that he was scheduled to make a ruling on the case, and a replacement judge sentenced the four journalists to three years in jail and a fine of $40 million. To produce the ruling, the replacement judge would have had to read through the five-thousand-page case file and write his sixty-page ruling in just two days.[43] As the case drew international condemnation by many U.S. and international newspapers, evidence emerged from another judge involved with the case that it was actually Correa's personal lawyer who wrote the verdict. To put it more clearly, Correa sued a newspaper's directors and their editorial page editor for an editorial that he didn't like and had his own lawyer write the verdict. After the immediate backlash from throughout the world, Correa issued a pardon for the four defendants, but not for the many other journalists whom he had also sued.[44]

Correa was utilizing what are called *desacato* (disrespect) laws in Latin America that were designed to prevent insults to the dignity of public officials but have mostly been used to silence government critics. Correa, for his part, had called journalists who criticized his government "human misery" and had ominously stated that "radio and TV frequencies have been granted in ways that are frequently dark and it's time to analyze the matter."[45] He later warned of a crackdown on media companies to combat what he called "corruption that has led to the awarding of radio and television frequencies," a charge that many saw as a veiled threat to critics of his government. To combat international critics of the move, Correa declared, "Be ready, because this fight against corruption . . . will be called an attempt against freedom of speech."[46]

A commission investigating corruption and the extent of narco-trafficking in Ecuador included in its findings that persistent attacks on the media by the Correa government and efforts to stifle freedom of expression had greatly affected free speech in the country. The commission also noted that the private media was one of the few centers of power in the country that Correa and his party did not control.[47]

Nicaragua, under its second presidency of Daniel Ortega and the Sandinistas, was already well schooled in the use of propaganda. During the first Sandinista government in the 1980s, Stephen Kinzer, a *New York Times* correspondent, quoted a Managua street vendor who let him know what most other reporters were either unaware of or were unwilling to report:

You Americans, I can't believe how stupid you are! . . . You come here for a couple of days or a week, you live in some nice hotel, and maybe you go up north to pick coffee for a day. . . . Then you go home to your little solidarity group or your church group and tell everyone how wonderful the revolution is. You people are so blind! You're forcing Communism on us Nicaraguans, don't you see? The Sandinistas are leading you around by the nose! You think everything looks so nice here, but we can't afford to eat in those places where you people eat. Poor people are suffering in this country! We don't have food for our children, but you don't see that because the Sandinistas don't show it to you! You're living in nice apartments in New York or Europe, and the idea of a revolution seems so nice to you from over there. Open your eyes! Don't keep telling lies! Don't be useful idiots![48]

In Nicaragua today, even though Ortega has changed his campaign rhetoric from communism to Christianity, his manipulation of the media has become far more strident since he returned to office. Though he was still denouncing the Yanquis in his campaign and even in subsequent presidential speeches, he had learned well the lesson of incremental politics. Since his second inauguration in 2007, he has rhetorically embraced both business interests and the Catholic Church while simultaneously consolidating his power at a slightly less startling pace than in his previous stint as president in the 1980s. Yet his treatment by the press, this time, has been more critical and ostensibly more difficult for him to accept.

During Ortega's previous administration, the Chamorro name was as prominent as Ortega's. Violeta Chamorro would defeat him in the first presidential election in which Nicaraguans got the chance to vote Ortega and the Sandinistas out of office. But Violeta's son, Carlos Fernando Chamorro, had been a full-throated supporter of the Sandinista regime during the 1980s when he ran its official news organ, *Barricadas* (*Barricades*). Carlos Fernando is also the son of Pedro Joaquín Chamorro, the famous publisher whose assassination in 1978 sparked the events that led to the ouster of Nicaragua's Somoza. The dictator's fall was the seminal event that had led to the Sandinistas' ascension to power in 1979.

Today Carlos Fernando says that he practiced "self-censorship in defense of the revolution" back then, and since Ortega's return to the presidency in 2007, he has become one of the regime's biggest critics. For this "treachery" to the Sandinistas, he has been targeted like no other journalist, having been prosecuted on trumped-up charges of money laundering. He has also been attacked relentlessly by those media outlets that have taken the place of *Barricadas* as party-line organs of the present-day Sandinista regime.

In the fall of 2008, Ortega sent government security forces to raid Carlos Fernando's office, taking computers, files, and equipment for a drawn-out political prosecution in which the Sandinista media accused him of being in league with narco-traffickers and organized crime. The Sandinista press got so carried away with its attacks that its supporters began attacking human rights activists and foreign critics of Ortega's government.

A report done for the United Nations by the Observatory for the Protection of Human Rights Defenders said that verbal attacks against anyone "who dared to criticise the policies of President Ortega or his Government . . . were systematically and continuously taken up by the official or pro-Government media." The report, issued in June 2009, stated:

> Furthermore, President Ortega's Government tried to silence dissident voices and criticisms of Government policies through members of the Government who verbally assaulted demonstrators and human rights defenders as well as the Citizens' Councils (*Consejos de Poder Ciudadano*—CPC) who hampered the NGOs' activities and physically assaulted defenders. In this context, 2008 saw numerous attacks against human rights defenders and attempts to obstruct their activities. In addition, the exclusion of human rights defenders from places and buildings devoted to the citizens' participation became commonplace. Many inter-institutional buildings used by civil servants, representatives of NGOs and social movements to discuss social problems were closed down and some were taken over by members of the CPC.[49]

These Citizens' Councils were taken directly from the "Revolutionary Brotherhood" plan and are close facsimiles of groups like the Bolivarian Circles in Venezuela. Ortega claimed in July 2007 that "more than 6,000 such [CPCs] had been formed," and "around 500,000 people participated in CPCs." Ortega also claimed that he expected that number to double by late 2007. According to Ortega, the CPCs were created only to "lobby local governments," but they have since proved to be vessels with which to replace existing statutory citizen participation and input organizations. They have also proved to be peopled mostly by members of Ortega's political party.[50] The report by the Observatory for the Protection of Human Rights Defenders stated that pro-government media branded Ortega's critics "puppets of imperialism" and "traitors to the country." These kinds of labels could endanger their lives, according to the report.[51]

Since then, phone numbers for the Nicaraguan presidential press office are no longer listed, and Ortega's cabinet members rarely, if ever, make public statements. Commenting on the media blackout, Sergio Ramírez, Ortega's vice president in the 1980s, told the *Miami Herald*, "It's the first time where we have a government where you say, 'Who's the minister of health? Who's the minister of education?' and no one knows."[52]

Honduras's Mel Zelaya worked closely with Ortega and began to follow his example after accepting financial support from Chavez. In June 2007 Zelaya ordered Honduras's privately owned media to run ten two-hour-long government-produced shows, telling reporters, "We find ourselves obligated to make this decision to counteract the misinformation of the news media about our 17 months in office." By Zelaya's diktat, all five hundred radio stations and hundred television stations in Honduras would be obligated to run the government-produced programming from 10 p.m. until midnight for ten days straight in order to counteract what the president claimed was a bias against his government and its accomplishments.[53] The ousting of Zelaya, though officials did it in a ham-handed manner by having him taken to Costa Rica rather than incarcerated at home, was the first constitutional stand taken by a Latin American country to stop the continental subversion by Chávez and his allies. The public relations battle that came afterward showed the vast difference in the propaganda operations of the two sides.

Zelaya supporters immediately set the tone by claiming, falsely, that he had been taken from his home in his pajamas.[54] This was repeated by the majority of media outlets, as well as the head of the OAS, José Miguel Insulza. It was only when Zelaya began making statements to the press members who were holed up with him in the Brazilian Embassy that "Israeli mercenaries" were torturing him with high-frequency radiation and "mind-altering gas" that the tide of elite opinion turned against him.[55]

9

MANAGING THE MASSES

Two days after Christmas of 1999, at the culmination of Chávez's first year in office, *Newsweek* published a retrospective in which it compared different predictions on the future of Venezuela under Chávez. One said that "critics warn of a secret agenda to transform one of Latin America's most enduring democracies into a thinly disguised authoritarian regime." The article quoted the now deceased Venezuelan congressman Jorge Olavarria, a former ally and adviser to Chávez who later denounced the president after he took office and revealed his plan for 21st Century Socialism. Olavarria warned, "We are heading toward catastrophe. This Constitution will set us back 100 years, and the military will become the armed wing of a political movement." The point of agreement that *Newsweek* found sounds even more prescient today: "There is . . . one thing about Chávez that his friends and foes agree on: he likes power and intends to hold onto it."[1]

Once the inevitable scarcity and economic malaise take hold under socialist economic systems, it becomes increasingly difficult to maintain motivation among voters who aren't directly dependent upon government jobs or its largesse. In order to ensure against voter apathy and desertion, several of the ALBA countries in Latin America have purchased hackable electronic voting systems and have vastly expanded the traditional vote-buying patronage systems that they once denounced as a tool of oppression for the oligarchy. The bedrock of incremental subversion has been to always maintain the facade of being democratically elected, so controlling the method with which elections are conducted is paramount. Yet election after election has been carried out with suspect voting equipment, blacklists of opposition candidates, and a lack of transparent electoral procedures to validate the vote.

Electronic voting systems were just starting to be accepted by the market about the time that Chávez was first elected, and it was actually members of the opposition who pushed for these systems in Venezuela in order to try to prevent fraud by the Chávez regime. He offered to accept the electronic voting systems as a concession to his opponents, but at the same time supporters in his government were forming a new company called Smartmatic.

Smartmatic's business history is somewhat murky. On the surface, it appears to be a rags-to-riches story of two Venezuelan computer entrepreneurs who provided technology services to banks in the late 1990s. But further investigation revealed that neither of the two had any election experience, even though their company miraculously received a $131 million contract in 2004 from Chávez's National Electoral Council (CNE) to replace Venezuela's voting equipment.

In March 2006 the Associated Press did a story on Smartmatic and its affiliate Bitza Software and reported that a Venezuelan state industrial development fund had an investment stake in Bitza. The company immediately released a statement saying that it would buy back the 28 percent was owned by the Chávez government.[2] It was also reported that, although the company had been described as a Florida corporation, it only had a small office in Boca Raton; its main operations were based in Caracas. It was also uncovered that the company was set up through a series of shell companies. The New York Times reported in October 2006 that the Committee on Foreign Investment in the United States (CFIUS) was investigating the Venezuelan government's connection to Smartmatic. And as independent journalists also investigated the company's background, it began to appear more and more like a typical shell corporation designed to hide ownership and assets.[3] Suspicions were further confirmed after Venezuela's electoral council removed the vote tallies it had posted online that were broken down by individual voting machines, after statisticians from Harvard, the Massachusetts Institute of Technology (MIT), and Venezuelan universities crunched the numbers and contested the results.[4]

Smartmatic had touted its security features as a way to "facilitate a transparent and secure right to vote." But without the proper auditing and controls, the system can be utilized by an ill-intentioned government to manipulate election outcomes and even to identify those who vote against the government's candidates.

When Venezuelans collected signatures in 2003 in order to demand a recall vote for Chávez's presidency, most of the signatories had little idea what their democratic action would cost them. Although the recall mechanism was included in the Venezu-

elan constitution by Chávez himself, he would use quite undemocratic means to retaliate against those who dared to invoke it against his rule. *The Economist*, writing
about the referendum process, noted the persecution suffered by those who signed
the petition:

> The first to suffer the consequences were military officers, subjected to dis-
> ciplinary hearings and even discharged for signing, though the 1999 consti-
> tution gives them almost the same political rights as civilians. Then came
> PDVSA [state-owned Petroleum of Venezuela (Petróleos de Venezuela, S.A.)].
> The oil corporation had already sacked over 18,000 workers for striking in
> December and January, and had forced its contractors to deny them jobs. Now
> PDVSA is using the referendum database to filter applicants for work. The
> man in charge of personnel is Asdrubal Chávez, the president's second cousin;
> he declined to answer questions.[5]

The list of names and identity card numbers from an earlier petition was leaked
to a Chavista congressman named Luis Tascón, who published it on his website.
Tascón threatened to publish the names for the 2003 petition as well. This was followed by a raid by police, in helmets and flak jackets and wielding assault rifles, of
the offices of the National Electoral Council, allegedly because of claims of a large
number of forgeries. The number of alleged forgeries would not have been enough to
be statistically significant among the 3.2 million signatures collected against Chávez.
But after the raid, many state workers began to claim that their signatures had been
forged, recalling how they had seen friends and family lose their jobs after the earlier
list of names was leaked. *The Economist* noted, "Those who dared to support the
recall are also being singled out for persecution by public-sector employers, including ministries, the armed forces and the powerful state oil corporation, Petróleos de
Venezuela. . . ."[6]

On an episode of Chávez's weekly television show *Alo Presidente!* later that
month, he called Congressman Tascón up onto the stage with him, asking the audience, "Do you remember Tascón's Web page? People are afraid of Tascón's Web page."
When Tascón got up on stage, Chávez smiled and asked, "Now I don't appear on your
list, do I?"[7]

After he received negative international attention for the blacklist, Chávez admitted that his government had indeed used the list to determine who got hired and

fired. He told his supporters, "There are still places that use Tascon's List to determine who gets a job and who doesn't. That's over. Bury Tascon's List. Surely it had
an important role at one time, but not now."[8] Chávez's appeal to his supporters was a
feint. Shortly afterward, what became known as the Maisanta List was made public.
Named for Chávez's great-grandfather, the Maisanta List expanded on Tascón's List,
incorporating information such as whether Venzuelan citizens actively participate in
Chávez's social programs.

Another Orwellian tenet of the 1999 Chávez constitution was the creation of
a new "moral branch" of government, which established a government ombudsman
who was purported to be a "defender of the people." The ombudsman during the
time of the recall referendum was Germín Mundaraín, a Chávez associate who, when
asked, claimed that he had received no complaints about persecution of state employees who signed the petition. It was later reported by members of his staff, both
former and current at that time, that he himself was purging his office of anyone supporting the opposition to Chávez.[9]

Once it was unable to stop the recall referendum by invalidating signatures, the
machinery of the Chávez government, militia, and political organization moved to
plan B—to control the election's outcome. If Chávez and his supporters could pull
it off, it would be a far greater feat than stopping the election, as it would allow them
to claim that "the people have spoken" and declare a further mandate to make sure
that Chávez would not be challenged again. Douglas Schoen, founder of the the
Penn, Schoen & Berland polling firm that did extensive polling in Venezuela, tells
the story of Chávez's election fraud in his book with Michael Rowan, *The Threat
Closer to Home*:

> Two Boston-based academics, Dr. Ricardo Hausmann of Harvard University
> and Roberto Rigobon of MIT, later examined the computer results and found
> statistical anomalies so striking and so unlikely that they concluded fraud was
> the most logical explanation for the announced result. Their conclusion was
> later corroborated by a multidisciplinary team, including a former rector of
> the CNE, as well as two academics.
>
> It appeared that results in certain voting tables had been changed through
> transmissions from the central computer so that neither [Jimmy] Carter nor
> the OAS observers noticed.
>
> When the questions raised by these academics were put to Jennifer Mc-
> Coy of the Carter Center at the Inter-American Dialogue in Washington,

D.C., while she defended the methods, practices and conclusions of the Carter Center she also acknowledged she did not have any certainty as to how Venezuela voted on the recall. Thereafter, President Carter went out of his way to criticize the PSB exit poll, and to reaffirm his support of Chávez's legitimacy.[10]

In a later interview in *Forbes*, Schoen elaborated on this and subsequent fraudulent elections under Chávez: "There's evidence that he switched the yes and no votes on a recall referendum in 2004, that he changed a 5% victory to a landslide 28% so he could claim a mandate for his revolution in 2006, and that he planned to rig a 13% margin rejecting his president-for-life referendum but then settled for a 1% loss when General Raul Baduel and hundreds of thousands of students demanded a fair count in 2007."[11]

Any remaining doubt about whether the Venezuelan elections were fraudulent was removed at a U.S. Election Assistance Commission field hearing in Orlando, Florida, in February 2009. There, CIA cybersecurity expert Steve Stigall gave a presentation that showed the methods that Chávez and his aides allegedly utilized to manipulate the 2004 election recount. Stigall told the attendees that the CIA had begun studying electronic voting systems a few years before, once it discerned that foreign governments might try to hack electronic voting equipment to affect election outcomes in the United States. After studying the voting systems in over thirty countries, Stigall had become the CIA's expert on electronic voting systems and how they can be compromised to affect a vote. Stigall mentioned that when Chávez won the 2004 recall election, mathematicians discovered "a very subtle algorithm" that could adjust the vote enough to give Chávez a win.[12]

When paper ballots were requested by election observers to check the count, Chávez agreed to allow 100 of the 19,000 voting machines to be audited. "It is my understanding that the computer-software program that generated the random number list of voting machines that were being randomly audited, that program was provided by Chávez," Stigall told the audience.

When there has been any doubt as to whether one method was sufficient to ensure the correct election outcome, Chávez has resorted to old-fashioned retail vote-buying. In September 2010, early polls showed Chávez not doing as well as he needed to maintain a rubber-stamp congress in the upcoming congressional elections. A news report just before the elections showed him unveiling shipping containers full of cheap appliances from China. Supporters were invited to purchase them at highly subsidized prices just a week prior to the vote.[13]

Further confirmation of these methods of election fraud and vote buying can be seen in their use by other autocratic governments both in the ALBA countries of Latin America as well as in the elections of their Middle Eastern allies. For example, statistical analyses by credible organizations showed that the Iranian elections of 2009, like recent Venezuelan elections, were rife with fraud.[14] Additionally, one of the revelations in the Wikileaks documents provides insight into the scope of Iran's election fraud.

A transmission from the U.S. Embassy in Turkmenistan on June 15, 2009, just three days after the Iranian election, elucidated the breadth of the fraud perpetrated by the Iranian regime. The embassy source reported on a conversation with an Iranian source who called Ahmadinejad's election a "coup d'état" and said that according to actual counts, he had received only about a fifth of the reported votes and actually finished third.[15]

Besides the similarities in election fraud, there have been eerily similar instances of voter intimidation in Iran and Venezuela. In November 2010, Maj. Gen. Henry Rangel Silva, head of Venezuela's Operational Strategic Command at the time, said in an interview that the thought of an "opposition government is hard to swallow, it would mean selling the country, and that is not going to be accepted, not by the Armed Forces and much less by the people."[16] A year earlier, Iranian government supporters published interviews just prior to the election in which Iranian Revolutionary Guard Corps personnel "implied that they would not accept victory by any candidate except Ahmadinejad."[17]

The militant rhetoric used to support their positions was strikingly similar as well. Rangel Silva stated that the opposition to Chávez acts "with the support of third countries," which, according to Rangel Silva, would affect Venezuelan nationalism and would not be accepted by its military. He also stated that the opposition in Venezuela is trying to get rid of Chávez loyalists in the Venezuelan armed forces because they are "inconvenient to their international interests."[18]

In Iran, Hossein Shariatmadari, a hard-liner loyal to Ayatollah Ali Khamenei and editor of the state-controlled newspaper *Kayhan*, told the press that Mir-Hossein Mousavi, the leading opposition candidate against Ahmadinejad in the 2009 election, was a "foreign agent" for the United States and part of a "fifth column" that wanted to topple Iran's revolutionary government. And an editorial for the same state-controlled newspaper said of Mousavi and his supporters: "That corrupt movement has been implementing a foreign mission in order to encourage unlawful activities, kill innocent people, create a rebellion, plunder public property and weaken the power of the Islamic system."[19]

As with the Chávez regime's cover-up after the Puente Llaguno shooting, the Iranian regime utilized state resources to try to place the blame on the opposition for the killings that took place after Iran's fraudulent elections. The *Washington Post* also quoted Shariatmadari as saying, "[Mousavi's] aim is to escape from definite punishment for the murder of innocent individuals, inciting riots and rebellions, hiring some thugs and ruffians to attack the lives, property and honor of the people, clear collaboration with foreigners, performing the role of the fifth column inside the country, and scores of other undeniable crimes." To further drive the point home, Shariatmadari said that Mousavi's main supporters were the United States and Israel, as well as the European Union, exiled Iranians, and even domestic "plunderers."[20]

Ahmadinejad called the election result a blow to the "oppressive system" ruling the world, referring to both the United States and capitalism.[21] Among the first to call and congratulate him after the fraudulent victory was Hugo Chávez, who said the victory "represents the feeling and commitment of the Iranian people to building a new world."[22]

Bolivia's Evo Morales also sent a congratulatory message to Ahmadinejad and evidently learned the lesson of reelection at all costs. In April 2009 Morales went on a "hunger strike" for five days to break a deadlock in the congress over a package of laws that would allow him to seek reelection and would implement a biometric electronic voting system. Morales had touted electronic voting systems as a way to prevent fraud after the opposition had protested earlier, when Morales's vote count vastly outpaced exit polling projections after Venezuela had supplied free ID cards to expedite Bolivia's voter registration drive. The biometric voting systems were, unsurprisingly, from Smartmatic.

10

MANAGING THE MILITARY

When the conquistadors landed on shore in the Americas, the first thing they would do upon encountering the natives was to unfurl and read a *requerimiento*, a legal document that invoked the king's and the church's legal right to expropriate the natives' lands and to enslave them. Most of the time the requerimiento was read without an interpreter, and the indigenous peoples didn't understand a word. This practice is said to have originated, ironically enough, from the Moorish conquest of Spain, when Arab conquerors would send *dawah* messages to infidel nations, before attacking, to demand that they submit to Islamic rule, a tenet of prior warning in warfare from the Koran. The admixture of this legal legacy with the Napoleonic code imported from Spain has left an unfortunate legal tradition in much of Latin America, where jurisprudence is wielded more often as a political tool than for settling disputes and enforcing the rule of law.

The modern use of the law as a political weapon in Latin America has been aimed at the military, a longtime nemesis of "revolutionaries" and the only bulwark that has stood between them and the democracies that they have sought to destroy. And today many of the erstwhile revolutionaries actually prosecute members of the military from positions within the institutions that were preserved only by military intervention against them. An ex-FMLN guerrilla leader turned Salvadorian statesman, Joaquín Villalobos, wrote in the foreword to a book about terrorism, "In 40 years, Latin America changed, the dictatorships and authoritarianism disappeared, and the leftist movements, even in Colombia, went from secrecy, exile, prisons, and the mountains, into governments and parliaments."[1]

Villalobos could have been referring to any number of Latin American countries that currently have high officials, from presidents on down, who are former members of terrorist groups. It has taken many years of political maneuvering to achieve this. While these actors were unable to overthrow their governments in their youth, they now control them in their adulthood. Worse yet, they enjoy close relations with many human rights groups and even with the U.S. State Department and the United Nations. This is not a solely Latin American construct. It has had the backing of a number of U.S. government officials going back to the Carter administration.

Shortly before Jimmy Carter was sworn in as president, Brady Tyson, who was later named to Carter's delegation to the United Nations, made the statement that "human rights would be used to support revolutionary forces in the hemisphere." Robert Pastor, a National Security Council staffer for Carter, made a similar statement once the Carter team was in office and began to radically change U.S. policy toward Latin America.[2]

An even more controversial Carter appointee, Patricia Derian, served as the assistant secretary of state for human rights and became the architect of the "disassociation" policy, which said that the United States should distance itself from countries that violated human rights, even if they were staunch allies. Derian won the right to review military aid and arms sales to countries in accordance with their human rights records. Author Ofira Seliktar remarked on Derian's use of this power: "Not surprisingly, she targeted a number of right-wing regimes, including Iran, South Korea and Argentina. Governments like Nicaragua and El Salvador, that fought Marxist insurgencies, incurred a particular censure of the Human Rights Bureau."

Seliktar wrote that "a number of insiders noted the left-wing bias of the human rights activists in the administration. David D. Newsom, Carter's undersecretary for Political Affairs, described them as people who 'came into the Department dedicated to the idea of seeing the overthrow of rightist regimes.'"[3] The late Richard Holbrooke, who served as the special representative for Afghanistan and Pakistan for the Obama administration, testified before Congress during the height of the Cold War that "in the name of human rights, a small but vocal group of people . . . sought to carry out far-reaching change in the world structure. . . . Their targets were almost without exception regimes of the right which happened to be anti-Soviet."[4]

At around the same time, human rights policy at the United Nations began a similar transformation. Democratic Party scion Daniel Patrick Moynihan, among others, loudly decried the UN's adulteration of human rights, stating, "Unless stan-

dards of human rights are seen to be applied uniformly and neutrally to all nations
. . . it will quickly be seen that it is not human rights at all which are invoked when
selective applications are called for, but simply arbitrary political standards dressed
up in the guise of human rights."[5]

Moynihan continued, "More and more the United Nations seems only to know
of violations of human rights in countries where it is still possible to protest such
violations. . . . Our suspicions are that there could be a design to use the issue of human rights to undermine the legitimacy of precisely those nations which still observe
human rights, imperfect as that observance may be."[6]

This new human rights–focused foreign policy originated with the publication of three policy studies, two by the Center for Inter-American Relations in 1974
and 1976 and one by the Transnational Institute, a project run by the Institute for
Policy Studies, arguably the most radical think tank ever to operate inside the Washington Beltway. The Transnational Institute document, titled *The Southern Connection*, became the working strategy for the Carter administration and many left-wing
congressmen at the time.[7]

Unlike the earlier Linowitz report, which was an attempt by establishment foreign policy circles to assuage the situation between the United States and the Soviets after Vietnam and Watergate, *The Southern Connection* was a coordinated effort
by far-left supporters of the Castro regime and other leftist governments in Latin
America to end the Monroe Doctrine or at least to deter Washington's policy of
intervention against communist expansion in the hemisphere. It advocated U.S. acceptance of the incipient Marxist-Leninist regimes in Latin America under what it
termed "ideological pluralism," relinquishment of U.S. sovereignty over the Panama
Canal and Guantanamo Bay, reconsideration of Puerto Rican statehood, elimination
of joint military aid to the region, and a complete withdrawal of U.S. forces from
military bases in and around the Caribbean.[8]

Shortly after the release of *The Southern Connection* in 1977, the Carter administration got its first chance to road test its new human-rights-as-foreign-policy
doctrine in the civil war raging in El Salvador. Frank J. Devine, U.S. ambassador to
El Salvador from 1977 to 1980, recounted his time as Carter's diplomat in the war-
torn El Salvador in his book *El Salvador: Embassy under Attack*: "To understand the
all-pervasive influence of this [human rights] factor, it is important to recognize the
size and power of the human rights lobby, which today exists and functions to defend
the persecuted and to promote the cause of justice, *as it defines these concepts* [empha-

sis added]." One human rights activist in El Salvador, according to Devine, stated, "The trouble with Ambassador Devine is that he is neither pro-government nor pro-opposition. He thinks his job is to be objective!"[9] Devine felt firsthand America's lessening influence in the region as the Carter administration's policy was implemented: "Many Latin American nations asked what right the United States had to constitute itself as judge and jury. . . . They protested that we were unilaterally redefining 'intervention' in such a way as to exclude any action we might take in the name of human rights. Some came to view our efforts more as zealotry than diplomacy."[10]

Devine, because of his lack of allegiance to the Carter policy, was relieved of duty as ambassador in February 1980. His replacement, Robert E. White, called himself during his confirmation hearing an advocate of the "passionate left." White commented that the business sector in El Salvador was a kind of capitalism embodied in an alliance of the military, business interests, and landowners "designed to reap maximum profits, give minimum benefits, prevent any kind of organization of the peasantry and workers, pay as little as possible in taxes and to the public treasury, and permit the corruption that was rampant in the government of El Salvador."[11] Ambassador Devine recalled that by 1977 many of these new types of human rights advocates had begun to concentrate their efforts on El Salvador, and many were even appointed to high positions in the government:

In addition to using their official positions to press for human rights improvement, these appointees were also viewed by many as breaking the rules of the game and misusing their positions, access to information, and power to push their cause. Some were criticized for making unauthorized public statements which were embarrassing to the United States government, under the justification that they contributed to the cause of human rights. Others were said to be leaking information to the press and to the human rights lobby for their own purposes. They completely outmaneuvered their opponents in dealing with members of Congress and their staffs. They were accused of engaging in skillful character assassination of those whom they saw as being unhelpfully loyal to interests of the United States government other than the cause of human rights. . . . One leader of the lobby even gloated publicly that he and his associates were now in a position to know, within forty-eight hours, of everything that went on within the Department of State, [which was] evidence of the shocking disloyalty and disregard for security rules and procedures which had by now become commonplace. It was impossible to run a coherent foreign policy under these conditions.[12]

El Salvador would reap the results of the new policy after Carter's single term in office and would see bloodshed for ten more years as it became a battleground for worldwide leftists versus a Reagan administration determined to stop another communist foothold in the hemisphere. El Salvador's civil war, from 1979 until 1992, was emblematic of the Cuba-instigated wars in Latin America. It was Fidel Castro who convinced the various left-wing guerrilla groups operating in El Salvador to consolidate under the banner of the DRU, officially formed in May 1980. The DRU manifesto stated, "There will be only one leadership, only one military plan and only one command, only one political line." Fidel Castro had facilitated a meeting in Havana in December 1979 that brought these groups together—a feat that has not been repeated since, as the historic tendency of most leftist terrorist groups in the region has been of splintering after fights over egos and ideological differences.

It was a Salvadoran of Palestinian descent, Schafik Handal, who helped found the Communist Party of El Salvador and who would serve as Castro's partner in the Central American wars of the era. Handal and Castro utilized the age-old littoral smuggling routes around the Gulf of Fonseca, whose coastline borders El Salvador, Honduras, and Nicaragua, to arm leftist terrorist groups from Costa Rica to Guatemala with Soviet-supplied weaponry. But it was when the insurgencies inevitably failed that Castro's instructions for winning the peace processes proved much more successful.

After a series of elections showed that the Salvadoran public was rejecting the FMLN as a political entity after it had converted from a guerrilla group, Handal and other leftist leaders tried to gain an advantage for a future insurgency in the Chapultepec Peace Accords that were signed in Mexico City in January 1992. Handal constantly insisted that "the demilitarization and the reduction of the army will be the principal theme. It is the 'Gordian Knot' to resolve the peace in our country."[13]

Many journalists reported at the time that the guerrillas' principal concern was to force the government to dismantle the military in order to remove any obstacles for a future insurgency. An editorial in the Costa Rican daily *La Nación* stated, "Schafik Handal, one of the five top leaders of the guerrillas, has made clear in each stage, a permanent mistrust of the remainder of the military and police, and what will remain of its military equipment. It has become apparent that Handal and the hard-liners of the *Frente* virtually insist that the Government is left defenseless."[14]

This tactic of using the law to dismantle the military, the traditional foe of left-wing subversives in the region, would become a perennial tactic throughout the hemisphere in the years to come. Ironically, when Fidel Castro named himself "maximum leader" of the revolution and commander in chief of all the armed forces in the spring of 1959, he also promised to cut the size of the Cuban military in half and to eventually replace it with a revolutionary people's militia. "The last thing I am," he said, "is a military man. . . . Ours is a country without generals and colonels." Soon afterward, the maximum leader instituted compulsory military service and thoroughly militarized the Cuban state.[15] Just twelve years after the signing of the Chapultepec Peace Accords, Handal ran unsuccessfully for president against Antonio "Tony" Saca, another Salvadoran of Palestinian descent. Handal would die of a heart attack in the airport coming back from the inauguration of Evo Morales in Bolivia, just three years short of seeing his party finally win the presidency in 2009.

Castro's El Salvador campaign is illustrative, because it was the last major offensive before the collapse of his Soviet sponsor. As a result of this failure in El Salvador, the Castro-directed insurgencies throughout the continent adjusted their tactics, as did Castro himself. Without Soviet sponsorship and weaponry, Castro turned to a stealthier approach to insurgency, utilizing asymmetrical and political warfare to achieve his ends. It can be argued that post-Soviet subversion in Latin America has been far more successful than the Soviet-sponsored attempts during the thirty years.

Stealth NGOs

One of the most effective asymmetrical tactics has been the use of dummy NGOs as front groups in Latin America. A number of nongovernmental organizations operating in the region that claim to advocate for human rights actually receive funding from radical leftist groups sympathetic to revolutionary movements in the hemisphere. Many of these groups derive much of their legitimacy from unwitting representatives of the European Union, the United Nations, and even the U.S. Department of State who often designate them as "special rapporteurs" for human rights reporting.

One of the most effective tactics of these NGOs is to use the justice system to immerse the military and security forces in endless lawsuits and false accusations, allowing seasoned soldiers to be pulled from the battlefield without a shot being fired. The military has been the historical bulwark against communist and terrorist subversion in Latin America, and one of the stated objectives of radicals in the region has been to destroy popular support for the armed forces. One of the earliest declarations of this was by the Communist Party of Peru in 1970 in *Bandera Roja* magazine: "We must energetically destroy the bourgeois military line and eradicate its venomous influence in Latin America."[16]

The results of this campaign are now becoming more profound, with many military officers suddenly finding themselves in jail under a civilian court system that assumes guilt upon incarceration, while unrepentant ex-terrorists fill government posts that oversee their jurisprudence. In Argentina, for example, an ex-Montonero was appointed by the Cristina Kirchner government to design a curriculum for the country's military academies that would stress a more "humanist" approach.[17]

The two Kirchner administrations may be the most blatant abusers of this type of "judicial warfare." Both Cristina Fernández de Kirchner, the current president, and her husband, the late President Néstor Kirchner, were far-left radicals in the 1960s and 1970s and filled both of their administrations with ex-terrorists and radicals. Many have accused the Kirchners and their allies of blatant double standards on human rights issues—especially in the prosecution of former military members who served during Argentina's Dirty War from 1976 to 1983.[18]

Since 2003, when Néstor Kirchner took office, the successive Kirchner administrations have aggressively prosecuted hundreds of ex-soldiers, many of whom served prior to the beginning of the Dirty War.[19] The double standard arises because not one of the ex-terrorists, who started the Dirty War in the first place, has been prosecuted. The Kirchners, along with far-left judicial activists in the region, have relied on a blatantly unjust tenet of "international human rights law" that says crimes against humanity only apply to representatives of the state, a group that includes military and police but excludes the terrorists who ignited the guerrilla wars.

According to advocates of these prosecutions, terrorist actions fall under "international humanitarian law" rather than "international human rights law." Even if one accepts the legal finery, there has still been no attempt to bring prosecutions against even the most bloody of the erstwhile terrorists. Still, the hypocrisy of this claim to legal strenuousness was belied by a September 30, 2010, decision by the Argentine government to grant asylum to Galvarino Apablaza, a Chilean terrorist responsible for a number of kidnappings, bombings, and murders, including the assassination of Chilean senator Jaime Guzmán.[20]

This decision came even after a fellow terrorist gave a televised interview in which he implicated Apablaza as the ringleader in the murder of Guzmán. The reason given for the decision seemed more of an attempt to invent a special protected legal class for terrorists, claiming that because Apablaza was a "political militant" and a "fighter against the dictatorship," he was not a common citizen. This, noted *The Economist*, was "an implicit argument that former guerrillas should be above the law forever." It was later revealed that Apablaza's wife, Paula Chain, was working on the presidential staff in Cristina Kirchner's press office.[21]

The double standard in human rights litigation shows up most vividly in Colombia, where President Álvaro Uribe turned the country from a war-torn "failing state" to a bastion of stability and growth. While this made him a hero to the United States and to countries that uphold the rule of law, he became a target of international activists who, by constant accusations of human rights violations, attempted to tie the hands of his administration while it fought FARC terrorists.

The double standard was starkly revealed when the Colombian military executed Operation Checkmate (Operación Jaque), the rescue operation in 2008 that freed three American and twelve Colombian hostages. Uribe's decision to undertake such a risky operation, coupled with the aggressive pursuit of the FARC throughout the country, led to a flood of desertions of FARC terrorists. Uribe had drawn the ire of the international human rights activists when he stated that some of the self-labeled human rights NGOs in the country were actually fronts for terrorists. But his assertion was backed up by the success of Operation Checkmate. FARC commanders were tricked into handing over their most highly valued hostages by telling them that a helicopter to transport the hostages was being loaned to them by an NGO sympathetic to their cause. The NGO was completely fictitious, but the ruse worked because the terrorists had become accustomed to getting help from such groups. Mary Anastasia O'Grady, the *Wall Street Journal*'s Americas columnist, noted in her weekly column at the time, "It may have taken years for army intelligence to infiltrate the Revolutionary Armed Forces of Colombia, and it may have been tough to convincingly impersonate rebels. But what seems to have been a walk in the park was getting the FARC to believe that an NGO was providing resources to help it in the dirty work of ferrying captives to a new location."[22]

The late Foreign Policy Research Institute scholar Michael Radu, talking about the pre-Uribe era, when the FARC was given a demilitarized zone that was supposed to foster a peace agreement, commented, "One has to be open and blunt about

this—far too many ordinary Colombians were demanding 'peace' at any cost—
exactly what [President] Pastrana was trying to deliver. These Colombians had been
encouraged by the burgeoning human rights NGOs—Colombia harbors half of
such groups in Latin America, virtually all leftist and subsidized from abroad, largely
by groups in Europe but also by U.S. organizations, and most are infiltrated by or
sympathetic to FARC and its smaller Castroite rival, the National Liberation Army
(ELN)."[23]

O'Grady, writing about the NGO practice of "judicial warfare," noted that
"since the late 1990s, the NGO practice of dragging the military into court on alle-
gations of human rights violations has destroyed the careers of some of [Colombia's]
finest officers, even though most of these men were found innocent after years of
proceedings."[24]

According to O'Grady, the enabling legislation that makes this judicial warfare
possible is what's been termed the "Leahy Law," after its sponsor, Sen. Patrick Leahy
(D-VT). Under this law, American military aid can be withdrawn if military officers are not immediately pulled from duty once charges of human rights offenses are
brought against them, even when the credibility of the charges is dubious. O'Grady
noted, "The NGOs knew that they only had to point fingers to get rid of an effective
leader and demoralize the ranks."[25]

The legislation that became the Leahy Law was first introduced in 1997 in the
Foreign Operations Appropriations Act, and similar language was inserted into the
2001 Foreign Operations Appropriations Act. It has since been used repeatedly
against Colombia, which has been a target ever since it became serious about taking on the FARC and took funding from the United States to implement Plan Colombia, an anti-drug-smuggling and counterinsurgency initiative. Sen. Christopher
Dodd (D-CT), in his capacity as a senior Democrat on the Senate Foreign Relations
Committee and as chairman of the Subcommittee on the Western Hemisphere,
Peace Corps, and Narcotics Affairs, sent a letter in May 2007 to Secretary of State
Condoleezza Rice complaining that members of paramilitaries and drug cartels were
serving in the Uribe administration. The Dodd letter expressed concern about the
killing of "trade unionists," which some speculated was a premise for then Speaker of
the House Nancy Pelosi to stop a vote on a free trade agreement with Colombia. The
charge was given greater import when an article in the *New York Times* showed that
trade unionists were far safer than was the average Colombian citizen.[26]

The same month that Dodd sent the letter, FARC commander Luis Edgar Devia Silva, better known by his nom de guerre Raúl Reyes, was killed by the Colombian military. The publicity about Reyes's death put the spotlight on the situation
in Colombia and led researchers to uncover the fact that many of the so-called trade
unionists in Colombia were moonlighting as FARC terrorists.

Raul Reyes was the prime example, having begun his career at age sixteen when
he joined the Colombian Communist Youth (JUCO), which led him to become a
trade unionist at a Nestle plant in his hometown of Caqueta. His position as a Nestle
"trade unionist" was a front for his real job, which was influencing, recruiting, and
radicalizing fellow workers at a plant for the Colombian Communist Party (PCC).

As Reyes performed well in his job with the Communist Party, he began moving
up the ranks and eventually reached the highest level of the party—the secretariat of
the FARC. Since the beginning of the FARC, and its collaboration and later split
with the party, a number of Colombian trade unions have served as way stations for
FARC members as they moved from union posts to the ranks of the FARC.[27]

The general bias against the security forces and in favor of the guerrillas was illustrated when FARC-friendly Ecuador continued to allow its border region to be
used as a FARC redoubt, leading President Uribe to call for an attack on a FARC
camp in Sucumbíos, about a mile inside Ecuador's border. The OAS and many others in the international community issued condemnations of the Colombian air
strike. But these same organizations had been relatively silent when the Colombian
government registered its complaints about Ecuador's open-border policy for terrorists. Covering the conflict in March 2008, *Time* pointed out that "it's no secret the
FARC often hides out in Ecuador as well as Venezuela" and quoted Colombian vice
president Francisco Santos as saying that the FARC "is a drug cartel that kills civilians. It's like al-Qaeda, Hamas, Hizballah—where are we supposed to draw the line
for our security?"[28]

According to *Time*, Colombia's long-stated position was "that it wouldn't have
had to violate Ecuador's border if Correa, like Chávez, hadn't been harboring FARC
militants in his territory." Colombian foreign minister Fernando Araújo, who had
been a hostage of the FARC for six years, told the magazine, "If the FARC can constantly take refuge outside Colombia, it becomes a threat to regional stability, too."[29]

The attack inside Ecuador not only killed Reyes, the FARC's international
spokesperson, but it also allowed the Colombian military to capture a cache of intelligence from laptop computers and portable hard drives that revealed suspected

ties between the FARC and Hugo Chávez. The information on the hard drives laid bare the connections among many of the groups that Uribe had earlier accused of collaboration.[30]

Uribe was able to turn the tide against the FARC because of help from the United States, initially through the antinarcotics funding in Plan Colombia. But the key difference was the strategic transition from the largely fruitless supply-control methods of Plan Colombia to the population-centric counterinsurgency (PC-COIN) methods of Plan Patriota, a later iteration of the original plan that put the focus on counterinsurgency. President Uribe, with U.S. help, transitioned from the counterproductive eradication of peasant coca crops to the successful eradication of FARC legitimacy. Where the previous policy had granted a vast demilitarized zone to the FARC in exchange for a proposed peace treaty, Plan Patriota utilized a counterinsurgency strategy that attacked the terrorists with physical force. But more importantly, it attacked their legitimacy by placing security personnel in remote areas where there had been no state presence before. What this accomplished, more successfully than any of the Colombian military's previous operational tactics, was to change the population's perception of the forty-year-old insurgency. What had been seen as a conflict between rival political parties was now looked upon as the battle of a legitimate, elected government against illegitimate narco-terrorists.

Revolutionizing the Military

Where left-wing leaders and militants have been unsuccessful in dismantling the military, they have fallen back on a contingency plan to "revolutionize" it. The purpose is to change the military in their own countries from an organization that exists to defend the country from external threats to one that aids the regime in cementing its hold on power. In Venezuela, Chávez's new constitution would eliminate civilian control and would concentrate more power under the executive. The new constitution would also remove the word "professionalism" from the description of the military's values and replace it with "patriotic, popular and anti-imperialist."[31] The 1999 constitution also added a provision for military suffrage, another harbinger of the coming politicization of the armed forces.

In 2001 the Venezuelan daily *Tal Cual* published a leaked document from the Directorate of Military Intelligence (Dirección de Inteligencia Militar, or DIM), which spelled out a plan to politicize the military.[32] According to the document, top military officers were to be divided into "revolutionists" who supported Chávez, "institutionalists" who were considered to be neutral, and "dissidents" who were opposed to the regime. It also advocated *catequesis* (Spanish for catechism) to proselytize these officers to accept Chávez's socialist governing program.

For those officers considered to be resistant to Chávez's governing vision, the DIM document suggested a "slow and voluntary segregation" from the military. In other words, the plan was to make those who wouldn't readily accede to 21st Century Socialism so uncomfortable and stagnated in their careers that they would voluntarily leave the military. The measures proposed in the plan, according to the document, were necessary to "strengthen the project of the Commander in Chief."[33]

11

MANAGING THE MILITIAS

Yuri Andropov, KGB director from 1967 to 1982, had always suffered from what his communist colleagues called his "Hungarian complex." During the Hungarian Uprising in 1956, Andropov "had watched in horror from the windows of his embassy as officers of the hated Hungarian security service were strung up from lampposts." It is said that Andropov was "haunted for the rest of his life by the speed with which an apparently all-powerful Communist one-party state had begun to topple" and was thereafter "obsessed with the need to stamp out 'ideological sabotage' wherever it reared its head within the Soviet bloc." This obsession made the Soviets much more eager to send in troops whenever other communist regimes were in jeopardy.[1] It also helped convince the politburo to initiate military intervention during the Prague Spring of 1968, and when problems began in Kabul in 1979, Andropov stated his obsessive view of "ideological subversion" at a KGB conference: "We simply do not have the right to permit even the smallest miscalculation here, for in the political sphere any kind of ideological sabotage is directly or indirectly intended to create an opposition which is hostile to our system . . . and, in the final analysis, to create the conditions for the overthrow of socialism." Again, in Warsaw in 1981, Andropov would also come to the conclusion that "only armed force could ensure [the Communists'] survival."[2]

Similarly, after the failed invasion at the Bay of Pigs in 1962 and after the 2002 two-day coup in Venezuela, both Castro and Chávez would develop a Hungarian complex as well, leading to a clampdown on "ideological sabotage" within their respective countries. In 1988 Castro stated, when speaking of the Sandinistas' use of civilian militias to defend their revolution in Nicaragua, that both Cuba and

Nicaragua needed a "committed . . . people's armed defense that is sufficient in size, training and readiness," adding that Salvador Allende hadn't had a big enough force to prevent the coup that drove him from power in Chile in 1973.[3] It was a rare moment of candor, as the militia is usually touted as a last bastion against a U.S. invasion. But in reality, it is a tool designed to accomplish the prime objective of an aspiring autocrat—to ensure the longevity of the regime. Max Manwaring, writing on Chávez's use of these civilian militias, stated:

> All these institutions are outside the traditional control of the regular armed forces, and each organization is responsible directly to the leader (President Chávez). This institutional separation is intended to ensure that no one military or paramilitary organization can control another, but the centralization of these institutions guarantees the leader absolute control of security and social harmony in Venezuela.[4]

Perpetuating the Regime

Other leaders within the ALBA countries have implemented similar plans to either purge the military or to check its power with militias and neighborhood committees that are loyal only to the regime. In Argentina what began as a protest group has turned into a civilian militia in the form of the piqueteros (picketers in English). Started as a jobless protest in 1996, the piqueteros have transformed into what are, according to *The Economist*, "government rent-a-mobs" consisting of "unemployed protesters receiving state welfare payments."[5] The piqueteros were co-opted by Nestor Kirchner's government, though some have splintered since his wife succeeded him.

In Bolivia President Evo Morales has developed a history of using violent mobs to attack the opposition. On March 7, 2009, a mob assaulted the home of former vice president Victor Hugo Cárdenas with his wife and children inside. Cárdenas, who had served as vice president for President Gonzalo Sánchez de Lozada (now living in exile in the United States) and who had led the campaign against approval of Morales's new constitution, was not home at the time of the incident.[6] The mob broke into the house and tried to set it on fire, then beat Cárdenas's wife and children as they tried to escape. They were hospitalized for two days. Cárdenas had asked the regional police for protection after receiving information that the attack was imminent, to no avail. The police, either fearful of or loyal to Morales, also failed to respond to numerous calls from the Cárdenas family as the incident took place.[7]

Since then, Morales has gone much further, turning Bolivia into a training center to professionalize these mobs from throughout the region. And he has enlisted Iran to help with the project. In 2008, Morales moved Bolivia's only embassy in the Middle East from Cairo to Tehran, and Iran reciprocated by opening a new embassy in Bolivia. In a trip to Tehran in October 2010, Morales said, "Iran and Bolivia have an identical revolutionary conscience which allows for the expansion of relations and accounts for the closeness of the two states."[8] By that time, this type of rhetoric had become so commonplace among the ALBA leaders, it hardly made news. But when it was discovered that the Iranian regime was actually financing a militia training facility in Bolivia, security analysts became much more concerned. On August 5, 2010, a Bolivian TV station broadcast a story showing video of civilians at a Bolivian military base receiving militia training. The participants even included young indigenous women wearing the traditional full-length skirts and bowler hats, bringing to mind the sordid history of radical groups exploiting indigenous populations for insurrections against Latin American governments. When questioned about the story, Vice President Álvaro García acknowledged that Morales's government was following the Chávez example by building a civilian militia "to help defend the Bolivian homeland." García, a former leftist guerrilla, said that it was "a citizen's duty" to join the militia. He added that the purpose of the training was to enable Bolivian civilians to assist in defending the homeland.[9] But the Bolivians had even bigger plans.

In November 2010 Bolivian defense minister Rubén Saavedra revealed that the militia training facility would be used to train militia members from throughout the region. He stated that "the formal establishment of the School of Defense will be the responsibility of the ALBA presidents. We consider that it is a very important advance." Saavedra added, "The goal is to train not only military personnel but also civilians who are interested in security and defense issues. The coordination is being established with all the ALBA countries."[10]

In February 2011 the gravity of the effort to militarize Morales's civilian supporters became far clearer. According to *ABC*, a Paraguayan daily, Iran was providing the financing for the militia training facility. Called the Military Academy of ALBA, it is located in Warnes, thirty miles north of Santa Cruz. *ABC* reported that the facility would train both military personnel and civilian militia members from all of the ALBA countries.[11]

Jack Terpins, the president of the Latin American Jewish Congress, stated that Iran's gesture of financing the military academy in Bolivia is "a confession that Iran is arming an army" in Latin America.[12] The most stunning aspect of Iran's boldness in inserting itself militarily in Latin America was that on the day that the militia training facility opened in Bolivia, Iran's minister of defense, Ahmad Vahidi, attended the ceremony. Vahidi was wanted by Interpol for his involvement in the deadliest terrorist bombing in Argentina's history, the 1994 AMIA bombing. When the Argentine government was made aware of his presence in Bolivia's capital, it loudly protested, but Vahidi was able to slip quietly out of the country because of diplomatic immunity.[13]

The involvement of Iran in training Latin American militias has brought far greater import to the threat that these militias may pose and augurs the possibility of much more aggressive and violent suppression of opposition groups. When the Iranian regime faced its greatest threat in the 2009 elections, it not only committed what was widely considered electoral fraud but also unleashed severe violence upon the opposition.[14] In 2002, when Hugo Chávez invoked Plan Ávila, giving government sanction to the use of deadly force against opposition protesters, he provoked his own ouster. Since then, he has avoided violent public confrontations and has relied much more on proxy groups to suppress the opposition.

Chávez has long used the Bolivarian Circles, the armed thugs on scooters and motorcycles who threw eggs at the U.S. ambassador's car in 2006 and shot at student protesters in 2008. But the Bolivarian Circles were not sufficient to stop the large protest march on Baralt Avenue in 2002, when the military refused to attack civilians. Since that time, Chávez has worked to develop a far larger militia to deter the opposition from thinking about expelling him from office again.

In October 2010 Chávez declared that his Bolivarian Militia members should be armed at all times, rather than just issued weapons for weekend drills. On one of his weekly TV shows, Chávez asked, "Who has seen a militia without weapons? . . . We need to break old paradigms because we're still seeing the militias as if they were a complementary force, some battalions that get together once a month over there, or go and march somewhere. No, buddy. The militia is a permanent territorial unit and it should be armed, equipped and trained. Campesinos, workers."[15]

Besides the Bolivarian Militia, Chávez can call on a number of other violent groups. The Alexis Vive Collective, a youth group based in a poor Caracas barrio, was used to attack the independent news station Globovisión, painting pro-Chávez

slogans on the walls and windows while police looked on. Chávez, instead of casti-
gating the lawlessness, took to the airwaves to accuse Globovisión of inciting violence
by broadcasting the violent Chavista demonstrations, and he threatened to close the
station down if it continued doing so.[16]

Building the Revolutionary Farm Team

In Venezuela, as well as in much of the rest of Latin America, universities have long
been the historial seat of radicalism and left-wing activism, providing a launching
pad for the careers of many young politicians whose families may not have been part
of the political elite. This university-based radicalism has often been exacerbated by
a concept in Latin American universities called *autonomia* (autonomy), which effectively means that there is a tacit understanding that law enforcement holds no juris-
diction on a university campus. Historically law enforcement personnel have been
prohibited from entering university grounds, even in pursuit of criminals, if they did
not get a search warrant first. Predictably this led to guerrillas and terrorist groups
utilizing campuses as escape routes to evade police during violent eras in the region.[17]

The concept of university autonomy is a colonial-era import from Europe. Universities in Spain, and later in Spanish Latin America, were designed after those of
medieval Bologna, where they were structured like corporate communities, with the
students serving as management. Unlike the French model of the era, where professors and rectors were the authority, Spanish students were allowed to elect their
university's administrators.[18]

The first instance of autonomia in Latin America began in 1918 at the National
University of Córdoba in Argentina, and the concept spread quickly throughout the
region. Shortly after Castro's guerrillas took power in Havana, Cuban embassies in
Latin America became recruitment centers and incubators for radical groups and terrorist subversives throughout the hemisphere. Organizing subversive student movements became a priority for Cuban "diplomats," and the autonomy of the campuses
provided easy access and impunity.

Venezuelan president Raúl Leoni called these autonomous universities "a state
within a state" that enjoyed "extraterritoriality."[19] An example was University City in
Caracas, the seat of the Central University of Venezuela. A comparison of the student vote to that of the general population at the time provides an illustration of the
radicalization of the student body. During the 1960s in Venezuela, students at the
Central University typically voted 50 to 60 percent for candidates from the Commu-

nist Party of Venezuela and the radical Castroite MIR, while these candidates never broke 10 percent among the general population.[20]

A Venezuelan MIR guerrilla noted that their near total domination of the *liceos* (secondary schools) and the universities led them to wrongly believe that this level of acceptance could be extrapolated to the general population. But in reality, noted the guerrilla, "there was absolutely no mass solidarity with the idea of insurrection." One MIR cofounder, Domingo Alberto Rangel, noted after renouncing the group's support for terrorism that "the Left enjoys support among students, but it is unknown among working-class youth, or the youth of the barrios."[21]

Before Fulgencio Batista was ousted as Cuba's president, students at the autonomous University of Havana organized a guerrilla front that fought out of the Sierra Escambray, though Castro quickly outlawed autonomy in Cuba's universities after taking power. In Colombia, the Industrial University of Santander in Bucaramanga was a haven for that country's ELN terrorists. In 1965 in Peru, the ELN based itself in the San Cristóbal of Huamanga National University in Ayacucho, and at the National University of Lima a number of leftist political parties set up operations for MIR terrorists.[22]

Just over twenty years later, after Shining Path and Túpac Amaru terrorists had gained control over a majority of the rural area of Peru and had begun to threaten the capital, the (first) government of President Alan García reluctantly decided to raid the University of San Marcos, the National University of Engineering, and a teachers' college—three schools that had long been known as terrorist havens.[23]

According to García's interior minister at the time, Abel Salinas, 4,000 police carried out the raids and arrested 793 people, but because so few of those arrested carried identification documents, they had no idea how many were actually students. Because the concept of university autonomy was so sacrosanct, the police were required by García to be accompanied by members of the attorney general's office to "prevent abuses." After the raid, Salinas showed reporters "one automatic weapon, 18 handguns, homemade explosives, dynamite and stacks of propaganda in support of the Shining Path and other terror groups"—all confiscated from the university campuses. Despite these weapon caches and wholesale infiltration by nonstudents, as well as students moonlighting as terrorists, García was strongly criticized for taking the decisive action. The rector of San Marcos University, Jorge Campos Rey, claimed that the raids added "to the escalation of the violence in the country." One senator who was even allied with García said, "I ask myself if what was found justified the intervention and its political repercussions."[24]

This kind of autonomy without accountability, a policy that invites terrorist infiltration among impressionable young people, continues today. In June 2010, the Peruvian newspaper *Peru 21* reported on the return of terrorism-supporting students in San Marcos University. The group of radical students had not only returned to campus, but they also had set up a table for the university's registration day and were greeting new students as they arrived. Shortly afterward, Manuel Fajardo, the lawyer for incarcerated terrorist leader Abimael Guzmán, gave a speech to a group of students that was followed by a protest march of about fifty students calling for amnesty for Guzmán and other Shining Path terrorists.[25]

When FARC terrorist Raúl Reyes was killed in 2008, five Mexican students were in the camp at the time. Four were killed in the bombing. Investigations by the Mexican press brought attention to the National Autonomous University of Mexico (UNAM), where they were enrolled. Investigations of UNAM found that parts of the university had been taken over by radical leftist groups, including Rebellion (Rebeldía), The Brigade Member (El Brigadista), Conscience and Freedom (Conciencia y Libertad), Front for Student Struggle Julio Antonio Mella (Frente de Lucha Estudiantil Julio Antonio Mella), and Collective Lucio Cabañas, Carlos Marx, and Ernesto Guevara (Colectivo Lucio Cabañas, Carlos Marx, and Ernesto Guevara). Another campus group, the Bolivarian Continental Coordinator (Coordinadora Continental Bolivariana), is dedicated to supporting Chávez's Bolivarian revolution.[26] A university strike in 1999 had provided the impetus for the radical groups to take over dozens of classrooms and other spaces. Because of an incident in 1968 in which three hundred radical students were gunned down by the Mexican army, the government had been reluctant to crack down on the student takeover of the university.

UNAM's School of Philosophy and Letters was singled out as the most accommodating to the student radicals. Its auditorium had been taken over by radical left-wing students, who renamed it the "Che Guevara Auditorium." In the Simón Bolívar section of the faculty office, students were found selling a documentary titled *Guerrilla Girl* by Danish filmmaker Frank Piasecki Poulsen, who is touted as a "former squatter and left-wing activist." The film follows the journey of "Isabel," a female college student who travels to Colombia with the approval of her radical father to join the FARC. A story in the *Miami Herald* about the radicals operating in UNAM reported, "The sign by the classroom door reads 'Video Library Fidel Castro.' Inside, a painted five-point red star with a black hammer and sickle at its center covers one wall. On the adjacent wall, posters with images of a young Fidel Castro, Argentine revolutionary Ernesto 'Che' Guevara and a militant Zapatista promote meetings and marches."[27]

A U.S. Embassy cable written at the time stated, "In 2003, Colombia's Ambassador to [M]exico publicly voiced concern over FARC's continued activities here, asserting that the organization worked through fellow travelers in UNAM's philosophy department, but he provided few details. Charges have also surfaced over the years that the organization has links to various indigenous guerilla [sic] groups, including the Popular Revolutionary Army (EPR)."[28]

Like guerrilla groups in many countries in Latin America, Mexico's also have a cadre of supporters in NGOs who purport to be human rights advocates. After the bombing of the FARC camp, instead of denouncing the FARC for hosting Mexican students in a war zone, one Mexican human rights NGO called the operation an "unjustified massacre" and announced that it was planning to sue the Colombian government.[29] The president of the group tried to excuse the students' presence in the FARC camp by making the claim that one of the students was working on a thesis "about the role in the insurgency of the folkloric music style Vallenato."[30]

This was reminiscent of a similar incident that occurred in Mexico in 1982. In the 1980s, Mexico, like Venezuela and Ecuador today, served as a haven for guerrillas who utilized border areas for evading authorities. Guatemalan guerrillas often escaped to Mexico after attacking government troops and civilians. And Mexico also housed training camps where terrorist tactics were taught to Latin American and even Palestinian terrorists. In February 1982 Nicaraguan citizen Ligdamis Gutiérrez Espinosa was captured crossing into El Salvador via the Guatemalan border. Gutiérrez Espinosa admitted to authorities that he had trained at the Technical Institute of Coahuila (later the Technical Institute of Saltillo) in Saltillo, Mexico. According to Gutiérrez Espinosa, of the forty terrorist trainees at the camp, twenty were from El Salvador, six were from Mexico, and the rest were from Nicaragua. The Mexican government adamantly denied the charge and claimed that Gutiérrez Espinosa was just a "college student on vacation."[31]

While Latin American universities have long been used as sanctuaries by terrorist groups, many nonradicals in the region still support university autonomy as a legal means to keep the government out of university curricula. But while autonomy has been utilized by leftist radicals and terrorists with little resistance, the law has not stopped autocrats in the region from encroaching on the universities' independence.

In the hastily approved raft of laws that Chávez pushed through in the lame-duck session in December 2010, just before he was about to lose his overwhelming congressional majority, there was one that looked as if it would bring a welcome end to this type of autonomy. The new law on education, while removing the universi-ties' autonomy, also allowed Chávez's government more control over not only boards of directors at the universities but also the elections of student leaders. This was not the first time that Chávez had attempted to codify the indoctrination of Venezuelan students. In February 2001, his supporters drew up new constitutional provisions to require all secondary schools to teach "Bolivarian principles." Chávez backed the provision, saying that education reform in Venezuela should focus on ensuring the "irreversibility" of his Bolivarian revolution. In January 2001 Chávez issued Decree 1.011, creating "itinerant inspectors" who were given the authority to close schools and fire teachers who weren't conducting classes according to the new government edict.[32] In November 2001, Chávez supporters with bricks and rocks attacked par-ents and teachers marching to the congress against the Chávez education edicts.[33]

On March 11, 2011, Chávez announced the creation of a new "Ministry of Youth and Students," a government agency that would be run by young people, who, according to Chávez, have enough "fire to make a revolution." He stated that the exact makeup of the new ministry was still being worked out, but he suggested that its members "flood the streets doing politics, culture, and with the socialist mes-sage."[34] The new ministry may have been superfluous, as a number of radical student movements already did the bidding of the Chávez regime on university campuses. *El Universal* reported on June 11, 2009, that the radical student movement M-28 had laid out a written plan, with support from Chávez's vice minister of student policy, Enry Gómez, to take over six universities that they described as "the epicenter of the Venezuelan right." The plan, called the "Movement for University Transformation," was designed to ensure that these universities would also "involve themselves in the movement for 21st Century Socialism."[35]

Venezuela has a history of student radicalism. And Chávez, rather than confront the student radicals, has instead chosen to co-opt them to build a "revolutionary farm team." From 2001 to 2003, at the University of the Andes in Mérida, Tarek El Aissami and Hugo Cabezas were "student leaders" in what was described as a dormitory that had been taken over by armed leftist guerrillas and Chávez-supporting radicals who vastly outnumbered actual students. Student leader Cabezas was one of the founders of Utopia, an armed radical group said to be affiliated with the Bolivarian Liberation Front. El Aissami served as student body president at the university, where it is alleged that he and a group of radical students turned the dorms into criminal sanctuaries, in which there were stolen vehicles, drug transactions, and members of guerrilla groups.[36]

According to *U.S. News & World Report*, supporters were "alleged to have consolidated their control of the . . . student dormitories and turned them into a haven for armed political and criminal groups."[37] The *Miami Herald* cited a report done by Oswaldo Alcalá, the vice rector of academic affairs at the university, that stated that "of 1,122 people living in the eight residences, only 387 are active students and more than 600 have no university connections." The vice rector also said of the residences where this group of radical students lived with other students, "There's always weapons there. This is something you see in the movies." According to the *Miami Herald,* El Aissami was born in Venezuela to Syrian parents, and his father, Carlos, was the president of the Venezuelan branch of the Baath Party and was an ardent supporter of Saddam Hussein. El Aissami's uncle, Shibli el-Aissami, whose whereabouts are unknown, was a top-ranking Baath Party official in Iraq.[38] After telling the reporter that his son was not a member of the Baath Party, Carlos showed an article that he (the father) had written just after 9/11, in which he called President George W. Bush "genocidal, mentally deranged, a liar and a racist" and praised Osama bin Laden as "the great Mujahedeen."[39]

Seeing the potential in the two student radicals El Aissami and Cabezas, Chávez appointed them director and deputy director of the National Office of Identification and Immigration (Oficina Nacional de Identificación y Extranjería, or ONIDEX), which controls identification cards and immigration. Both El Aissami and Cabezas have been reported to have illegally issued Venezuelan passports and identification documents to operatives of Hezbollah and Hamas.[40]

Reporting on ONIDEX in 2003, *U.S. News & World Report* quoted "an American official with firsthand knowledge of the ID scheme," who said that there were spreadsheets categorized by nationality that contained "several thousand" individuals from terrorism-sponsoring countries who had been issued Venezuelan IDs by ONIDEX under Chávez. The unnamed official stated that "Colombians were the largest group; there were more than a thousand of them. It also included many from

Middle Eastern 'countries of interest' like Syria, Egypt, Pakistan, Lebanon. It was shocking to see how extensive the list was."[41]

After seeing the performance of El Aissami and Cabezas, Chávez has looked for ways to produce more students like them. Every education decree since Decree 1.011 has sought to make the entire education system similar to the environment created under El Aissami and Cabezas. And all have been similar to the decree in calling for "reeducating" university graduates "in order to implement and execute state social action programs under the leadership of Commander Chávez."[42]

Reeducating the young has long been a priority in autocratic regimes. Chávez understands that his international image is as important to his survival as his domestic approval ratings, and having young faces as ambassadors for the regime can only help, especially if they can also be called out to the streets to defend it when needed. Moreover, military and police crackdowns on civilians don't play well on international news channels. As the *New York Times* reported on the Basij in 2009, the Iranian government "decided to invest in a force that could take over the streets that didn't look like a military deployment."[43] After Iran's fraudulent elections in 2009, it was the IRGC and the Basij militias that kept Ahmadinejad in office. The lesson was not lost on Chávez or his ALBA allies.

12

EXPORTING
THE REVOLUTION

La Revolución, as Fidel Castro calls his life's mission, has narrowly escaped several near-death experiences. But it wasn't until Chávez came along and provided ready access to Venezuela's oil wealth that it was truly resuscitated. Long before he began his quest to undermine the United States, Castro had initiated a number of ill-fated expeditions against neighboring countries in Latin America. Even before he took power in Cuba, Castro joined a group when he was attending university in the late 1940s called the "Caribbean League," which consisted of members of the "democratic left" who wanted to overthrow the authoritarian governments in Nicaragua and the Dominican Republic.[1]

After coming to power in 1959, Castro chose as his first foreign junket a visit to Venezuela, where he asked President Rómulo Betancourt for a $300 million loan to help with his "master plan against the gringos." President Betancourt later related the story of Castro's plan:

> This consisted in the government of Venezuela lending $300 million dollars to the government of Cuba. I replied that this was impossible, that at the beginning of this period of constitutional government, our treasury was in a bad state. Its reserves were depleted, and the public debt, though undetermined, was estimated to exceed four billion bolivars. I told Dr. Castro that because of Venezuela's serious financial situation, my financial advisers and I were considering the need of taking advantage of a negotiation already advanced by the provisional government for contracting a $200 million dollar short-term loan in the United States.[2]

Within weeks of Betancourt's rebuff, Castro was training guerrillas to assassinate him and to invade Venezuela in order to join up with guerrilla groups there to take over the country and its oil resources.[3] But Castro's plan would have to wait a few decades. In 2004 Hugo Chávez would welcome Castro and several thousand Cubans in through the front door, as he filled his security and military headquarters with Cuban Intelligence Directorate agents who now manage the most sensitive areas of the Venezuelan government.[4]

Chávez would also replenish Cuban coffers that had suffered since the Soviets were forced to cut off subsidies, providing approximately $3.5 billion a year by sending an estimated 115,000 barrels of oil per day. To maintain his increasingly fragile regime, Castro then resells Venezuelan oil to other Central American nations for hard currency.[5]

From its inception, Castro's Cuba has served as an incubator for subversives and terrorists with an array of nationalities and ideological pedigrees. Long after Che Guevara's ill-fated mission in Bolivia, Castro has continued to hone the skills of subversion and has utilized those skills both in Latin America and in the United States.[6]

Castro declared early on that he would "turn the Andes into the Sierra Maestra of Latin America," referring to the mountains where his guerrilla group began its insurrection in Cuba. Eyewitnesses have reported that as early as February 1959, just weeks after Castro and his guerrillas ousted Batista, guerrilla camps in Cuba were training foreigners—mostly Nicaraguans, Haitians, and Panamanians—to invade their own countries in replication of the triumph of the Cuban revolution.[7]

The extent of Cuban subversion was investigated and reported to Congress as early as 1963, when the Senate Judiciary Committee released a report detailing the activities of Cuban operatives in the hemisphere. The report concluded: "A 'war of liberation' or 'popular uprising' is really hidden aggression: subversion . . . the design of Communist expansion finds in subversion the least costly way of acquiring peoples and territories without exaggerated risk."

The report elaborated on the goals of Cuban subversion:

Its aim is to replace the political, economic, and social order existing in a country by a new order, which presupposes the complete physical and moral control of the people. . . . That control is achieved by progressively gaining possession of bodies and minds, using appropriate techniques of subversion that combine psychological, political, social, and economic actions, and even military operations, if this is necessary.

In March 1963, CIA director John McCone reported to the House Foreign Affairs Subcommittee that approximately fifteen hundred people had been trained in terrorist tactics in Cuba in 1962 alone. McCone told the committee:

> The Cuban effort at present is far more serious than the hastily organized and ill-conceived raids that the bearded veterans of the Sierra Maestra led into such Central American countries as Panama, Haiti, Nicaragua, and the Dominican Republic during the first eight or nine months Castro was in power. . . . Today, the Cuban effort is far more sophisticated, more covert and more deadly. In its professional tradecraft, it shows guidance and training by experienced Communist advisers from the Soviet bloc, including veteran Spanish Communists.[8]

McCone stated that Castro's terrorist trainings lasted as long as a year and included intensive courses in infiltration, sabotage, propaganda, and psychological warfare. The participants were also used as mules for Soviet money laundering and for passing clandestine information among the worldwide terrorist diaspora.[9]

Once he had subdued the population of Cuba, Castro set his sights on Venezuela, an obvious target for leftist revolutionaries looking for financial support for their hemispheric revolution. In July 1966 Castro sent a small force of Venezuelans and Cubans into the eastern coast of Falcón State in a guerrilla invasion ironically dubbed Operation Simón Bolívar. The group was detected within twenty-four hours of landing and nearly wiped out by Venezuelan troops.

Undeterred, on May 10, 1967, a dozen more Cuban and Venezuelan guerrillas landed on the Venezuelan coast in two rafts at the town of Machurucuto. *Time*, writing about the incident in 1967, stated, "Two men were captured —the first uniformed Cuban army men that the Venezuelans have ever nabbed. . . . The Venezuelan episode was a blatant example of the way Fidel Castro is attempting to export his revolution to other Latin American countries. Though he so far has met with little real success."[10]

Though the Caribbean League would fail in its mission to overthrow Somoza, Castro would be welcomed by the top echelon of Nicaragua's government in 1979. Like the Chavistas in Venezuela today, the Nicaraguan Sandinistas were also amenable to handing control over key positions to Castro's Cubans. Beginning in 1979, the first time that Daniel Ortega was at the helm in Nicaragua, Castro sent an "international brigade" to fight with the Sandinistas, along with about five hundred tons of weapons and supplies.[11] It was reported by a defector that all Sandinista military plans were sent first to Havana to be vetted by Raúl Castro and a Soviet handler before any action was taken against the contras.[12]

The first Cuban nonmilitary advisers arrived in Managua the same day that the Sandinistas took power. The Sandinista leadership, in fact, was reported to be holding secret meetings with Fidel Castro in Somoza's abandoned beach house, Montelimar, in the first days of the Sandinista takeover, at which Castro made many of the important decisions for the new Sandinista government.[13] On July 18, 1979, Julián López Díaz, one of Castro's top covert operatives, arrived in Nicaragua to become a key adviser and would stay on to become the Cuban ambassador.[14]

In June 1983, the *New York Times* reported that Arnaldo Ochoa Sánchez, Castro's top military commander, who had led Castro's first attempt to invade Venezuela in 1966 and had been put in charge of Cuba's forays into Angola and Ethiopia in the 1970s, was said to be "secretly assigned to duty" in Nicaragua.[15] And by the end of 1983, it was reported that there were three thousand Cuban military and security advisers in Nicaragua, as well as five thousand nonmilitary technicians.[16] A State Department background paper also reported that besides the influx of thousands of Cuban "advisers," nearly all of the members of the new state police organization, the General Directorate of Sandinista State Security, were trained by Cubans.[17]

Alfonso Robelo, one of the original members of Nicaragua's five-man junta, told reporters, "This is something you have to understand, Nicaragua is an occupied country. We have 8,000 Cubans plus several thousand East Bloc people, East Gemans, PLO, Bulgarians, Libyans, North Koreans, etc. The national decisions, the crucial ones, are not in the hands of the Nicaraguans, but in the hands of Cubans. . . . And, really, in the end, it is not the Cubans, but the Soviets."[18]

A May 1983 State Department report said there were around fifty Soviet military advisers and around a hundred economic advisers in Nicaragua. According to the report, "About twenty-five of the Soviet personnel are assisting the security services, and the others are attached to the Nicaraguan General Staff and the headquarters of various military services."[19]

While many foreign policy experts and officials in the Carter administration scoffed at the idea of either Soviet or Cuban steering of the Sandinistas, numerous defectors later confirmed it. Victor Tirado, one of the original Sandinistas, wrote in 1991 that "we allowed ourselves to be guided by the ideas of the Cubans and the Soviets." Alvaro Baldizón, a chief investigator of the Sandinista Ministry of the Interior, said after defecting, "The ones who give the orders are the Cubans. . . . Every program, every operation is always under the supervision of Cuban advisers."[20] The former chief of police for internal order under the Sandinistas, Miguel Urroz Blanco, also declared, "A suggestion made by the Cubans is an unbreakable order."[21]

The only successful and sustained Marxist insurgency in Latin America has been that of Fidel Castro and that was only after the United States openly withdrew support from Fulgencio Batista's government. Not since 1959 has another left-wing insurgency actually accomplished its goal of overthrowing the existing government by force and installing its governing vision for any extended period of time. But Castro has been behind almost every attempt at leftist subversion in the hemisphere since taking power in 1959.

After cheering the 1959 ousting of the autocrat Batista, the Castro regime quickly removed the delusion that leftist suitors to the throne might be any better than the military juntas that had typically been the ones to throw them out. Military governments in Latin America have at least been persuaded at some point to hold elections and have given up power when they were defeated at the ballot box.

Chávez often refers to Cuba as "a sea of happiness" for average Cubans and says that his Bolivarian socialism plan will develop a similar model for Venezuela.[22] But for Venezuela's immediate needs and to help him implement his plan, Chávez has imported between thirty thousand and sixty thousand Cubans to work in jobs ranging from coaching soccer and serving in neighborhood health clinics all the way up to advising the military at the highest levels.[23] Gen. Antonio Rivero, a Venezuelan general who spent time in jail with Chávez after participating in his failed 1992 coup attempt, caused some consternation in a June 2010 press conference when he announced that Chávez was allowing Cubans free rein over the army, including access to state secrets. Rivero told reporters that Chávez was "remodeling the army along Cuban lines" and that Cuban advisers had enjoyed "free run of the country since 2007."[24]

A long-term Chávez ally, Rivero served as head of emergency services in his government until 2008, when he resigned after a twenty-five-year career. Rivero also reported that Cubans were present in the Strategic Operational Command, Venezuela's highest military planning department, and while they were not officially in the chain of command, their advice often overruled that of Venezuelan military officers. "One thing is to learn from them, another to receive instructions," Rivero lamented.[25]

Chávez's relationship with Castro goes back to the 1990s, when he was personally invited by the Cuban dictator for a hero's reception in Havana after being released from prison for leading the failed 1992 coup. It would be less than a decade before the overture would pay dividends.

In April 2003, Castro sent the first Cuban doctors to Venezuela as part of a program called "Misión Barrio Adentro" (Mission Inside the Barrio). According to Castro's autobiography, *My Life*, Chávez paid for these Cuban doctors (and soccer coaches et alia) by sending 53,000 barrels of oil per day, at preferential prices, and on a payment plan.[26] These "community doctors" are actually at the medical training level of some emergency medical technicians or paramedics in the United States and only complete three years of medical school and one year of a pseudo-residency. They are then sent with the dual purpose of treating patients in poor communities while indoctrinating the community in Cuban-Marxist dogma. Because of Cuban doctors' high defection rate, minders are sent along to dissuade them from fleeing. They are also prohibited from fraternizing with local people outside of work, though this rule has proved hard to enforce.[27] In 2007 the medical journal *The Lancet* wrote that "growing numbers of Cuban doctors sent overseas to work are defecting to the USA" and that "Cuban doctors working abroad are reported to be monitored by 'minders' and subject to curfew." In February 2010 a group of seven Cuban doctors who defected and made it to the United States filed an indictment against both Cuba and Venezuela, as well as the PDVSA, for putting them in "conditions of indentured servitude" and turning them into "economic slaves."[28]

The indictment alleged that the agreement between Cuba and Venezuela to send doctors to work in slave-like conditions "constitutes a flagrant conspiracy comparable to the slave trade in colonial America."[29] The chairman of the Venezuelan Medical Federation reported in July 2007 that 70 percent of the Barrio Adentro branches had either been abandoned or their construction had never been completed.[30]

Since the Barrio Adentro program began in Venezuela in October 2000, the number of Cubans in the country has grown to somewhere between forty thousand and sixty-five thousand, depending on the source. In the last two years, Cuban influence has reached much higher levels of the Venezuelan government, including the security and military establishments, as well as within the bureaus that issue identity documents. Since 2005, when Cuba and Venezuela signed an agreement for the automation of personal identification systems, the number of Cubans working in the bureaucracy that controls and issues identity documents has grown significantly.[31] In a 2006 embassy cable, the U.S. ambassador to Venezuela, William Brownfield, wrote that Cuban agents had direct access to Chávez and provided him with information unvetted by Venezuelan intelligence officials. "Cuban agents train Venezuelans on both Cuba and Venezuela, providing both political indoctrination and operational instruction," wrote Brownfield.[32]

According to the Spanish newspaper *El Pais*, a cable sent in 2010 reported that Cubans were in control of espionage against the U.S. Embassy in Caracas. Brownfield noted that Cuban espionage had become so expansive inside Venezuela that it was causing rivalry between the Cuban and Venezuelan intelligence operations, which "appear to be competing with each other for the Venezuelan government's attention." Brownfield also commented that "Venezuelan intelligence services are among the most hostile towards the United States in the hemisphere, but they lack the expertise that Cuban services can provide."[33]

At the time that Ambassador Brownfield wrote the cable, he noted that he had received no credible evidence of Cuban infiltration of the Venezuelan military. But over the following years, a number of high-ranking Venezuelan officers either resigned their commissions or took early retirement after being told that they must now, after lengthy and distinguished military careers, defer to recently arrived Cubans.

Retired general Francisco Usón, a former defense planning director and finance minister in the Chávez government, told the *Washington Times* in April 2010, "There are indications that agents of the Cuban G-2 [military intelligence] are operating openly at all the main military installations, principally the Ministry of Defense, the strategic operations command, the joint chiefs of staff headquarters, command centers of the army, navy, air force and national guard, as well as the military intelligence directorate." General Usón also said that the "sports instructors" who were attached to military battalions were tasked with reporting on any soldiers who expressed any disloyalty to Chávez and the socialist doctrine now taught to the military.[34]

According to the *Washington Times* report, a Colombian security analyst backed General Usón's assertions, stating that Cubans were operating at the "tactical unit level," meaning that they decided on deployments and even recommended promotions. "Their recommendations are generally supported by the high command and considered orders," the Colombian analyst stated. One of the programs instituted by the Cubans that has driven out many of the professional officers is a new system that allows sergeants to be promoted to the rank of colonel simply by what they call "technical merit"—which most officers define as a high level of fealty to the Chávez political program. The Cubans who serve as informers report suspected disloyalty among soldiers to senior advisers at Venezuela's command centers. According to Usón, "There is much ill feeling about the presence of these agents, but my comrades in arms generally show genuflection and passivity towards these individuals." And sailors in the Venezuelan merchant marine have also reported that during the 2002 oil strike, it was Cuban agents who took control of the ports in order to protect tankers bound for Havana with vital oil supplies.[35]

Perhaps the greatest indignity for apolitical Venezuelan soldiers has not only been having to take orders from Cubans but also having to do so with the knowledge that terrorists who have always been their main enemy were most likely trained by those same Cubans now giving them orders.

Crossing the Andes

Prior to the 2006 presidential election in Peru, Hugo Chávez set his sights on the country to try to bring it into the ALBA orbit. Besides sending letters of invitation to mayors near the border areas of his allies, Chávez underwrote a number of ALBA houses in rural areas of Peru. The Peruvian government became concerned enough about the ALBA houses that a congressional committee investigated them and issued a report in March 2009 recommending they be shut down. The committee report concluded that Chávez was trying to influence Peruvian politics via the ALBA houses, which had been established without any government-to-government agreement.

The ALBA houses offered air travel to Caracas, eye surgery, and room and board during recovery—all for free—to poor Peruvians. Peruvian politicians had allowed the houses to operate for fear of a backlash that might occur if the free services were shut down. But a June 2009 incident in the Amazon city of Bagua ended the détente. The incident, called the *Baguazo*, ended in a bloodbath when members and supporters of a radicalized "indigenous rights" group slit the throats of police officers who had been sent to end the group's roadblock that had closed the city's only highway for over a month. Leaders of the Interethnic Association for the Development of the Peruvian Rainforest (Asociación Interétnica de Desarrollo de la Selva Peruana) were revealed to have ties to Chávez and Morales and had previously traveled to Caracas to participate in a meeting of radical indigenous groups.[36]

Peruvians were so appalled by the incident that Cardinal Juan Luis Cipriani, the archbishop of Lima, addressed the subject in his sermon on Peru's Independence

Day, saying, "Peru needs an iron front to stamp out foreign meddling and interference in the country's internal affairs." The archbishop declared, with President García and most of his cabinet in the congregation, "Peru is an open country and is always ready to initiate dialogue with those willing to collaborate in good faith. But we are implacable and firm with those who plan to destroy us."[37] The archbishop's remarks reflected those of García's at the time, that Chávez and Morales were encouraging social unrest among indigenous groups and the Peruvian poor in order to cause instability in the country. This was a serious subject in a country that had pacified the terrorism of the Shining Path and Túpac Amaru terrorist groups only a decade earlier.[38]

Morales, who came to power by radicalizing a coalition of coca growers and indigenous Bolivians, has had the most success in this area. The Red Ponchos (Ponchos Rojos), consisting of indigenous Bolivians who live in the country's high plains, have been radicalized by Morales to defend his government and to agitate in the areas of the country where he enjoys less support. In 2007 the Ponchos Rojos called local TV reporters to Achacachi, where they hung two puppies by the neck, shouted slogans in support of Morales and his political party, and then grabbed the puppies by their feet. While the animals writhed and struggled in front of the cameras, the Ponchos Rojos sawed their heads off with a knife. A video of this disturbing event is widely available online.

La Razon, a Bolivian daily, reported on the macabre spectacle: "Amid the howls of pain from the animals, the enraged Aymaras screamed a threat: 'This is how the dogs of the half moon will suffer!'" The half moon refers to the *media luna*, which includes Tarija, Santa Cruz, Beni, and Pando—four industrialized areas where opposition to Morales is concentrated.

As the men performed the torture and beheading, dozens of women and children watched and celebrated, many wielding rifles that they proudly displayed to members of the press. The mayor of Achacachi, along with a leader of the Ponchos Rojos, Eugenio Rojas, announced that a thousand peasants would march to Sucre and warned, "If they oppose we will have to attack."[39]

Financing the Continental Revolution

Like Soviet communism, Chávez's 21st Century Socialism can only survive by spreading and enveloping its neighbors, lest too much of a distinction be shown in economic outcomes by its nonsocialist neighbors. To facilitate the loyalty necessary to achieve that goal without force of arms, Chávez has had to spread Venezuela's oil wealth around the region. In a July 2008 hearing of the Western Hemisphere Sub-committee of the House Foreign Affairs Committee, Dr. Norman Bailey, a former official of the National Security Council whose specialty was monitoring terrorism by tracking finances, testified that Chávez had spent "$33 billion on regional influ-ence." Bailey further stated that corruption in the Chávez regime was "nothing less than monumental, with literally billions of dollars having been stolen by government officials and their allies in the private sector over the past nine years." Bailey also testified that a Chávez government official had his bank accounts closed by HSBC Bank in London, which had deposits of $1.5 billion.[40]

Although Venezuela's state-owned oil company, PDVSA, had to borrow $16 billion in 2007, a large amount of the money collected by oil sales has continued to be used to influence policy and elections outside the country. One of the many ways in which this is done is by buying billions of dollars' worth of Argentine bonds at usurious interest rates. In 2001 Argentina lost its ability to access international credit markets because it had defaulted on its international debt. Bailey reported to the committee that Chávez had funded elections in Argentina, Bolivia, Ecuador, Nica-ragua, Peru, and some of the Caribbean countries. Bailey added that, besides funding elections, Chávez has also financed terrorist groups, including the FARC in Colom-bia, ETA in the Basque territory of Spain, and even Hezbollah, Hamas, and Islamic Jihad via their networks in Latin America. Bailey mentioned that this work was done through the Islamic Center on Margarita Island through the networks maintained by the Iranians and the Arab diaspora elsewhere in the hemisphere.[41]

Bailey also discussed the money laundering that was taking place in Venezu-ela, facilitated by the Iranian-owned Banco Internacional de Desarollo that was suspected of choosing its name to confuse it with the Spanish initials (BID) of the Inter-American Development Bank. Much of the corruption and money laundering in Venezuela, according to Bailey, is connected to narco-trafficking, which has in-creased considerably since Chávez took office. A large portion of the income derived from both the narco-trafficking and money laundering is funneled to Venezuelan entities and officials and "is facilitated by the Venezuelan financial system, includ-ing both public and private institutions."[42] In Nicaragua, President Daniel Ortega talks the talk of a Marxist revolutionary, often condemning the "failed imperialist model" and the evils of "savage capitalism," but he walks the walk of a monoplist con-glomerate head. In October 2009 the *Christian Science Monitor* published an article that carried the headline "Nicaragua's Newest Tycoon? 'Socialist' President Daniel Ortega," and that catalogued the business empire that the self-described Marxist revolutionary has built in poverty-ridden Nicaragua.[43] According to the *Monitor*,

> Ortega has created a network of private businesses that operate under the auspices of the Bolivarian Alliance for the Americas (ALBA). . . . Ortega's "ALBA businesses"—known by an alphabet soup of acronyms, including ALBANISA, ALBALINISA, and ALBACARUNA—have cornered Nicaragua's petroleum import and distribution markets, become the country's leading energy supplier and cattle exporter, turned profits on the sale of donated Russian buses, and purchased a hotel in downtown Managua, among other lucrative investment moves.[44]

At the same time that he has shut out the independent media in the country, Ortega has dropped a curtain of secrecy over his business empire as well. But it is impossible for the regime to completely hide the profits that these business enterprises generate. The *Christian Science Monitor* article stated that while "secrecy has cast a long shadow over the business operations, the light that gets through reveals profits registering in the hundreds of millions of dollars, despite the economy's slip into recession." It was also reported that in 2008, Venezuela gave the Nicaraguan Central Bank $457 million in "aid," all of which was managed privately, and with no independent oversight, by Ortega's ALBA holding company.[45]

Opposition critics complain that Ortega is blurring the lines between state, party, and family, as he has mixed confidants from the FSLN with family members in his business empire. As an example, critics mention Francisco López, who is both the treasurer of the FSLN as well as a personal confidant of Ortega's. López also was the president of the state-owned Petronic oil company; president of ALALINISA, which manages luxury hotels and cattle; and vice president of the privately owned ALBANISA, which handles oil distribution. He also serves as the Ortega regime's representative to Unión Fenosa, a Spanish power distribution company in which the government bought a minority share.[46] These types of interrelated and corrupt business, government, and personal relationships have compounded the lack of transparency in the Ortega regime and have made it almost impossible for any type of oversight of government coffers. It has also enabled the Ortega family and friends of his government to become fabulously wealthy.

Even though Chávez is aware of Ortega's business empire, the experience of losing Honduras in 2009 has caused him to keep the money flowing to maintain his ally in Nicaragua. A Wikileaks cable released in December 2010 revealed that Ortega had been given "suitcases full of cash" in Caracas. "We have firsthand reports that GON [government of Nicaragua] officials receive suitcases full of cash from Venezuelan officials during official trips to Caracas," a 2008 diplomatic cable written by Ambassador Paul Trivelli stated. The embassy cables also said that Ortega was believed to have used drug money to underwrite a massive election fraud.[47]

A May 8, 2008, embassy cable called Ortega a "Chávez 'Mini-Me'"—a reference to the character in the Austin Powers movies—for his fawning praise of Chávez's governance and for Ortega being a "willing follower" of the Venezuelan president. The cable also stated that, according to "several unconfirmed reports," Ortega would have "as much as 500 million dollars at his disposal over the course of 2008."[48] The cables also revealed that Ortega had allegedly bribed Ricardo Mayorga, a famous Nicaraguan boxer, to campaign for him in exchange for getting rid of sexual assault charges. The bribery accusation against Ortega would be highly contentious, as he himself had been famously accused of long-term sexual abuse by his stepdaughter. According to the embassy cable, Ortega only escaped facing her charges by stacking the courts and the legislature with his supporters.[49]

The money that Ortega was accused of receiving from Chávez was never accounted for through normal campaign funding channels, according to embassy officials. More importantly, the Venezuelan cash allowed him to dole out campaign funds to those legislators and judges who would eventually help bury the case against him. These supporters also helped the Sandinistas win a majority of legislative seats in an election that was condemned as fraudulent by a number of international authorities. The cable also spoke of Ortega's "anti-democratic tendencies," which included political harassment, unannounced government audits, and even violent attacks.[50]

A May 5, 2006, embassy cable said that money from international narco-traffickers is "usually in return for ordering Sandinista judges to allow traffickers caught by the police and military to go free." In one case in 2005, according to the embassy official, a Supreme Court judge "coordinated a complicated scheme to make 609,000 dollars in drug money seized from two Colombians 'disappear' from a Supreme Court account."[51]

The accusation of suitcases of Venezuelan money going to Nicaragua match very closely with an August 2007 case in which a Venezuelan American businessman,

Antonini Wilson, was caught at the Ezeiza Airport just outside Buenos Aires with a suitcase packed with $800,000 in cash. According to U.S. prosecutors who ended up in charge of the case, the money was intended for Cristina Fernández de Kirchner, who was campaigning for (and eventually won) the presidency of Argentina. The probable reason that the case was not covered up by both Venezuelan and Argentine officials was that when Wilson flew home to Key Biscayne immediately after the incident, he reported it to the FBI, fearing (rightly) being set up as the "fall guy," according to his court testimony.[52] Wilson agreed to wear a wire during his subsequent meetings with Venezuelan officials and to record his phone calls. Three of the officials involved were indicted in the United States and pleaded guilty. Another fled and is still at large. During courtroom testimony, Venezuelan businessman Carlos Kauffman called PDVSA the "cash register of Venezuela." He confirmed that the money was from a PDVSA slush fund and was indeed for Kirchner's campaign.[53]

Kauffman also testified that the Venezuelan ambassador to Bolivia, Julio Montes, told him that he had "$100 million to spend on Bolivia" in order to get Morales supporters elected. Additionally he testified that Montes mentioned that, as an incentive to help spread the Venezuelan campaign cash to other countries, he might let Kauffman and an associate manage the multimillion-dollar slush fund and make money off of the interest. Another stunning revelation that came out at the Miami trial was that there was far more money involved than the $800,000 confiscated by customs officials. According to Wilson's testimony, the PDVSA representative in Argentina asked him where "the rest of the money was" and then mentioned "$4.2 million."[54]

Cristina Kirchner initially called the entire case a "trashing operation," but it was hard for the Argentine presidential candidate to protest too much. Just before leaving office, her husband was involved in a similar scandal. His economy minister, Felisa Miceli, was found to have hidden a bag containing $60,000 cash in her office bathroom.[55]

A separate purpose for the theft of state monies in the ALBA countries, besides the outright greed of their leaders, is to establish the notion in the minds of the public that it is the head of state who is the arbiter of wealth distribution in the country. This idea is then further emphasized by the regime's subsequent property and business expropriations from the entrepreneurial class. In October 2005 Chávez delivered a message to private property owners who had begun to organize themselves to legally resist the regime's arbitrary expropriations of farms and land: "We don't believe in threats, and we won't be threatened. If you take that road, be aware of the consequences, because we will act with the greatest assertiveness and we won't allow the country to be set ablaze. The permissive Chávez of 2000 is gone. I will not allow it." Since that time, all property confiscations have been accompanied by Venezuelan army and national guard soldiers.[56]

Revolutionary Terrorism and Organized Crime

A 2009 Freedom House report titled *Undermining Democracy: 21st Century Authoritarians* stated:

> The Venezuelan regime also seems to rely on a practice that is more peculiar to Chavismo, as the Chávez phenomenon is commonly known, or at least to a small subset of semi-authoritarian states: the promotion of disorder. Whereas many nondemocratic governments—such as those in Russia, China, and Saudi Arabia—seek political legitimacy by attempting to deliver order, the rulers of Venezuela and their ilk do nothing to stop lawlessness. Consequently, ordinary citizens live in fear of random crime, oppositionists face targeted attacks by thugs, and businesses are subject to violence by government-sponsored labor groups. This intimidation through third parties, rather than through direct state pressure alone, helps to discourage collective action by regime opponents. It also produces discontent, but not among the protected class of Chavistas.[57]

The "promotion of disorder" that the report describes has long been the subject of debate among security analysts. Whether the escalation in street crime under Chávez's tenure is due to incompetence or design may be unknowable while he remains in office. But the regime's connection to and collaboration with international terrorism and organized crime leave far more clues. The *New York Times* reported in December 2010 that in one of the Wikileaks cables, U.S. Embassy personnel revealed that Chávez government officials had infiltrated local U.S. Drug Enforcement Agency (DEA) operations and had even hired a computer hacker to intercept U.S. Embassy e-mail traffic.[58]

In a 2006 congressional hearing before the Subcommittee on International Terrorism and Nonproliferation titled "Venezuela: Terrorism Hub of South America?," Rep. Brad Sherman (D-CA) questioned Charles Shapiro, U.S. ambassador to Venezuela from February 2002 until August 2004 and then the principal deputy assistant secretary in the State Department's Bureau of Western Hemisphere Affairs:

Mr. SHERMAN. Mr. Shapiro, have we confronted the Venezuelan Government with our concerns?

Ambassador SHAPIRO. Over the past 2 years, our Embassy in Caracas has sought on 20 different occasions to have meetings with Government of Venezuela officials who have responsibility for counterterrorism. We have not had a single meeting with the government on these issues over the past 2 years.

Let me go a little bit further than that, sir. The bread-and-butter work of counterterrorism cooperation is the exchange of information regarding bank accounts, people coming in and out of countries, phone numbers, e-mail accounts. Over the past 3 years, the Embassy in Caracas has submitted roughly 130 written requests for different types of biographical or immigration-related information on potential terrorist suspects and, to date, has not received one single substantive response. These include requests for entry and exit information from the Venezuelan immigration authorities.

Mr. SHERMAN. Ambassador, if I can interrupt, because the Chairman has been very generous with the time, I want to kind of crystallize this for the Venezuelan press that is in the audience. What this means is Hezbollah is proud that they have killed Americans. Chávez is proud to help fund Hezbollah. On September 11th, we lost nearly 3,000 people. There is a Venezuelan citizen, Mr. Hakim Mamad al Diab Fatah, who attended school with the hijackers and we have asked for cooperation and, in every respect, the response is that the Venezuelan Government won't even meet with our people.[59]

Frank Urbancic, principal deputy coordinator for the Office of the Coordinator for Counterterrorism at the State Department, also testified about Venezuela's lack of cooperation on counterterrorism:

Earlier this year, the Secretary of State determined that Venezuela demonstrated a near complete lack of cooperation with the United States Government and with our efforts to fight terrorism. This determination reflected a view of Venezuela's overall actions against terrorism, the Venezuelan Government's public statements in international fora addressing terrorism, Venezuela's conduct toward terrorist organizations, and the Venezuelan Government's relations with state sponsors of terror.[60]

Terrorism and organized crime has long been associated with despotic regimes, where corruption is inherent. But what is rarely discussed is whether these two phenomena must necessarily coexist. Over the last thirty years, the drug trade has had a tendency to move to the path of least resistance in the hemisphere. In that same time frame, the path of least resistance has inevitably been those countries under the thrall of Marxist "revolution."

In a 1985 joint hearing of the Senate Foreign Relations and Judiciary Committees, Deputy Assistant Secretary of State Clyde D. Taylor told the panel that Cuba was a "way station on the trade routes of drug smugglers," adding that "evidence continues to mount that boats and planes carrying drugs have enjoyed Cuban airspace, territorial waters, and refueling facilities without hindrance."[61]

Cuba was not the only "way station" at the time. The year 1985 was the midpoint of the first Sandinista reign in Nicaragua, and numerous federal drug trials in the 1980s and 1990s elicited evidence of drug trafficking under the aegis of Nicaragua and Cuba. In the 1991 trial of Panamanian general Manuel Noriega, for example, star witness Carlos Lehder testified about Cuban and Nicaraguan officials helping the Medellín cartel traffic drugs into the United States during the 1980s.

Lehder provides one of many examples of a pattern that emerges among drug traffickers over the last forty years: their sanctuaries have most always been wherever there was a Marxist "revolutionary" government at the time. After the assassination in April 1984 of Colombian minister of justice Rodrigo Lara, the political winds in the country suddenly shifted, and Colombia decided that it would honor extradition requests by the United States. Lehder's name was the first on the list.

Most Colombian cartel members took refuge in General Noriega's Panama, but when Noriega was discovered to be cutting a deal with U.S. officials, the cartel members went to the friendliest country that they could find for protection— Nicaragua under the Sandinistas. Lehder testified in Noriega's trial that high-level Cuban and Nicaraguan officials, including Raúl Castro, helped the Medellín cartel smuggle cocaine into the United States in the 1980s and that he met twice with Raúl in Havana to gain overflight permission in Cuban airspace for drug planes moving cocaine from Colombia to Florida. Lehder also testified that the cartel set up a drug-smuggling route out of Nicaragua that had the approval of top Sandinista leaders as well as assistance from Cuba's top intelligence agent in Managua.[62] "The Cubans were in charge of that cocaine conspiracy in Nicaragua," Lehder told the court, adding that "it was not the Sandinista Government, it was the Cubans" who were in charge of organizing and running the Nicaragua-to-Florida operation.[63] Lehder's testimony supported statements by former Sandinistas that the Cubans were in charge. Nicaraguan defectors had long reported the drug-trafficking habits of the Sandinista government. Antonio Farach, a defector who had worked as a Sandinista minister in Nicaragua's embassies in Honduras and Venezuela, told U.S. officials in 1983 that Humberto Ortega, brother of the president and then Nicaragua's minister of defense, was "directly involved" in drug trafficking.[64]

Farach repeated an oft-reported rationale used by Marxists who moonlight in the drug trade as a sideline to revolution. He stated that Sandinista officials believed their trafficking in drugs was a "political weapon" that would help to destroy "the youth of our enemies." According to Farach, the Sandinistas declared, "We want to provide food to our people with the suffering and death of the youth of the United States."[65]

Convicted drug smuggler George Jung (the subject of the movie *Blow*) would say the same thing about Carlos Lehder, testifying in court that Lehder "hoped that by flooding the country with cocaine he could disrupt the political system." Lehder, like many in radical movements, would straddle the worlds of far-left and far-right hate. In Colombia, Lehder founded a neo-Nazi political party, National Latin Movement (Movimiento Nacional Latino), which he also used to try to reverse Colombia's decision to extradite drug suspects.[66]

Lehder's father was a German transplant to Colombia, and according to the *Los Angeles Times*, Lehder "grew up with a passion for things German, particularly the Third Reich, and was a strong anti-Semite." He "idolized late Beatle John Lennon and Che Guevara and considered Adolf Hitler a genius." Lehder also greatly admired fugitive financier Robert Vesco, whom Lehder credited with teaching him how to launder drug money. Vesco was also the one who introduced Lehder to Fidel Castro.[67]

Vesco's history is also telling. When he fled the United States for Costa Rica in 1973, Vesco found protection under socialist president José Figueres, who was a supporter of the Sandinistas and had been on the payroll of the Soviet Union.[68]

Once Figueres left office in 1974, Vesco moved to Nicaragua. When the Sandinistas were voted out of office, Vesco moved to Cuba, where he made deals with the Castro brothers and would eventually die in prison after trying to swindle them.[69]

The promotion of societal disorder is also necessary to ensure that no one notices when certain friends of the regime are not prosecuted for crimes. As Venezuela has become more and more of a drug-trafficking hub and has refused to cooperate with U.S. and international antinarcotics agencies, its justice system has become less and less interested in prosecuting drug traffickers.

Since drug kingpin Pablo Escobar was killed on a rooftop in Bogotá in 1993, leaving the Colombian cartels temporarily debilitated, the DEA began focusing its interdiction efforts on the Caribbean. Since the 1990s, narcotics traffic has been routed through Central America and Mexico, and much of the cocaine production has moved from Colombia to Peru and Bolivia. During that time, Venezuela has become the principle launching point for smuggling. On July 13, 2010, *USA Today* reported that "drug smuggling through Venezuela has exploded since President Hugo Chávez severed contacts with U.S. law enforcement agencies in 2005, U.S. and United Nations officials say in reports."[70] A June 2010 report by the UN Office on Drugs and Crime stated that, between 2006 and 2008, 41 percent of all cocaine shipments to Europe originated in Venezuela, and half of all ships interdicted in the Atlantic Ocean carrying cocaine had originated in Venezuela. As a comparison, only 5 percent had originated in Colombia. The report traced a vastly increased amount of trafficking by small planes and fast boats that moved drugs from Venezuela to the Dominican Republic, Haiti, and Honduras that were mostly bound for the United States and Europe.[71]

The *USA Today* article reported on a gathering of drug smugglers in Monrovia, Liberia, in May 2010 to plan the logistics of a massive cocaine shipment operation across the Atlantic Ocean. According to an unsealed U.S. indictment, cocaine shipments were destined for Russia, Europe, Ghana, and New York by jet, prop plane, and ship, and all were leaving from one place—Venezuela.

A major scandal in 2008 involving the president of Sierra Leone resulted from a plane that landed in that country's capital with 600 kilograms of cocaine. The plane had arrived illegally at Freetown's Lungi Airport with a fake Red Cross insignia. More ominously, it had taken off from Venezuela.[72] It was not the first time. The UN Office on Drugs and Crime warned about transatlantic drug planes in November 2009 after a Boeing 727 was found burned in the desert in Mali. The plane had taken off from Venezuela, and cocaine smugglers had set the plane on fire after unloading the drugs.[73]

Other recent U.S. court cases have included a ring that operated between Colombia and Liberia that was busted in May 2010 as it prepared to fly two tons of cocaine from Venezuela to Liberia. Prosecutors said that the ring was planning to take two massive loads of cocaine per month, and one of the defendants claimed to manage five other planes that were making similar smuggling runs. Another antinarcotics operation busted the Valencia-Arbeláez Organization after it purchased a $2 million plane to allow the group to make monthly flights between Venezuela and Guinea. The group claimed to have six other planes already flying between South America and West Africa.[74]

Since Chávez came to office, there has been an escalating amount of internal corruption as well as a wholesale increase in major drug trafficking. Recently Venezuela analysts began looking into those who were surrounding Chávez to discern whether an increasingly autocratic government was either oblivious to or accommodating these illicit activities.

The first place that opposition officials began looking was at the family of Tarek El Aissami, who was alleged to have facilitated drug dealing from his dorm room at the University of the Andes. Since going to work in the Chávez government, he has faced charges of corruption and of collaborating with terrorist groups. But investigators began looking into nepotism when a report came out in November 2010 about El Aissami's family. His sister, Haifa El Aissami, had been appointed ambassador to the Netherlands, although she had no diplomatic experience. Another sister, Amin Obayda El Aissami, worked as an executive at Intevep, a Venezuelan oil technology firm.

But what tied the family to drug trafficking was when brother Firaz El Aissami and cousin Aiman El Aissami were reported to have been involved in the case of Walid Makled, a notorious drug trafficker arrested in late 2010 in Colombia.[75] Makled, a Venezuelan "businessman" of Syrian lineage, was designated by the U.S. government as an international drug kingpin in 2009 under the Foreign Narcotics Kingpin Designation Act. Makled has also worked extensively with the FARC, according to sources.[76]

In January 2011, the *Washington Post* reported that Makled admitted to making payments of around $1 million a month to high-level civilian and military officials and to paying $100,000 to the brother of Tarek El Aissami. Makled was quoted as

saying, "If I'm a drug trafficker, everyone in the Chávez government is [a] drug trafficker."[77] And according to the indictment, Makled rationalized his actions just like
the others: "If the gringos want the poison, keep sending it their way."[78]

Unfortunately, because the Obama Justice Department did not hastily pursue
the extradition of Makled, Colombian president Juan Manuel Santos agreed to
extradite him to Venezuela, which had put in an extradition request first. This elim-
inated the chance for U.S. officials to properly interrogate a major drug trafficker
who had been behind the considerable increase in drug trafficking tied to Venezuela.
Mildred Camero, the top antinarcotics official in the Venezuelan government until
she got into a dispute with Chávez in 2005, said of Makled, "It's a shame he's coming here. . . . Absolutely nothing is going to happen here. He will arrive. They will
sentence him. They will isolate him, but we won't find out anything" about narco-
trafficking and corruption at the highest levels of the Chávez government.[79]

PART IV
Gauging the Threat

13
THE THREAT TO AMERICA'S
"SOFT UNDERBELLY"

On October 5, 1969, a heavily armed, Soviet-built MiG-17 fighter buzzed the tower at Homestead Air Force Base, just south of Miami. The jet had skirted the meager defenses and radar coverage of the southern United States and flown in undetected. Because the pilot was speaking in Spanish and broken English, it took the stunned controllers in the tower several minutes to understand that he was a Cuban pilot defecting to the United States.

What made the incident even more alarming was that Air Force One was sitting on the tarmac at the time, waiting for President Richard Nixon to make a return trip to Washington. The story caused much consternation within the U.S. defense establishment, because it exposed America's "soft underbelly," as one U.S. senator called it at the time. Over forty years later, the southern part of the country, especially our border with Mexico, continues to be a soft underbelly that is exposed to anyone wishing to cause us harm.

Peripheral Asymmetric Warfare and the Border Threat
In January 2011, two nearly simultaneous incidents occurred on the border with Mexico that illustrated well the threats posed by peripheral asymmetric warfare. In one a catapult was utilized to launch bales of narcotics over the border fence from Mexico into Arizona—a thoroughly modern use of ancient technology in order for criminals in a lawless region to circumvent the rule of law in another.[1] Reported on the same day was the arrest by the Border Patrol of a radical Muslim imam found hiding in the trunk of a BMW while trying to illegally cross into California. He had previously been arrested in France for forming an illegal group and later deported

from Canada for having lied in immigration documents about a separate conviction for assault.[2] Neither of these incidents were lethal attacks, but they represent examples of the comprehensive aspect of asymmetric warfare, where a much longer-term view is coupled with a stealthier approach and where terrorists and narco-traffickers find mutually beneficial reasons to work together to further one another's objectives. Nevertheless, there has been a tendency in policy circles to treat warnings about the threat of Islamist terrorism plots launched from south of the border as overwrought—at least until an astoundingly brazen one was uncovered later in 2011.

On October 11, two Iranians—Manssor Arbabsiar, a naturalized U.S. citizen with Iranian and U.S. passports, and Gholam Shakuri, an Iran-based member of the Quds Force—were charged with plotting to assassinate Adel al-Jubeir, the Saudi ambassador to the United States. According to court documents, the two men had planned to pay members of the Zetas, a Mexican drug cartel, $1.5 million to plant a bomb to murder al-Jubeir while he lunched in a crowded Washington restaurant. According to a Justice Department press release, when asked by a government informant about the hundreds of potential casualties that might even include U.S. congressmen, Arbabsiar said, "They want that guy [the Ambassador] done [killed], if the hundred go with him f**k 'em."[3]

Inside Washington's foreign policy establishment, the alleged plot was met with incredulity. Secretary of State Hillary Clinton said, "The idea that they would attempt to go to a Mexican drug cartel to solicit murder-for-hire to kill the Saudi ambassador, nobody could make that up, right?" And the *New York Times* published four stories within the first two days after the news broke that questioned the notion that Iran would attempt such a brazen attack on U.S. soil.[4]

But this was not the first time that Iran had planned something so audacious. In 1980 the Iranian regime solicited Dawud Salahuddin, an American who was named David Theodore Belfield until he converted to Islam in 1969, to murder an Iranian exile in Bethesda, Maryland. Salahuddin, who was working as a security guard at an Iranian diplomatic office, fatally shot Ali Akbar Tabatabai, then fled to Iran, where he has since worked on the website of the government-sponsored propaganda station, Press TV.[5]

Along with blowing up the restaurant in Washington, Arbabsiar and Shakuri also planned to simultaneously bomb the Saudi and Israeli Embassies there, as well as in Buenos Aires. The familiar sound of this last part of the plot should have removed some of the skepticism about whether the Iranian regime would attempt such a destructive act. In 2009 Iran and Argentina were back in the news when Mahmoud Ahmadinejad named as his defense minister Ahmad Vahidi, the man wanted by Interpol for planning the 1994 bombing of a Jewish community center in Buenos Aires, that of the Argentine Israelite Mutual Association.[6]

Despite the skepticism within officialdom of the notion that Iran or its allies would work with Latin American narco-traffickers and guerrillas, numerous instances of this type of collaboration have been reported. On January 25, 2011, Border Patrol agents found a copy of *In Memory of Our Martyrs*, a book published by the Iranian Ministry of Islamic Guidance. It is typically used to venerate suicide bombers and Basij martyrs of the Iran-Iraq War, as is done in other countries of the Middle East with posters and murals of those who have strapped bombs to themselves to kill innocents.[7] In 2004 Border Patrol agents had found a discarded jacket on a smuggler's trail in Jim Hogg County, Texas, that proved to be even more alarming. On the sleeves were two patches. One was similar to a U.S. Army Airborne patch, with wings, a parachute, and a lion's head. The caption, in Arabic, read, "Martyr—way to eternal life." The other patch needed no caption. It depicted a plane flying into the Twin Towers.[8]

Sigifredo Gonzalez, Jr., the sheriff who reported the find to the Subcommittee on Investigations, told a reporter in January 2011 that both Homeland Security as well as the FBI "summarily" dismissed the find as unimportant. But prior to the sheriff's report, Homeland Security had issued "officer alerts," warning that they had received intelligence about cartels on the border planning to kill their personnel.

The Border Debate

A surprising number of security officials have gone to great lengths to downplay the threat of spillover violence from Mexican drug cartels as well as the probability of a Middle Eastern terrorist utilizing the services of a Mexican *coyote* to cross the border into the United States. Others insist on separating the larger war on narco-trafficking in Mexico from the threat of terrorism.[9] But it may be a better strategy to look at both wars together.

Louise Shelley, founder and director of the Terrorism, Transnational Crime and Corruption Center at George Mason University, calls the simultaneous globalization of crime, terrorism, and corruption an "unholy trinity" that is "more complex . . . than terrorists simply turning to crime to support their activities or merely the increased flow of illicit goods internationally. Rather, it is a distinct phenomenon in which globalized crime networks work with terrorists and both are able to carry out their activities successfully, aided by endemic corruption."[10]

This "unholy trinity" began to appear at the end of the twentieth century, but according to Shelley, it is not a new phenomenon. She mentions that in the 1930s, members of the Mafia in the United States traveled to Kobe, Japan, and Shanghai, China, to buy narcotics and that members of American crime gangs escaped to China to avoid capture and punishment by U.S. authorities. A similar collaboration has been seen in recent years in the so-called Tri-Border Area (TBA) of South America where Argentina, Brazil, and Paraguay meet—a modern-day Casablanca where authorities have tracked groups ranging from neo-Nazis to al-Qaeda to Hezbollah.

U.S. court dockets are full of examples of collaboration between crime syndicates and terrorist groups, yet the phenomenon is still often misunderstood. Shelley describes as follows:

> The artificial distinction made between crime and terrorism is based on an antiquated concept of both. The adage that criminals engage in crime for profit and terrorists operate exclusively for political motives belies the contemporary reality of these two groups. Criminals no longer belong to hierarchical organizations that do not threaten the state itself—as was true of the Sicilian Mafia or the Japanese Yakuza. Terrorists, often supported by crime, frequently move between identities as criminals and terrorists. The network structures of both allow them to hook up, conscious or unconscious of each other's identities: The two groups may work directly together, or they may connect through their facilitators. For example, in Los Angeles, the same language school that provided some of the 9/11 hijackers their visa documents also provided them for the prostitutes of a major trafficking-in-persons ring. In turn, the trafficking ring engaged in stolen identities that could facilitate terrorist activities.[11]

According to the Congressional Task Force on Terrorism and Unconventional Warfare, Pablo Escobar, the late kingpin of the Medellín cartel, flew to Larnaca, Cyprus, in 1989 to meet with senior Syrian military and intelligence officers to discuss the terms of a collaboration between the groups. What they worked out was that the cartel would help Syria to develop its Lebanon-based cocaine operations, and the Syrians would provide the cartel members with terrorist training and equipment to enable it to fight a terrorist offensive against state security forces and against any U.S.

intervention in Colombia.[12] After the agreement was concluded, members of the Basque separatist group ETA who were based in the Ta'lbaya and al-Marj camps in the Bekkaa Valley were sent to Latin America to conduct terrorist training there. In exchange, a cocaine operation was set up in the Bekkaa in January 1990 with materials sent from Colombia and other parts of Latin America.[13]

Soon afterward, the Medellín cartel would utilize its newly acquired skills to wreak havoc in Colombia. On November 27, 1989, Avianca flight 203 from Bogotá to Cali exploded in midair five minutes after takeoff, killing all 107 people on board. The investigation revealed that the bomb was made of Semtex and that the detonator was very similar to the one used in the Libyan bombing of Pan Am flight 103 over Lockerbie, Scotland, in December 1988. Two of the passengers were Americans, which prompted the George H. W. Bush administration to initiate intelligence activity in Colombia to find Escobar.[14]

This type of collaboration is still occurring today. Edgardo Buscaglia, a government researcher at the Autonomous Technological Institute of Mexico, recently reported that Mexican drug cartels have begun collaborating with narco-traffickers in Afghanistan to help them with their supply for the European Union and the United States. The report in *El Pais* said that the Sinaloa cartel, along with others, had set up "ghost companies" with the help of Turkish and Indian smugglers in Afghanistan to aid them with heroin trafficking.

Buscaglia stated, "The Mexican organizations have penetrated the Turkish market through contacts established principally with firms and companies that are dedicated to illegal activities, where they also serve as minor stockholders." According to Buscaglia, this collaboration has allowed the Mexican cartels that had always served only as "mules" when Colombia ruled the cocaine trade to become international operations. "It is in the interest of these Mexican groups (specifically the Sinaloa alliance) that they open smuggling routes for the distribution of heroin to the U.S. market," he said. "Furthermore, they are not only focusing on the movement of Afghan heroin through Mexico; they are also taking positions of power as major players in the international world of the heroin trade."[15]

More ominously, to avoid being traced by the movement of money through bank accounts, the cartels often trade the drugs for arms and other illicit military equipment, which also allows them to militarize without having to make the purchases from traceable sources. Said Buscaglia, "These emissaries often exchange drugs for arms, or for other items. Nothing is out of the question, it really just depends on the region."[16]

As far back as 1985, Rep. Glenn English (D-OK), then chairman of the House Government Information, Justice, and Agriculture Subcommittee, said, "There is an inescapable correlation between arms and drugs. There's a threat both ways. The same people who deal in drugs traffic in the weapons of terrorism. The drug money buys arms, the arms buy revolutions."[17]

As of 2008, nineteen of the forty-three groups that are officially designated "foreign terrorist organizations" were all linked to the international drug trade, and as much as 60 percent of all terrorist organizations were believed to be linked to the drug trade.[18] What adds to the danger of this nexus is the monetary incentive of the highly profitable drug trade, as it leads to more and more creative ways to cross the southern border undetected. The Society for Risk Analysis did a study in 2009 that used statistical modeling to predict the likelihood that a terrorist would successfully enter the United States via the southern border. Based on current methods of immigration enforcement, the study predicted that the probability of a non-Mexican terrorist crossing the border was 97.3 percent.[19] The available immigration statistics indicate that there is certainly a need for concern. From fiscal year 1999 through March 2010, 329 Iranian nationals have been caught by U.S. Customs and Border Protection.[20]

In March 2005 FBI director Robert Mueller testified before the House Appropriations Committee that "there are individuals from countries with known Al Qaeda connections who are changing their Islamic surnames to Hispanic-sounding names and obtaining false Hispanic identities, learning to speak Spanish and pretending to be Hispanic."[21]

In 2010 the Department of Homeland Security had thousands of what are called "OTMs"—Other Than Mexicans—incarcerated for illegally crossing the southern border. The OTMs consisted of individuals from Afghanistan, Egypt, Iran, Iraq, Pakistan, Saudi Arabia, Yemen, and elsewhere. Though Homeland Security doesn't usually release these statistics, an Atlanta TV news station acquired documentation in 2010 that showed that there were 108,025 OTMs detained in 2006, compared to 165,178 in 2005 and 44,614 in 2004.[22]

But border-crossing jihadis are not the only concern. Of equal or greater importance are the training, arming, and radicalizing of the Islamic diaspora in Latin America by Middle Eastern terrorist groups with the imprimatur of Latin America's anti-American regimes. To gauge the problem, it is important to understand the differences between long-term migration and strategic infiltration in the hemisphere. The first Muslim to arrive in the Americas, Estevanico, or "Stephen the Moor," traveled to Cuba and Hispaniola (present-day Dominican Republic and Haiti) in 1527 with Pánfilo de Narváez's futile expedition to colonize Florida. In the nearly five hundred years since, only Suriname, where Muslims make up 21 percent of the country's small population of some 510,000 people, boasts a Muslim population greater than 10 percent of the general population.[23] Just thirty years ago, nearly 90 percent of the total population in Latin America was Roman Catholic. Today that figure has dropped to 55 to 65 percent. While there has been a large increase in *"evangelicos,"* or non-Catholic Christians, there has also been an effective recruiting effort by various Muslim groups.

Whereas the influence of Islam in the past in Latin America was mostly based on smaller immigrant Muslim enclaves, there has been some recent success in proselytizing indigenous tribes and remote populations by both Shiite and Sunni preachers and activists. Significant Muslim populations exist today in Argentina, Panama, Guyana, Trinidad and Tobago, and Brazil, which contains the largest Muslim community in South America, with estimates of its size ranging from 250,000 to nearly a million. The most successful Islamic proselytizing movement in Latin America is believed to be Spain's al-Murabitun.

An Islamist revival movement founded by a Scottish convert to Islam who goes by the name Shaykh Dr. Abdalqadir as-Sufi, al-Murabitun draws inspiration from the Almoravids, a Berber dynasty of the western Sahara that ruled North Africa and Spain in the eleventh and twelfth centuries and included a significant population of converts to Islam from Spain and other European countries. Al-Murabitun advocates a "collective reversion to Islam and a return to the region's true heritage," as opposed to what most Muslims would consider a true conversion to Islam. The members of al-Murabitun preach a form of Islam that is not imbued with "imperialism" but instead claims to serve as a "remedy for the oppression and destruction brought by Spanish conquest."[24]

It has been reported that al-Murabitun made an attempt, though unsuccessful, to form an alliance with Mexico's Subcomandante Marcos, the head of the Zapatista Army of National Liberation (Ejército Zapatista de Liberación Nacional) of Mexico, after his unsuccessful 1994 uprising in Chiapas. Although Subcomandante Marcos refused the offer, many of the Zapatista insurgents who belong to the Tzotzils, a

Yucatan tribe, did convert to Islam. This fact alarmed Mexican president Vicente Fox enough to accuse them of having links to al-Qaeda.[25]

Since the 1980s, Hezbollah has been recruiting and raising money from Lebanese and Syrian immigrants living mostly in three specific areas—the TBA; the Caribbean coast of Colombia, concentrated in the towns of Maicao and San Andrés; and Margarita Island.

An Egyptian Islamic group linked to al-Qaeda, al-Gama'a al-Islamiyya, has operated in Brazil since 1995. According to Brazilian authorities, one member of the group, Mohammed Ali Hassan Mokhles, flew from Egypt to Foz do Iguaçu, Brazil (one of the three cities of the Tri-Border Area), in 1993 to raise money and to carry out logistical support for fellow jihadis, including forging documents and passports.

Authorities claim that Mokhles was involved in the first World Trade Center bombing in 1993 and had attended a terror training camp in Khost, Afghanistan. He was arrested in Uruguay in 1999 for trying to illegally cross the border from Brazil with fake documentation and was extradited to Egypt. Mokhles also was said to have been involved in the 1997 terrorist attack that killed fifty-eight tourists in Luxor, Egypt.

Another member of the al-Gama'a al-Islamiyya terrorist group, Abed Abdel Aal, was arrested trying to cross from Ecuador into Colombia by bus in October 1998. He was also extradited to Egypt, being suspected of involvement in the Luxor massacre and an April 1996 attack in Cairo that killed twenty Greek tourists. Additionally, authorities reported that Abdel Aal had been working to establish a working relationship with the FARC.

In 2002 authorities in Brazil captured members of an al-Gama'a al-Islamiyya cell, which included Mohammed Ali Soliman, another of those suspected of involvement in the Luxor attack. Brazil released him in 2002, citing insufficient evidence from Egypt of his involvement in the massacre. Ali Soliman was also reported to have been trained in a terrorist camp in Afghanistan and to be associated with Mokhles.[26]

The only Islamic group in the Latin America or Caribbean region that has ever attempted a coup d'état in order to establish an Islamic government was Jamaat al-Muslimeen, a Sunni terrorist group based in Trinidad and Tobago. The group held the country's prime minister and members of the government hostage for six days in 1990. And though the coup failed, the group was able to negotiate an amnesty for its members.

This type of amnesty, obtained under duress, would normally be declared invalid once hostages were released. But the courts in Trinidad and Tobago astoundingly upheld it after the incident, so none of the terrorists were prosecuted. Instead, they aligned themselves with the United National Congress and later the People's National Movement, both left-wing political parties, and began trying to manipulate the country's politics. The attempted coup had been led by the head of Jamaat al-Muslimeen, Yasin Abu Bakr, who has since been arrested numerous times for other crimes. Born Lennox Philip, Abu Bakr converted to Islam while studying in Canada and returned to found the terrorist group with support from Muammar el-Qaddafi.

In his Eid ul-Fitr message (to mark the end of Ramadan) on November 3, 2005, Abu Bakr called for war against any Muslim who did not pay the *zakaat* tax, a type of tithe, in the upcoming year. Listeners took the threat to mean that all Muslims in the country must pay the tax directly to Jamaat al-Muslimeen, and Abu Bakr was subsequently arrested on charges of inciting extortion and sedition. Authorities subsequently found a cache of weapons, ammunition, and hand grenades at the group's headquarters. In March 2007 three of the group's members confessed to involvement in the kidnapping, rape, murder, and dismemberment of Indo-Trinidadian businesswoman Vindra Naipaul-Coolman. Jamaat al-Muslimeen also has been suspected of being involved in a kidnapping and extortion ring, as well as in narco-trafficking.[27]

In June 2007 the Department of Justice charged four people with conspiring to blow up fuel tanks and a pipeline at JFK Airport in New York. Two of those charged were from Guyana, one was a U.S. citizen of Guyanese origin, and one from Trinidad and Tobago named Abdul Kadir was a business partner of Abu Bakr's. Kadir, a former member of the Guyanese parliament, was convicted and sentenced to life in prison in December 2010.[28]

Evidence uncovered in the trial established that Abdul Nur, one of the Guyanese terrorists involved in the plot, had tried to locate al-Qaeda operative Adnan Shukrijumah, a Saudi-born fugitive terrorist suspect who grew up in Miramar, Florida. He had also introduced the other terrorists and shown the plan to Abu Bakr.[29] Another pair of terrorists from Trinidad and Tobago, Barry Adams (aka Tyrone Cole) and Wali Muhammad (aka Robert Johnson), are members of a Pakistan-based terrorist group, Jamaat al-Fuqra. The two were arrested in 1994 in Canada for conspiracy to bomb a Hindu temple in Toronto. According to Canadian prosecutors, the two terrorists had lived in Texas under aliases for several years before hatching the Toronto plot. After serving their full sentences, Canada deported them to Pakistan.

Tri-Border Terrorism

In the Middle East, Hamas and Hezbollah, like the Sunnis and Shia, are typically at each other's throats on most matters. But in the Tri-Border Area, they cooperate fully. Intelligence officials have reported observing meetings between Hezbollah and Hamas inside the mosques there.[30] From this notoriously ungovernable area, criminal gangs, international mafiosi, and terrorist groups have long conspired in numerous criminal activities—from pirating DVDs, shoes, and handbags to plotting and practicing terrorist attacks.

Tri-border regions such as this have always attracted crime because of the ease with which jurisdictional restrictions can be exploited to escape law enforcement. There have long been congregations of the Arab diaspora within free trade zones, because during times of Arab emigration the historically entrepreneurial sects tend toward areas of commercial opportunity. Many have assimilated fully into their host cultures, even becoming presidents and reaching other heights of government and industry.

It is only recently that family ties and clan loyalties back home have been exploited to support terrorism. The clan culture that has been radicalized back home can count on family ties in the free trade zones of the TBA, the canal area of Panama, Margarita Island, and the free trade zone in Iquique, Chile, among other places. These high-traffic commercial areas serve the interests of these groups because they provide opportunities for money laundering by the use of overinvoicing inventory and underinvoicing merchandise.

Profits made in free trade areas, both legitimate and not, can then be transferred easily and quickly by the age-old Arab tradition of person-to-person money transfer called *hawala*. Consequently, it was the entrepreneurial tradition of many of the Arab clans that originally developed the system of hawala, which is believed to have begun in the medieval period to facilitate trade over very long distances. It remained in place until it was supplanted by a formal banking system in the early twentieth century. This system has remained in place in modern times because of the migrant workers' need to send remittances back home to their families.[31]

The TBA has become a one-stop shop for all of these activities. It has developed a competitive advantage because of its remoteness and because of its producers' access to the U.S. market for their counterfeit goods.

In the 1970s Brazil and Paraguay were looking to promote the TBA for tourism and to establish it as a free trade zone where Argentine and Brazilian citizens could buy cheap electronics and appliances. When customs policies were changed in Argentina in the 1990s, the tourist traffic dried up, leaving the inhabitants with no domestic market. They filled the vacuum by producing knockoffs that could be exported to external markets. This illicit trade attracted those looking for a way to raise and launder money—which coincided with the growth of al-Qaeda, Hezbollah, and other terrorist groups during the late 1990s.[32]

The Arab presence in the TBA is highly visible, most notably in its Paraguayan section, Ciudad del Este. Ubiquitous hummus and shawarma kiosks dot the city, as do Koranic verses on signs and Lebanese flags flying from buildings and homes—a result of the Lebanese immigration wave that started in 1944 and picked up again during the civil war in Lebanon in the 1970s. A well-known Shiite cleric in the city, Hamid Nasrallah, is a relative of Hassan Nasrallah, the Hezbollah leader in Lebanon. His mosque, which bears a nondescript sign saying, "Mezquita" (Spanish for mosque), has been identified by various intelligence services as a ganglion of Hezbollah activities on the continent. Nasrallah is a gun-toting fund-raiser and enthusiastic supporter of Hezbollah, which he calls "a respectable political movement."[33]

In 2003 several Brazilian news sources, as well as the *Washington Post*, reported that Osama bin Laden was filmed at a mosque in Foz do Iguaçu in 1995 and that 9/11 mastermind Khalid Sheik Mohammed was documented to have been in the area the same year.[34] According to the *Final Report of the National Commission on Terrorist Attacks upon the United States*, one of the top al-Qaeda leaders, Mohammed Atef, provided Mohammed with his contact person in Brazil.[35]

Khalid Sheikh Mohammed is said to have spent nearly three weeks in Brazil, visiting members of the Muslim community. Authorities say that while in Brazil, he helped found a charity designed to generate funds for al-Qaeda. When in the TBA, Mohammed reportedly stayed with Khalid Rezk El Sayed Take El Din, a representative of the infamous Holy Land Foundation—a group that was found to be funding Hamas and other terrorist groups.

Brazilian police discovered in 1996 that Marwan al-Safadi, an explosives expert who was reported to have participated with Khalid Sheikh Mohammed's nephew Ramzi Yousef in the 1993 terrorist attack on the World Trade Center, had been living in the TBA. And in 1997 authorities in Paraguay discovered a joint al-Qaeda–Hezbollah plot to bomb the U.S. Embassy in Paraguay on the first anniversary of the bombing of the Saudi National Guard headquarters in Riyadh.[36]

When authorities raided Safadi's Ciudad del Este apartment, they discovered explosives, firearms with silencers, fake U.S. and Canadian passports, and a large amount of cash. After being extradited to Canada, Safadi was sentenced to nine years in prison on drug-trafficking charges. He managed to escape three times, the third time reportedly making it back to South America with a fake passport.[37]

Throughout the TBA, an array of weapons is available for unlicensed purchase, with no questions asked. Uzi submachine guns go for around $2,500 and can be delivered dismantled, in several different packages, so they can make it across the border more easily. More serious armaments, such as antitank missiles, rocket-propelled grenades, and explosives, can be purchased as well. These are either smuggled by land or flown in to one of the hundreds of private airstrips in the area. A short drive north of the TBA in Brazil is the city of Guaíra, the hub of weapons and drug smuggling in the region. And according to police, it is the hemispheric headquarters for the highly profitable enterprise of cigarette smuggling.[38]

Sheikh Akhram Ahmad Barakat, a well-known city councilman in Ciudad del Este, is said to also be the unofficial representative of Iran in the region. He is the brother of Assad Ahmad Barakat. According to the Paraguayan newspaper *ABC*, Assad Barakat is the military commander of Hezbollah in the TBA. Assad has also been linked to al-Qaeda by his ownership of the Mondial Engineering and Construction Company, which has reportedly given money to the terrorist group.

Assad Barakat kept his cover as a business owner in the TBA until he was arrested in 2002 for tax evasion. His brother Hattem was also his business partner and had business interests in Iquique, Chile, another terrorist enclave populated by a number of Paraguayans of Lebanese descent with reported links to Hezbollah. Since the governments of the Tri-Border countries and the United States began monitoring the TBA after 9/11, the Paraguayan émigrés in Iquique are reported to have set up a shakedown operation that extorts payoffs from local businessmen and sends money to Lebanon to fund Hezbollah.[39]

Hattem was also arrested later in Paraguay for document fraud. During the arrest, police found a number of documents in his possession that connected him to Hezbollah, including a letter from Hezbollah leader Hassan Nasrallah thanking Assad for a $3,534,149 transfer sent to the "martyrs program." The Barakats have another brother who is a sheikh in Lebanon at a Hezbollah mosque.[40]

In 2002 the name of a well-known Sunni leader in the TBA, Mohammad Dahrough, was found in an address book of Abu Zubaydah, a high-level al-Qaeda operative apprehended by U.S. officials and put through enhanced interrogation. Darhough is reported to have left the TBA in September 1998 to rejoin al-Qaeda operatives in the Middle East. He was also reported to have transferred $10 million during 2000–2001 from fund-raising efforts in the TBA to dummy corporations in the United States that were used as fronts for al-Qaeda and Hamas. Dahrough's nephew, Ali Nizar Dahrough, was captured in the TBA in 2002 and sentenced to five years for Paraguayan tax evasion in 2003. Paraguayan officials contend that both men were high-level al-Qaeda operatives in the TBA.[41]

The most infamous terrorist operation to originate in the TBA was the bombing of two Jewish targets in Argentina: the Israeli Embassy in 1992 and the AMIA community center in 1994. Though the investigation has been a decades-long fiasco of incompetence and corruption by the Argentine government (for instance, Argentine investigators dumped a human head, thought to be that of a bomber, into a trash can, rather than preserve it for forensic and DNA evidence[42]) parallel U.S. and Israeli investigations have uncovered evidence of Iranian involvement at the highest levels. The consensus of the intelligence communities of the United States, Israel, and Argentina is that the embassy bombing was financed, planned, and carried out by members of the Shi'ite community of Ciudad del Este, acting on the orders of Iran. It has been established that those who have been identified as the perpetrators were present in Ciudad del Este prior to the bombing, then left the area, but returned to the area after the terrorist act.[43]

And in November 2007, Interpol announced a red notice with the names of six individuals accused of involvement in the AMIA bombing: Imad Fayez Mughniyah, Ali Fallahijan, Mohsen Rabbani, Ahmad Reza Asghari, Ahmad Vahidi, and Mohsen Rezai. In February 2008 Mughniyah, who was thought to have also been behind the 1983 Marine barracks bombing in Lebanon, was killed by a car bomb in Damascus. In August 2009 Vahidi was named by Mahmoud Ahmadinejad as Iran's defense minister. At the time of the AMIA bombing, Vahidi was the leader of the Quds Force, the Iranian proxy group that has been building its presence in Venezuela in the last few years.

Mohsen Rabbani's activities were highlighted in a December 2011 documentary by the Spanish-language network Univision. Rabbani served as the cultural attaché at the Iranian Embassy in Argentina at the time of the bombings, and he fled to Iran ahead of the Interpol Red Notice being issued. He is currently working at the al-Mustafa Al-Alam Cultural Institute in Qom, a Shiite ideological institution whose purpose is to export Shia Islam.

Because his travel is limited due to the Red Notice, Rabbani has enlisted two Argentine operatives, Sheik Suhail Assad and his brother-in-law Sheik Karim Abdul Paz, to serve as his ambassadors in Latin America. Both Suhail Assad and Abdul Paz were under the tutelage of Rabbani when he was working in Argentina and were chosen for their ability to proselytize and to convert young Latin Americans into recruits for radical Islam. The Univision documentary featured one of those young recruits, José Carlos Garcia Tolentino, who was sent to Qom for a two-month indoctrination course on Islam. Garcia Tolentino, rather than becoming a militant, turned informant and told investigators that his instructors in Qom were actually Suhail Assad and Abdul Paz, who were "more well versed than those from Iran" in the ways of radical Islam, despite their upbringing in Argentina.

From the groundwork that was laid in the 1990s by Rabbani, Suhail Assad and Abdul Paz are now creating networks between radical Islamists in Latin America and radical leftist supporters of Chávez. The two were recently reported to be in Puno, Peru, where they were honored guests at an event sponsored by "Casas del Alba," an affiliate organization of radical leftist supporters of Hugo Chávez in Peru. The two are also alleged to be setting up operations in another tri-border area at the intersection of Peru, Bolivia, and Chile, where operations can be moved when there is too much publicity or enforcement pressure in the other TBA.[44]

Despite the negative publicity garnered by the terrorist presence in the TBA, Islamic radical groups have continued to operate there in various capacities. The Galeria Page Mall, a shopping center in Ciudad del Este, has been labeled a Specially Designated Global Terrorist, because its owner and many of the businesses within it are reported to fund Hezbollah. In October 2009 a federal indictment was issued against Khaled T. Safadi, Ulises Talavera, and Emilio González-Neira after a three-year investigation of their export and freight-forwarding businesses.

The investigation, carried out by U.S. immigration and FBI agents in a joint terrorism task force, found that the men had falsified invoices and export paperwork and utilized a network of false addresses to hide the true destination of their products, which consisted mostly of digital cameras and PlayStations.[45] Paraguayan authorities have also fingered Mohamed Tarabain Chamas, the manager of a five-story commercial building in Ciudad del Este, as not only a Hezbollah member but also a counterintelligence operative for Hezbollah in the TBA.[46]

Horacio Calderón, a former government minister in Argentina, stated that the United States had worked with Argentina, Brazil, and Paraguay to create "technical teams" to share information about import-export data in order to detect illegal commerce and terrorist financing operations. The United States donated a high-end data-mining computer system to the Trade Transparency Unit, the task force's oversight entity that oversees the technical teams. According to Calderón, "a very important Lebanese source" provided confidential information that Venezuela may be helping to thwart the ability of these technical teams to identify new arrivals to the TBA. According to a confidential Lebanese source, "Venezuela is supplying original personal identification cards and documents with Spanish names to Near and Middle Eastern citizens." Calderon mentions two pending cases in the Fifth Office of Paraguay's public prosecutor against business owners with Venezuelan citizenship who speak Arabic and English but not Spanish.[47]

Hugo Chávez's placement of individuals with known ties to terrorist groups in charge of his immigration and identification bureau has long been documented. But his strategy to exploit the border areas of his enemies is much more complex. As mentioned in the introduction, in 2009 Chávez sent letters of invitation to several small-town mayors near another tri-border area at the intersection of Brazil, Peru, and Colombia. One of the towns whose mayor received a letter to visit Caracas was Requena, Peru. Requena is just downriver from Leticia, Colombia, and Tabatinga, Brazil—port cities that are the gateways to enter the remote corners of both countries.

Analysts in the region speculated that Chávez was searching for friends on the border with Colombia, but officials of Peru's National Counter-Terrorist Directorate (Dirección Nacional Contra el Terrorismo, or DINCOTE) have speculated that Chávez may also be seeking to ease the movement of cocaine from Peru's Huallaga Valley, one of the most productive areas for cocaine cultivation.

In 2006 Peruvian president Alan García pulled ahead of the Chávez-backed candidate in the presidential race by aggressively denouncing Chávez's meddling in Peruvian politics and by portraying his opponent, current president Ollanta Humala, as a Chávez proxy. Prior to the election, Chávez had been infiltrating parts of Peru by opening ALBA houses throughout the country.[48]

Chávez's collaboration with the FARC on the Colombia-Venezuela border was highlighted in a July 22, 2010, presentation to the Permanent Council of the Organization of American States by Colombia's ambassador to the OAS Luis Alfonso

Hoyos. Hoyos revealed that Venezuela was allowing the FARC a safe haven within its territory. His two-hour presentation included intelligence reports, satellite photos, and witness testimonies that laid out the case with incontrovertible evidence.[49]

At a hearing in March 2010, Gen. Douglas Fraser, commander of U.S. Southern Command, also mentioned the increasing presence in Venezuela of the IRGC's Quds Force. General Fraser's remarks helped to put Islamist infiltration on the radar within policy circles in Washington, though the issue received far less attention in the media.

The issue received greater scrutiny after June 23, 2010, when Rep. Sue Myrick (R-NC) wrote a letter to the director of Homeland Security, Janet Napolitano, requesting a task force be set up to address the cooperation between Islamic terrorist groups and Mexican drug cartels. Myrick's letter quoted former DEA chief of operations Michael Braun: "Hezbollah relies on the same criminal weapons smugglers, document traffickers and transportation experts as the drug cartel. . . . They work together; they rely on the same shadow facilitators. One way or another they are all connected."[50]

Myrick commented on the threat: "Our intelligence sources have really clarified that they are in Mexico, that there is an operation that is quite large in place there, and it's very frightening to me because this is national security." Elaborating on Hezbollah's collaboration with Chávez, Myrick stated, "We know some of them have gotten across the border in the past, and now we know that there are people from Iran who are going to Venezuela. They are actually learning Spanish, and then they come up through Mexico to cross our border. So they're working in cahoots with Venezuela as well."[51]

In September 2010, a spokesperson for the Simon Wiesenthal Center told DPA, a German press agency, that "a reliable official US source with which we held a meeting last week confirmed to us the existence of dormant terrorist Hezbollah cells in South America, who await signals to come into action in Argentina."[52]

Besides the itinerant travelers to the TBA, Hezbollah has had two main centers in Latin America, based in Argentina and Venezuela, although they have been branching out lately into Peru and Chile. The Venezuelan contingent was centered among the Wayuu tribe located in the La Guajira Peninsula in the northwestern region of Venezuela and the northern part of Colombia. The Wayuu are recent converts to Islam, and the tribe's leader, Teodoro Darnott (aka Mario Morales Meza and Daniel José González Epieyu), quickly became radicalized.

On October 3, 2006, the group placed a bomb in front of the U.S. Embassy in Caracas. It failed to go off, but it did help get the group's propaganda out to the public, as pro-Hezbollah pamphlets were found with the undetonated bomb.[53] Immediately after the failed bombing, Darnott claimed responsibility and posted on the group's website that the bomber, José Miguel Reyes Espinosa, had been assassinated by the CIA and Mossad. In retaliation, Darnott suggested that U.S. ambassador to Venezuela, William Brownfield, was "worthy of death" and posted his photo on the site.[54]

While later serving a ten-year sentence, Darnott would entrust the undercover author of the book *El Palestino*, Antonio Salas, to run his official website. ("Antonio Salas" is the nom de plume of a Spanish journalist known for his earlier book, *Diario de un Skin*, for which he infiltrated a skinhead group. He then repeated the exploit by going undercover as a Muslim terrorist-in-training in Venezuela and reported on terrorist training camps located there.[55])

Adnan Shukrijumah

In January 2005 it was reported that a Boston branch of the street gang Mara Salvatrucha (also known as MS-13) had been meeting with al-Qaeda members to help smuggle terrorists into the United States via the southern border. One of their contacts was reported to be Adnan Shukrijumah, who is said to have been regarded as the successor to 9/11 terrorist Mohammed Atta.[56]

Shukrijumah was alleged to have trained in explosives with "dirty bomb" plotter José Padilla in Pakistan. The two had planned to go to Florida, rent several adjacent apartments in high-rise buildings, seal the doors and windows air tight, and ignite the natural gas lines to cause a massive explosion. The only reason that the terrorist duo didn't carry out the plan was that they had "personality conflicts" and parted ways before they could execute the plan.[57]

Shukrijumah's father had been the imam at the Miramar-based Al-Hijrah Mosque. The father (now deceased) was fired after his son's plot was made public, but he was hired shortly afterward as an assistant director of the Shamshuddin Islamic Center in North Miami Beach. The center was run by Sofian Abdelaziz Zakkout of AMANA, the American Muslim Association of North America.[58]

After Khalid Sheik Mohamed was apprehended in March 2003, he gave U.S. forces confirmation that Shukrijumah was a member of al-Qaeda. It was later learned that Shukrijumah had been in Panama surveying the Panama Canal for a potential

terrorist attack in April 2001, and Honduran officials confirmed that Shukrijumah
had met with Mara Salvatrucha members in their country in May 2004. Later that
year Shukrijumah was reported to have been spotted in Costa Rica and was supposedly planning to reenter the United States via the Mexican border. According to a
June 2007 report, he had been personally chosen by Osama bin Laden "to detonate
nuclear bombs simultaneously in several U.S. cities."[59] Shukrijumah was formally
indicted in July 2010 in a federal case for being one of three al-Qaeda operatives
plotting to attack targets inside the United States. These charges were in addition
to an earlier indictment for plotting to bomb New York's subway system. Today, his
whereabouts are unknown.[60]

14

A POTENTIAL FAILED STATE NEXT DOOR

In Mexico security officials have been concerned about collaboration between the FARC and Mexican drug cartels. A U.S. Embassy cable in 2008 stated:

> [FARC] members have been tied loosely to several Mexican drug trafficking organizations in the past in drugs for guns deals according to DEA. In 2001, Colombian Carlos Ariel Charry Guzman was arrested in Mexico for acting as an intermediary for a drugs and weapons deal with the Arellano Felix Cartel. According to the DEA, he was a doctor for the FARC and came to Mexico to buy medical supplies to take back to the camps of the FARC. At the time, Mexico's Attorney General publicly denounced the link between the FARC and the Tijuana-based organization. DEA also reported that in October 2007 a plane piloted by known Mexican narcotraffickers ran large quantities of cocaine between Ecuador's border region (near a FARC stronghold in Colombia) and Mexico. After the killing of [FARC commander Raul] Reyes on March 1, media carried an unsubstantiated report that one of the computers seized at the site contained information relating to a February 18, 2008, shipment of drugs to a cartel in Mexico.[1]

The undersecretary of the U.S. Army, Joseph Westphal, commented in February 2011 that the United States might need to send troops to Mexico to defend Americans against the cartels. Westphal described the narco-trafficking problem in Mexico as an "insurgency" that had the potential to overthrow the Mexican government, adding, "This isn't just about drugs and about illegal immigrants. This is about, potentially, a takeover of a government by individuals who are corrupt."[2]

The Mexican government strongly condemned the undersecretary's comments, and Westphal apologized, saying he "mistakenly characterized the challenge posed by drug cartels to Mexico as 'a form of insurgency.'" But his words were telling. Answering an audience question about foreign policy, Westphal stated that he would never want to see a situation in which "armed and fighting" American troops would be sent to fight an insurgency "on our border, in violation of our Constitution, or to have to send them across the border."[3]

Westphal was referring to spillover violence from drug traffickers on our border and the potential of Mexico becoming a "failed state," a connotation that had first appeared in the Department of Defense's 2008 Joint Operating Environment report, which mentioned Mexico's domestic problems in its "Weak and Failing States" section. While the report did not classify Mexico as a failed state, it did warn that "two large and important states"—Mexico and Pakistan—"bear consideration for rapid and sudden collapse."[4]

While many chose to downplay the comments as overblown, it is worth noting how close Mexico had already come to becoming an ally of Hugo Chávez and hence of Iran. In the 2006 presidential election, Andrés Manuel López Obrador, better known as AMLO, came within 0.5 percent of defeating President Felipe Calderón. Influenced by Chávez and radical leftist groups in the region, López Obrador staged a populist sit-in in the central square of Mexico City for nearly two months, claiming to be the "legitimate president."

Rep. Jim Kolbe (R-AZ) told several Mexican legislators at the time that he had received intelligence reports that Chávez had been funding AMLO's Party of the Democratic Revolution (Partido de la Revolución Democrática).[5] Had López Obrador won, the nefarious influences of Chávez and Ahmadinejad would have moved to America's doorstep, and the nexus of drug trafficking and terrorism that were already on the border would be an order of magnitude greater.

But the greater concern among security analysts in recent years has not been the probability of a failing Mexican state but of a terrorist crossing the border into the United States. In March 2009, the commander of U.S. Southern Command, Adm. James G. Stavridis, told the House Armed Services Committee that the connection between illicit drug trafficking and Islamic radical terrorism was a growing threat to the United States. He stated that the previous August, "U.S. Southern Command supported a Drug Enforcement Administration operation, in coordination with host countries, which targeted a Hezbollah-connected drug trafficking organization in the Tri-Border Area." Stavridis also mentioned that an interagency operation the previous October had led to the arrest of dozens of Colombians associated with a Hezbollah-connected narco-trafficking and money-laundering ring that funded Hezbollah terrorism worldwide.[6]

In recent years, numerous cases have been reported of Hezbollah agents operating on the border with Mexico. In 2008 Salim Boughader Mucharrafille, a Mexican of Lebanese descent, was sentenced to sixty years in prison on charges of organized crime and immigrant smuggling. Boughader Mucharrafille had been arrested six years earlier for smuggling immigrants into the United States, some of whom were connected to Hezbollah. A year before that, in 2001, Mahmoud Youssef Kourani illegally crossed the Mexican border and traveled to Dearborn, Michigan, where he was later charged and convicted for "material support and resources . . . to Hezbollah," according to the indictment.[7] In July 2008 the Venezuelan daily *El Universal* reported that a DEA document suggested that since 2005, two Mexican drug cartels had been sending operatives to train in Iran with the IRGC. Reportedly the training included instruction in sniper tactics and use of rocket launchers.[8] Though the DEA would not confirm the report, it clearly indicated that there was now a link between Latin American narco-traffickers and Middle Eastern terrorists.

On February 21, 2011, Fox News investigative reporter Adam Housley quoted DEA chief of operations Michael Braun:

Hezbollah are absolute masters at identifying existing smuggling infrastructures. I don't care if it's along our southwest border, if it's in North Africa, on the Afghanistan/Pakistan border; they are masters at identifying those existing infrastructures. Hezbollah is developing relations with those responsible for operating those smuggling operations and then forming close relations with them, so that they can move anything they have an interest into virtually anywhere in the world.[9]

Housley mentioned that military and Department of Homeland Security contacts had told him that drug tunnels are becoming much more sophisticated and "strikingly similar to tunnels being used by terror organizations to smuggle weapons into the Gaza Strip" and that there was "real concern" within Homeland Security that "bombing techniques used in the Middle East to promote terror are now also being used inside Mexico" in the battle for power among the drug cartels. Braun, according to the report, said that Hezbollah is "rubbing shoulders" with drug cartels internationally and that other officials confirmed that "it's not if Hezbollah operatives have been smuggled into the U.S. . . . but how many."[10]

In a speech in Mexico in 2007, Robert Grenier, the former head of the CIA's Counterterrorism Center, warned that the United States was concerned that Hezbollah or Hamas would try to set up operations in Mexico in order to infiltrate America's southern border and carry out terrorist attacks.[11] His warning proved prescient when, as recently as July 2010, a Hezbollah cell was busted by Mexican police in Tijuana, where Mexicans of Lebanese origin had been recruited to set up a cell to train for attacks against Israel and the West. The head of the operation, Jameel Nasr, had been under Mexican police surveillance as he traveled frequently back and forth to Lebanon and spent two months in Venezuela in the summer of 2008.[12]

ETA, FARC, and Venezuela

Spain's former president, José Luis Zapatero, demanded in March 2010 that Venezuela explain its assistance to Basque ETA terrorists plotting attacks on Spanish soil. That month, Spanish High Court judge Eloy Velasco had issued warrants for thirteen ETA and FARC terrorists, one of whom was a Venezuelan government employee born in Spain. The warrants declared that the Venezuelan government had served as a go-between for ETA and the FARC and that, after the contact, the FARC had sought logistical assistance from ETA as it sought possibly to assassinate Colombian officials visiting Spain. Colombia's President Álvaro Uribe, the court said, was one of the targets. According to the magistrate, several ETA terrorists had traveled to Venezuela to train members of the FARC to use cell phones as detonators for bombs containing the explosive C-4, and members of Venezuela's armed forces had accompanied them on at least one occasion. Several ETA terrorists had also traveled to FARC camps in Colombia, via Venezuela, to receive guerrilla training. The same day that the magistrate's report was released, Spanish police disclosed the names of three ETA terrorists captured the day before. One, José Ayestaran, had been wanted by Spanish authorities in connection with ten killings. Ayestaran had lived in Venezuela for many years.[13]

On January 10, 2011, a joint operation between French police and Spain's Guardia Civil led to the arrest of two members of ETA. Twenty-seven-year-old Iraitz Guesalaga Fernández, said to be in charge of ETA's Internet operations, and his girlfriend and accomplice Itxaso Urtiaga, who is accused of playing a supporting role in her boyfriend's operations, were arrested in Ciboure on the French side of the border.[14] According to reports, the couple had traveled to Venezuela to train FARC and ETA members in Venezuela on how to encrypt computer documents and communicate securely over the Internet. Guesalaga's name first appeared in a cache of documents that were captured from the former leader of ETA, Javier López Peña, also known as Thierry, when police arrested in him 2008. The documents showed that Guesalaga had traveled to Venezuela in 2007 and again in September and October 2008 accompanied by his girlfriend.

In Judge Velasco's indictment issued in February 2010, it was alleged that "there is evidence that the Venezuelan government is co-operating in the illegal association between FARC and ETA" and that ETA terrorists were given a military escort in 2007 to a jungle hideout where they trained FARC terrorists in explosives. According to the Spanish daily *El Mundo*, Guesalaga had met with Arturo Cubillas, an ETA member whom Spanish antiterrorism authorities sought and whom Chávez had appointed as head of the National Lands Institute (Instituto Nacional de Tierras, or INTI), a branch of the Venezuelan Ministry of Agriculture. Cubillas, who moved to Caracas after being deported from Algeria in 1989, was suspected of being the head of ETA in South America and in charge of coordinating the terrorist group's relations with the FARC.[15]

El Universal also reported that six additional ETA members work in the Chávez government, three of whom are in the same agency (INTI). The Spanish newspaper *20 minutos* reported on its website that "counter-terrorism officials have a list of 180 ETA members who have fled to foreign countries over the past three decades, many of which have ended up in Venezuela. It is suspected that that is where two of the heavyweights of the ETA political apparatus could be."[16] The pro-Chávez newspaper *Ciudad Caracas* quoted Cubillas as saying, "I have never provided any explosives training. In fact, I have never been to Guasdualito." Cubillas added that the two ETA terrorists who had confessed to being trained in explosives in Venezuela had confessed under torture by Spanish authorities.[17]

In September 2011, *El Universal* reported that a Spanish court had prosecuted five members of Askapena, the international wing of ETA. Court documents showed that Askapena had been instructed to set up an international relations network by organizing seminars and creating "solidarity committees" in Europe and North and

South America. It had established one of the first of these solidarity committees in Venezuela. This Caracas-based solidarity committee released a communiqué on September 11, 2010, in support of ETA's announcement of its "cessation of offensive military actions" that was released a week before.[18]

Remarkably, it was a member of ETA living under the aegis of the Sandinistas in Nicaragua who provided the Islamic terrorists behind the 1993 World Trade Center bombing with Nicaraguan passports and IDs. Also, among the passports found in the terrorists' apartment, one had been falsified with the photo of El Sayyid Nosair, who was connected to the 1990 murder of Rabbi Meir Kahane in New York.[19]

In fact, the *New York Times* reported on January 28, 1996, that during the last two months that the Sandinistas were in power, they had granted Nicaraguan citizenship and documentation to over nine hundred foreigners, including terrorists from ETA and Italy's Red Brigades, three dozen Arabs and Iranians from Islamic terrorist groups, and terrorists from "virtually every guerrilla organization in Latin America."[20]

This information was uncovered after the May 23, 1993, explosion of a hidden vault in Managua located under a mechanics' shop that belonged to Miguel Antonio Larios Moreno—a fake identity for Eusebio Arzalus, an ETA operative. The arsenal also contained "several tons of weapons, explosives, 19 surface-to-air missiles, 310 passports from 21 countries, many of them blank." After the explosion, Sandinista interior minister Tomás Borge was the first to arrive on the scene, wearing only pajamas. It was later discovered that three members of ETA had been working for Borge under false identities in the Sandinista government.[21]

In a letter to the UN secretary-general sent in June of 1993, the Salvadoran commander of the FMLN (now a political party), Salvador Sánchez Cerén, admitted that the weapons found in the vault belonged to the FMLN. Under a disarmament agreement that the Salvadoran guerrilla group had negotiated with the UN, the weapons were explicitly illegal. Today Sanchez Cerén is the vice president of El Salvador.[22]

15

VENEZUELA: STATE SPONSOR
OF TERRORISM

Even as Hugo Chávez consolidated power in Venezuela and used his country's oil wealth to spread anti-Americanism to other countries in the region, both the Bush and Obama administrations made it a policy to ignore him in order to minimize his influence. But today, his ability and willingness to both abet terrorists and serve as a sanctions buster for Iran make him a much bigger problem and one that will only become worse as Iran gets closer to becoming a nuclear power. It may be time to change strategy.

As far back as May 2008, Jackson Diehl, deputy editorial page editor and foreign policy writer for the *Washington Post*, wrote that Chávez belonged on the State Department's list of State Sponsors of Terrorism (SSOT):

> His reported actions are, first of all, a violation of U.N. Security Council Resolution 1373, passed in September 2001, which prohibits all states from providing financing or havens to terrorist organizations. More directly, the Colombian evidence would be more than enough to justify a State Department decision to cite Venezuela as a state sponsor of terrorism. Once cited, Venezuela would be subject to a number of automatic sanctions, some of which could complicate its continuing export of oil to the United States. A cutoff would temporarily inconvenience Americans—and cripple Venezuela, which could have trouble selling its heavy oil in other markets.[1]

Since Diehl's article was published, revelations about the extent to which the Chávez regime is collaborating with terrorist groups has continued to accumulate.

On February 16, 2011, Radio Free Europe published a report that quoted Assistant Secretary of State for Western Hemisphere Affairs Arturo Valenzuela saying that the State Department was investigating the issue to "determine if in fact there is a violation." The report said that PDVSA had sent to Iran at least 600,000 barrels of reformate, a component of hich-octane gasoline, in two shipments of 300,000 barrels each to the National Iranian Oil Company in late December 2010.[2] This clear violation of the sanctions placed on Iran would normally trigger the listing of a country as an SSOT. But violations do not stop there. In the Chávez regime, there are a large number of advisers and bureaucrats with ties to Hezbollah and other terrorist groups in positions that allow them to aid not only Iran but other terrorists in the region as well. Roger Noriega, former assistant secretary of state for Western Hemisphere affairs, has reported on the number of Chávez regime officials with connections to Hezbollah, Iraq's Baath Party, and other terrorist and radical groups. The list is not comprehensive:

> Tarek William Saab Halabi, governor of the province of Anzoategui; George Kabbou Abdelnour, who heads Bariven, the purchasing arm of state-owned Petroleos de Venezuela, SA (PDVSA); Imaad Saab Saab, Venezuela's ambassador to Syria; Radwan Sabbagh, president of a mining company operating in the province of Orinoco; Aref Richany Jimenez, a brigadier general in the Venezuelan army who heads the military's industrial company and is a director of PDVSA; Fadi Kabboul Abdelnour, PDVSA's director of planning; the minister of interior's sister, Amin Obayda El Aissami Maddah, an executive in PDVSA's technology arm; Kamal Naim Naim, president of the Bolívar provincial assembly.[3]

Patricia Poleo, an investigative journalist who had to flee Venezuela to exile in Miami, wrote in the Venezuelan daily *El Nuevo Pais* that Ghazi Nasr al Din, his brother Ghasan Atef Salameh Nasr al Din, and Tarek El Aissami recruited young Venezuelan Arabs affiliated with Chávez's United Socialist Party of Venezuela (PSUV) to travel to Hezbollah camps in Lebanon for guerrilla warfare training and to prepare for asymmetric warfare against the United States. After returning to Venezuela, they were received by radical PSUV members affiliated with the National Experimental University of the Armed Forces (Universidad Nacional Experimental Politécnica de la Fuerza Armada Nacional) and the Venezuelan Bolivarian University, where they continued their training in firearms and demolition. The recruits are supervised by Hezbollah in Venezuela, Iraqi al-Qaeda members, and the Democratic Front for the Liberation of Palestine, whose office is located in Caracas. Poleo also identified a known Hezbollah explosives expert, Abdul Ghani Suleiman Wanked, as living in Venezuela and helping with the training. Suleiman Wanked is also known to be a close confidant of Hezbollah leader Hassan Nasrallah.[4]

In June 2008, the U.S. Treasury Department announced that it had designated two Venezuelans, the aforementioned Ghazi Nasr al Din and Fawzi Kan'an, as supporters of Hezbollah and had also designated two travel agencies owned and controlled by Kan'an as illegally supporting Hezbollah.[5] According to Poleo, Raymundo Kabchi, a Venezuelan lawyer born in Lebanon, is an "adviser" to Venezuela's foreign minister and is the one who recommended Nasr al Din for the post in the Venezuelan Embassy in Damascus.

According to the Treasury report, Nasr al Din, while serving as a Venezuelan diplomat and simultaneously managing a Shiite Islamic center in Caracas, conspired to provide financial support to Hezbollah. He had previously served as the chargé d'affaires at the Venezuelan Embassy in Damascus and was later named the director of political affairs at the Venezuelan Embassy in Lebanon. He allegedly met with donors to Hezbollah and briefed them on the status of fund-raising efforts for the terrorist group. More specifically, he provided these donors with bank information so that their donations would go directly to Hezbollah.

Nasr al Din allegedly flew to Lebanon to meet with senior-level Hezbollah leaders "to discuss operational issues" and provided logistical support for their members' travel to Venezuela. In January 2006 he aided two members of Hezbollah, who were also members of the Lebanese parliament, so they could fly to Venezuela and do fund-raising for Hezbollah under the guise of opening a Hezbollah office and "community center" in Caracas. In 2005 Nasr al Din had also arranged for members of Hezbollah to travel to Iran to attend a terrorist training camp.

The other Treasury Department designee, Fawzi Kan'an, is also a fund-raiser for Hezbollah based in Venezuela. He allegedly arranged the travel of Hezbollah members and helped move money raised in Venezuela for Hezbollah to its coffers in Lebanon. According to the press release from Treasury, Kan'an met with Hezbollah senior officials in Lebanon "to discuss operational issues, including possible kidnappings and terrorist attacks." Moreover, Kan'an is said to have traveled along with others to Iran for training.[6]

On March 20, 2011, Ghasan Atef Salameh Nasr al Din's name showed up in another *Washington Post* article. Roger Noriega reported that Nasr al Din actually runs the Hezbollah network in Latin America, including terror operations and drug trafficking.[7]

Noriega also obtained a document from a senior Venezuelan diplomat that said Nasr al Din was connected to four businesses that had been operated by the incarcerated drug kingpin Walid Makled. Since his capture, Makled has given a number of media interviews in which he admitted his involvement in narco-trafficking and told reporters that he has documentation and video proving the complicity of Henry Rangel Silva, Chávez's top-ranking military commander, as well as other officials in the Chávez administration.[8] Despite that the United States had designated Rangel Silva a "drug kingpin," Chávez named him defense minister in early 2012. Noriega also reported a clandestine meeting that Chávez hosted on August 22, 2010, at Fuerte Tiuna, the military intelligence headquarters in Caracas. The secretary-general of Palestinian Islamic Jihad, Ramadan Abdullah Mohammad Shallah, was present, along with the supreme leader of Hamas, Khaled Meshal, and the chief of operations of Hezbollah, whose identity is not publicly known.

According to Noriega, the meeting was prompted by an earlier meeting between Ahmad Mousavi, the Iranian ambassador to Syria, and Imad Saab Saab, his Venezuelan counterpart, at Venezuela's embassy in Damascus on May 10, 2010. In a report given to Venezuela's foreign minister, the content of the session was said to discuss a meeting between their presidents and Hasan Nasrallah, the head of Hezbollah. Mousavi had suggested that the three could travel to Caracas to rendezvous with Chávez. The arrangements were made, according to documents provided from within the Venezuelan regime, by Ghazi Nasr al Din, now Chávez's second-ranking diplomat in Syria. Noriega, commenting on the meeting, said, "That these infamous criminals left their traditional havens demonstrates their confidence in Chávez and their determination to cultivate a terror network on America's doorstep."[9]

A Venezuelan government source reported to Noriega that two Iranian terrorists were training an eclectic group of terrorists from around Latin America that had congregated on Margarita Island. And, Noriega added, "radical Muslims from Venezuela and Colombia are brought to a cultural center in Caracas named for the Ayatollah Khomeini and Simon Bolivar for spiritual training, and some are dispatched to Qom, Iran, for Islamic studies. Knowledgeable sources confirm that the most fervent recruits in Qom are given weapons and explosives training and are returned home as 'sleeper' agents."[10]

More ominously, Noriega reported that the U.S. Embassy in Caracas was evacuated on January 31, 2011, due to "credible threats" that two known al-Qaeda operatives in Venezuela were plotting a "chemical" attack on it.[11]

16

THE EMERGING THREATS

By the time you read this, an election will have taken place in Mexico. The results of that election and the policies that it produces will determine much about the threat level that the United States will face in the next few years. Although Mexico is an ally, its hands will be full fighting the drug cartels or possibly cutting a deal with them. Mexico has also demonstrated a penchant for downplaying the threats from terrorist elements that may use its territory as a staging area.

In early 2005 a Mossad agent code-named Manuel visited the security services in Bolivia, Colombia, the Dominican Republic, and Peru, where each country's intelligence service briefed him on the extent of al-Qaeda's infiltration of their countries. According to intelligence sources, al-Qaeda operatives had met with the FARC in Colombia and with Shining Path members in Peru.[1]

During CIA operations in Pakistan, agents found documents showing considerable collaboration between al-Qaeda and Mexico's EPR terrorist group. The recovered documents also showed al-Qaeda had ties to Muslim students in Dominica and with Arabs living on the border area of Chile and Peru. The documents also revealed that Mexico's EPR guerrillas helped smuggle al-Qaeda operatives into the United States through the border crossing at Tijuana.

There is also evidence that Ayman al-Zawahiri, reported in 2011 to be the new head of al-Qaeda, made several visits to Latin America. Yet, when Mossad agent Manuel asked the head of Mexico's intelligence and national security agency, Eduardo Medina-Mora, if he could help confirm al-Zawahiri's presence in Mexico, he demurred, saying, "Purely media speculation." Medina-Mora would deny that his service had any reason to believe that not only al-Zawahiri but any al-Qaeda members had any presence in Mexico.[2]

In February 2009, Michael Scheuer, former head of the CIA's Osama bin Laden unit, stated in an interview on Fox News about al-Qaeda's intentions in Mexico:

> They've been studying the Mexican border since 2002, if you look at their electronic journals. They're fascinated with the fact that America doesn't protect its borders, and they're particularly interested in how many trucks get across the border without being inspected. As you can see as what's going on in Afghanistan, they're very good at using unprotected borders to move their people in to attack.[3]

Al-Qaeda's desire to infiltrate the border was further confirmed in the June 2009 video that was mentioned in chapter 4. The video, which was authenticated by U.S. counterterrorism officials, showed recruiter Abdullah al-Nafisi telling an auditorium of supporters about al-Qaeda's aspirations of smuggling a biological weapon into the United States across the southern border.[4]

> Four pounds of anthrax—in a suitcase this big—carried by a fighter through tunnels from Mexico into the U.S. are guaranteed to kill 330,000 Americans within a single hour if it is properly spread in population centers there. What a horrifying idea; 9/11 will be small change in comparison. Am I right? There is no need for airplanes, conspiracies, timings and so on. One person, with the courage to carry 4 pounds of anthrax, will go to the White House lawn, and will spread this "confetti" all over them, and then we'll do these cries of joy. It will turn into a real celebration.
>
> The Americans are afraid that the [weapons of mass destruction] might fall into the hands of "terrorist" organizations like al Qaeda and others. There is good reason for the Americans' fears. . . . [Al Qaeda] had laboratories in north Afghanistan. They have scientists, chemists and nuclear physicists. They are nothing like they are portrayed by these mercenary journalists— backward Bedouins living in caves. No, no, by no means. This kind of talk can fool only naive people. People who follow such things know that Al Qaeda has laboratories, just like Hezbollah.[5]

Al-Nafisi then spoke glowingly of the neo-Nazi groups that he says are planning terrorist attacks on nuclear plants inside the United States:

These militias even think about bombing nuclear plants within the U.S. May God grant them success, even though we are not white, or even close to it, right? They have plans to bomb the nuclear plant at Lake Michigan. This plant is very important. . . . May God grant success to one of these militia leaders, who is thinking about bombing this plant. I believe that we should devote part of our prayers to him.[6]

Security planners have hardened security at nuclear plants since 9/11 and have drastically increased precautions against anthrax attacks since the anthrax-laced letters were sent to congressmen and others shortly afterward. But the greatest threat to the continental United States may be from a little-noticed but far more dangerous weapon.

EMP: The Ultimate Terror Weapon

A November 2010 article in *Die Welt*, a German daily, reported that Hugo Chávez had agreed to give Iran a "military base manned by Iranian missile officers, soldiers of the Iranian Revolutionary Guard [Corps] and Venezuelan missile officers." The military base inside Venezuela would reportedly be armed with ballistic missiles, the short-range Scud-B and -C , as well as the medium-range Iranian Shahab-3. While the Scuds have the capability to threaten only nearby Latin America, the Shahab-3 would have enough range to hit many parts of the United States.[7] However, the report has not been verified, and such a move by Chávez would probably represent a risk that he is not yet prepared to take, though it should not be discounted. It would, however, violate one of the major tenets of asymmetric warfare—plausible deniability.

At an event at the Heritage Foundation on August 15, 2011, called "National EMP Recognition Day: The Threat That Can't Be Ignored," Rep. Roscoe Bartlett (R-MD) told the story of being in a hotel in Vienna in 1999 while working on the framework for a final agreement to end the Kosovo conflict. He was with nine members of Congress, three Russians, and a personal representative of Serbian leader Slobodan Milošović.

According to Congressman Bartlett, the senior Russian official, Vladimir Lukin, who was the chair of the Duma's foreign affairs committee at the time, was angry.

He said to Bartlett, "You spit on us, now why should we help you? If we really wanted to hurt you, with no fear of retaliaton, we'd launch an SLBM, which would shut down your grid, your communications, for six months or so." The third-ranking Russian present, Alexander Shibanov, supposedly smiled and said, "If one weapon won't do it, we have some spares."[8]

What Lukin was referring to by "SLBM" was a submarine-launched ballistic missile, which can also be launched from a commercial container ship. The most probable scenario that has been promulgated for this type of attack is an SLBM launched from a commercial cargo ship in the Gulf of Mexico. This would allow detonation above one of the major hubs of the U.S. electrical grid, knocking out power for an extended period of time.

According to Bartlett, a tramp steamer using a Scud missile purchased on the open market for around $100,000 and any crude nuclear device would allow any state or non-state actor to send the United States back in a time-machine ride to the 1800s in the blink of an eye. With this inexpensive maritime missile-launch capacity, a missile detonated above the continental United States could be a threat greater than any we have faced in modern times for three reasons:

- A missile defense system, in order to have maximum effectiveness, requires "lead time" in order to be able to shoot down incoming missiles. A ship-launched missile just off the coast would cut that lead time down considerably.
- Even if there was enough time for a missile-defense response, a generic Scud missile, fired from a ship, could also be launched with no "fingerprint," because generic Scuds are found in the inventories of numerous countries in the Middle East. Moreover, it would not have been launched from any country's territory.
- A country such as Iran could commandeer another country's ship and launch a generic Scud and force a retaliation against that country. This makes a ship-launched attack the most compatible with asymmetrical proxy warfare as practiced by Iran, Venezuela, and other hostile countries.

An EMP blast over an area that contained one of the hubs of the electrical grid could be more devastating to the country overall than a standard nuclear attack on a major city. More importantly, a ship-launched ballistic missile carries an even greater threat. The generic Scud-type missile has no "return address," as earlier mentioned. There is no way to discern which country or group launched it. This eliminates the normal deterrent of retribution should a rogue regime decide to launch a nuclear attack.[9]

To compound this anonymity, the Iranians have been conducting midair detonation tests of their Shahab-3 inventory over the Caspian Sea since 2005. The test launches were fired from the deck of Iran's navy ships rather than from land bases.[10] According to Dr. Peter Pry, who served on the Commission to Assess the Threat to the United States from Electromagnetic Pulse Attack, "A nuclear missile concealed in the hold of a freighter would give Iran or terrorists the capability to perform an EMP attack against the United States homeland without developing an ICBM and with some prospect of remaining anonymous."[11]

During a March 2005 hearing of the Senate Subcommittee on Terrorism, Technology, and Homeland Security, Pry said, "Iran's Shahab-3 medium range missile is a mobile missile and small enough to be transported in the hold of a freighter. We cannot rule out that Iran, the world's leading sponsor of international terrorism, might provide terrorists with the means to execute an EMP attack against the United States."[12]

An article published in an Iranian military journal in 2005 titled "Electronics to Determine Fate of Future Wars" examines how an EMP attack on the United States would devastate the country. It states:

> Once you confuse the enemy communication network you can also disrupt the work of the enemy command- and decision-making center. Even worse today when you disable a country's military high command through disruption of communications, you will, in effect, disrupt all the affairs of that country. If the world's industrial countries fail to devise effective ways to defend themselves against dangerous electronic assaults then they will disintegrate within a few years. American soldiers would not be able to find food to eat nor would they be able to fire a single shot.[13]

If the United States decided to harden its coastline protections to intercept a short-range missile to protect against this type of threat, there is an alternative delivery method available to a determined terrorist. As far back as January 1998, a Swiss newspaper reported that the Swedish National Defense Research Institute had purchased a Russian "suitcase bomb" that utilized high-power microwaves to destroy any electronic circuits within its blast radius. The article stated that the device was sold commercially and that one had been purchased by the Australian military for around $100,000.[14] Today, a quick Internet search turns up commercial sellers of "suitcase EMPs" that will get smaller and cheaper over time. A few of these devices would only need to be carried and deployed near one or a few of the electrical hubs in the United States.

This threat has been quietly studied over the past decade in the U.S. Congress by the Commission to Assess the Threat to the United States from Electromagnetic Pulse Attack, chaired by Dr. William R. Graham. Besides the technical findings about the vulnerability of civilian infrastructure, the commission studied previous blackouts that showed a glimpse of how quickly the social order would break down. Any larger EMP attack that knocked out just two or three electrical hubs would have an almost inconceivable effect. The commission described it vividly:

> A massive EMP attack on the United States would produce almost unimaginable devastation. Communications would collapse, transportation would halt, and electrical power would simply be non-existent. Not even a global humanitarian effort would be enough to keep hundreds of millions of Americans from death by starvation, exposure, or lack of medicine. Nor would the catastrophe stop at U.S. borders. Most of Canada would be devastated, too, as its infrastructure is integrated with the U.S. power grid. Without the American economic engine, the world economy would quickly collapse. Much of the world's intellectual brain power (half of it is in the United States) would be lost as well. Earth would most likely recede into the "new" Dark Ages.[15]

Such apocalyptic rhetoric, and possibly the fact that the subject of EMPs has been taken up by an unpopular politician or two, has caused many officials to write it off as overblown or as a means of causing fear in order to generate support for an aggressive posture against Iran. But it deserves a sober analysis. As technology and time keeps producing smaller and cheaper tools with which to construct and deploy an EMP, it will undoubtedly enter the arsenal of some determined terrorist group. What remains is whether the decision is made to harden the grid to defend against it.

Conclusion

Maj. Stephen Coughlin opened his master's thesis "To Our Great Detriment: Ignoring What Extremists Say about Jihad" with an 1862 letter from Brig. Gen. William Tecumseh Sherman to President Abraham Lincoln:'

> North design to conquer the South, we must begin at Kentucky and reconquer the country from there as we did from the Indians. It was this conviction then as plainly as now that made men think I was insane. A good many followers now want to make me a prophet. I rather think you now agree with me that this is no common war. You must now see that I was right in not seeking prominence at the outstart. I knew and know yet that the northern people have to unlearn all their experience of the past thirty years and be born again before they will see the truth. Though our armies pass across and through the land, the war closes in behind and leaves the same enemy behind.... I don't see the end or the beginning of the end, but suppose we must prevail and persist or perish.... We cannot change the hearts of the people of the South, but we can make war so terrible that they will realize the fact that however brave and gallant and devoted to their country, still they are mortal and should exhaust.[16]

What Sherman was proffering is that an enemy who seemed to be so doggedly determined was still fighting a battle of will, and of legitimacy. It was not just tactics but also what those tactics signaled about the will of those utilizing them that would determine the outcome of the war.

Today we seem to be irreconcilably at odds over how best to take on the current threat. There tends to be two opposite reactions to the specific threat of Islamist terrorism—one that takes the enemy at their word and another that discerns a greater threat in painting the religion with too broad a brush.

Of these two mind-sets, the latter precludes the necessary peer pressure that might be brought to bear on the radical elements within Islam, as it becomes more empowering to don the mantle of victimhood and discrimination than to cajole fellow parishioners to reform. The requisite pushback from the vast majority of peaceful Muslims becomes instead tiptoeing caution when they are castigated as "inauthentic" and criticism is deemed "Islamophobic"—a term of propaganda developed specifically for the purpose of preventing reform.

Coughlin's thesis has underscored the need to conduct a "doctrine-based threat assessment"—to simply analyze the threat based on the enemy's declared strategic doctrine. While security analysts have been cognizant of the Islamists' kinetic warfare doctrine, many have ignored the more pernicious "political Islam"—sometimes called "civilization jihad"—that is designed to use the institutions of modern democracies in order to undermine them. This "democratic subversion" now regularly claims formerly free countries in the Middle East and in Latin America, with operatives from both regions even sharing tactics for subverting one another's democracies. Coughlin observed: "In an ideological struggle, controlling the terms of debate goes a long way towards controlling the debate itself. . . . It is through the language we use to define the WOT [War on Terror] that we understand it. Language that does not align with the enemy's doctrine will cause decision making to miscalculate."[17]

As of late, we have seen an abrogation of the duty to fight the ideological war that is as much a part of asymmetric warfare as are suicide bombings and guerrilla warfare. Homeland Security Secretary Janet Napolitano, after giving her first address to Congress without mentioning the word "terrorism," actually supplanted it with "man-caused disaster"—a catch-all phrase that, according to her, was supposed to "move away from the politics of fear toward a policy of being prepared for all risks that can occur."[18]

It is this irrational reluctance to properly describe the threat we face from declared enemies that validates those enemies' contrived grievances. Almost inversely proportional to our increased prowess in kinetic warfare, we have continually ceded the ideological war that has become the only battlefield on which our enemies are able to make an impact. As Max Manwaring and others have stated, today's battles are fights for legitimacy. To allow political correctness or misplaced deference to alter the terminology of war is to cede our most valuable territory. To our enemies, deference equals weakness, not civil accommodation.

Another tenet shared by political Islam in the Middle East and 21st Century Socialism in Latin America is that its adherents have declared war not only on the United States and the West in general but on capitalism and free societies as well. To most of us in the West, this is the equivalent of declaring war on gravity, as free exchange and free enterprise are the bases of life and the engines of progress throughout the world.

But, like communism's "fatal conceit" during the Cold War, this ideological flaw presents the West with a tactical advantage. In both Kandahar and Caracas, the inhabitants have long seen the squalor produced by enforced communism, socialism, and mercantilism. If nation-building has now become a required part of the U.S. arsenal, proving the legitimacy of the Western way of life—of individual freedom, entrepreneurship, and the rule of law—should be as important an aim as providing civilian security.

In our own hemisphere, the United States is confronting not only the infiltration of Hezbollah and IRGC elements intent on fomenting terrorism but also the erosion of individual freedom under the rubric of Bolivarian socialism. How the United States confronts this threat will have repercussions, either good or bad, in other trouble spots in both Latin America and the Middle East.

The Hoover Institution scholar and historian Victor Davis Hanson has equated our accommodationist tendency toward our enemies with "feeding the Minotaur," after the mythical Athenians who were content to sacrifice fourteen of their best young citizens every year to the Minotaur to appease King Minos. It is an apt analogy.

We enjoy the advantage that our enemies are not only fighting against us but are also fighting against the trajectory of human progress. Our duty is to decide whether we are going to continue to accommodate their superstitions or whether we will confront them before further carnage provides them with false validation. That decision will also determine whether we are able to *choose* to respond as an act of prevention or whether we are *forced* to respond as an act of retaliation.

Notes

Preface
1. Bernard Brodie, *War and Politics* (London: Longman, 1974), 83.

Introduction
1. Amir Taheri, "Tehran's Price for 'Solidarity,'" *New York Post*, October 12, 2007, http://www.nypost.com/p/news/opinion/opedcolumnists/item_ubd6fA2Xym8hXeqCjb zdtL#ixzz1EqPauFp5.
2. Deniz Ozdemir, "In Venezuela It's Chavez O'Clock," *Foreign Policy*, September 26, 2007, http://blog.foreignpolicy.com/posts/2007/09/26/in_venezuela_its_chavez _oclock.
3. U.S. Office of Research and Policy, U.S. Information Agency, Voice of America–Radio Martí Program, *Cuba Annual Report, 1988* (New Brunswick, NJ: Transaction, 1991), 212.
4. Gen. Vo Nguyen Giap, *To Arm the Revolutionary Masses: To Build the People's Army,* (Moscow: Foreign Languages Publishing House, 1975).
5. James P. Harrison, *The Endless War: Vietnam's Struggle for Independence* (New York: Columbia University Press, 1989), 157.
6. U.S. Office of Research and Policy, *Cuba Annual Report: 1988*, 209. For good measure, Risquet also utilized this concept to justify the large expenditures—and tacitly Cuba's perennial budget shortfalls and scarcity of foodstuffs—on the necessary construction of fortifications, training, continuation of salaries during training exercises, and the ongoing costs and loss of production during training exercises and fortification building. For these ancillary reasons, the theory has also proved quite useful to despotic regimes seeking to justify the inevitable scarcity that their economic policies produce.
7. Christon I. Archer, John R. Ferris, Holger H. Herwig, and Timothy H. E. Travers, *World History of Warfare* (Lincoln: University of Nebraska Press, 2002), 354.
8. John A. Nagl, *Learning to Eat Soup with a Knife: Counterinsurgency Lessons from Malaya and Vietnam* (Westport, CT: Praeger, 2002), 132.
9. William C. Westmoreland, *A Soldier Reports* (New York: Doubleday, 1976), 38.
10. Lawrence Kaplan, "Clear and Fold: Forgetting the Lessons of Vietnam," *The New Republic*, December 19, 2005.

11. Conrad C. Crane, *Avoiding Vietnam: The U.S. Army's Response to Defeat in Southeast Asia* (Carlisle, PA: Army War College Strategic Studies Institute, 2002), 12.
12. Linda Robinson, "The Book on Bad Apples: A New Army Manual Shows the Smart Way to Beat Insurgents," *U.S. News and World Report*, July 24, 2006, http://www.usnews.com/usnews/news/articles/060716/24counter.htm.
13. William S. Lind, Keith Nightengale, John F. Schmitt, Joseph W. Sutton, and Gary I. Wilson, "The Changing Face of War: Into the Fourth Generation," *Marine Corps Gazette*, October 1989, 22–26.
14. Thomas E. Ricks, "Army Historian Cites Lack of Postwar Plan," *Washington Post*, December 25, 2004.
15. Rod Nordland, "Can This Man Save Iraq?," *Newsweek*, July 2004, http://www.prnewswire.com/news-releases/newsweek-cover-can-this-man-save-iraq-75166612.html.
16. Linda Robinson, *Tell Me How This Ends: General David Petraeus and the Search for a Way Out of Iraq* (New York: PublicAffairs, 2009), 74.
17. Ibid., 78.
18. Ibid.
19. Kelley Beaucar Vlahos, "One-Sided COIN: The Military-Industrial Complex Surges Washington," *The American Conservative*, August 1, 2009, http://www.theamericanconservative.com/article/2009/aug/01/00038.
20. Sarah Sewall, "He Wrote the Book: Can He Follow It?" *Washington Post*, February 25, 2007, http://www.washingtonpost.com/wp-dyn/content/article/2007/02/23/AR2007022301741.html.
21. Ibid.
22. John Boyd, *Patterns of Conflict*, presentation to Command Staff, 1986, slide 108.
23. "Gaddafi, Chavez Sign Anti-terrorism Declaration," Associated Press, September 29, 2009, http://www.ynetnews.com/articles/0,7340,L-3782632,00.html.
24. Jorge Verstrynge, *La Guerra Periférica y Islam Revolucionaria: Orígenes, Reglas y Ética de la Guerra Asimétrica* (Barcelona: El Viejo Topo, 2005), 158.
25. Simon Romero, "Chávez Seeks Tighter Grip on Military," *New York Times*, May 29, 2009, http://www.nytimes.com/2009/05/30/world/americas/30venez.html.
26. Max G. Manwaring, *Latin America's New Security Reality: Irregular Asymmetric Conflict and Hugo Chávez* (Carlisle, PA: Strategic Studies Institute, 2007), 23–24.
27. Greg Myre and Steven Erlanger, "Clashes Spread to Lebanon as Hezbollah Raids Israel," *New York Times*, July 12, 2006, http://www.nytimes.com/2006/07/13/world/africa/13iht-web.0713mideast.2188501.html?_r=1.
28. Dore Gold, *The Rise of Nuclear Iran* (Washington: Regnery, 2009), 276–77.
29. Mayoral aide in Loreto region of Peru, interview by author, October 2009.
30. Representative of DINCOTE (Peru's counterterrorism directorate) in Lima, interview by author, August 2009.
31. "'Kill Those Gringos!': Armed Pro-Chavez Civilians Train for Battle at Boot Camp in Venezuela," Associated Press, May 2, 2010, http://www.foxnews.com/world/2010/05/02/kill-gringos-armed-pro-chavez-civilians-train-battle-boot-camp-venezuela/.

Chapter 1: Assessing the Enemy

1. John Bulloch and Harvey Morris, *The Gulf War: Its Origins, History and Consequences* (London: Methuen, 1989), 281.
2. *Iranium*, a 2011 documentary directed by Alex Traiman and produced by the Clarion Fund.

3. Stephen Collins Coughlin, *"To Our Great Detriment": Ignoring What Extremists Say about Jihad* (Washington: International Assessment and Strategy Center, 2007), 7.

4. Douglas Farah, "Venezuela and the Threat It Poses to U.S. and Hemispheric Security," Center for Security Policy Capitol Hill Briefing, December 8, 2008, http://www .youtube.com/watch?v=c_2L7-3ZHUw&feature=relmfu.

5. "Mexico: Troubles on the V," *Time*, April 19, 1971, http://www.time.com/time /magazine/article/0,9171,905026,00.html#ixzz1FCGewp00.

6. John Barron, *KGB: The Secret Work of Soviet Secret Agents* (New York: Reader's Digest, 1974), 230.

7. "Mexico," *Time*.

8. Barron, *KGB*, 248.

9. Ibid., 316.

Chapter 2: Checking the Record

1. Steve Rosenberg, "Computers to Solve Stasi Puzzle," BBC News Berlin, May 25, 2007, http://news.bbc.co.uk/2/hi/europe/6692895.stm.

2. Mary Williams Walsh, "Terrorist or Model Citizen," *Los Angeles Times*, February 27, 1996, http://articles.latimes.com/1996-02-27/news/mn-40629_1_model-citizen/2.

3. Jonas Bernstein, "When in Need, Terrorist Groups Turned Eastward," *Insight*, January 21, 1991.

4. John O. Koehler, *Stasi: The Untold Story of the East German Secret Police* (Boulder, CO: Westview, 1999), 387.

5. Allan Hall, "How Carlos the Jackal Was Feted and Pampered by Stasi Backers," *Daily Mail*, October 30, 2010, http://www.dailymail.co.uk/news/article-1324950/How -Carlos-Jackal-feted-pampered-Stasi-backers.html#ixzz1EFMthaiJ.

6. Ibid.

7. Ibid.

8. Patrick Donahue, "Germany Releases Files on Lawmakers Ensnared by Stasi (Update 1)," August 2, 2006, http://www.bloomberg.com/apps/news?pid=newsarchive&sid =aT8cF_v57e88&refer=germany.

9. Philip Pomper, "Lenin's Brother: 'Scientific' Ethics, Terrorism and Suicide," (paper, Connecticut Academy of Arts and Sciences meeting, Wesleyan University, February 8, 2006).

10. V. I. Lenin, *Left-Wing Communism: An Infantile Disorder*, vol. 31 (Moscow: Progress Publishers, 1972), 33.

11. V. I. Lenin, *Collected Works*, vol. 5 (Moscow: Progress Publishers, 1972), 19.

12. Ibid., 35:238.

13. Karl Marx and Frederick Engels, "The Victory of the Counter-Revolution in Vienna," *Collected Works*, vol. 8 (New York: International Publishers, 1977), 506.

14. Ariel Merari, ed., *On Terrorism and Combating Terrorism: Proceedings of an International Seminar*, Tel-Aviv, 1979 (Westport, CT: Praeger, 1985), 107–8.

15. UN General Assembly, UN DOC A/C 6/SR 1389, December 13, 1972, 4–5.

16. UN General Assembly, UN DOC A/AC 160/I,Add. I, June 12, 1973, Ad Hoc Committee on International Terrorism (July 16–August 10, 1973), 26.

17. Benjamin Netanyahu, *International Terrorism: Challenge and Response* (Jerusalem: Transaction, 1982), 92.

18. Ibid., 93.

19. Ibid., 94.

20. Allen Weinstein and Alexander Vassiliev, *The Haunted Wood: Soviet Espionage in America—the Stalin Era* (New York: Random House, 1999); and Yevgenia Albats, *The State within a State: The KGB and Its Hold on Russia—Past, Present and Future* (New York: Farrar, Straus and Giroux, 1994).

21. Stephen W. Stromberg, "Documenting the KGB," *Oxonian Review of Books*, Winter 2005, http://www.oxonianreview.org/issues/5-1/5-1stromberg.html.

22. Brian Crozier, ed., *Annual of Power and Conflict, 1973–1974* (London: Institute for the Study of Conflict, 1974), 230–58.

23. Netanyahu, *International Terrorism*, 94.

24. Crozier, *Annual*, 230–58.

25. Juliana Geran Pilon, *At the U.N., Soviet Fronts Pose as Nongovernmental Organizations* (Washington: Heritage Foundation, 1986), http://www.heritage.org/research/reports/1986/12/at-the-un-soviet-fronts-pose-as-nongovernmental-organizations.

26. Hearings on Soviet active measures, Subcommittee on European Affairs, Committee on Foreign Relations, U.S. Senate, September 12–13, 1985.

27. Ibid.

28. Albats, *State within a State*, 227–29.

29. Ibid., 229.

30. Ibid., 230.

31. Ibid.

32. Yonah Alexander, *International Terrorism: National, Regional, and Global Perspectives* (New York: Praeger, 1976), 120.

33. Brian Crozier, *Strategy of Survival* (London: Temple Smith, 1978), 43; and Barron, *KGB*, 257.

34. Christopher Story, *Arab-Asian Affairs*, vol. 28 (New York: World Reports Limited, 2004), 8.

35. *Soviet World Outlook*, University of Miami, Center for Advanced International Studies, November 15, 1979, 5–6.

36. Ernesto Guevara, *Venceremos! The Speeches and Writings of Che Guevara*, ed. John Gerassi (London: Littlehampton, 1968), 380.

37. *Tricontinental Conference of African, Asian, and Latin American Peoples: A Staff Study*, U.S. Senate Committee on the Judiciary, Subcommittee to Investigate the Administration of the Internal Security Act and Other Internal Security Laws (Washington: Government Printing Office, 1966), http://www.latinamericanstudies.org/tricon/tricon4.htm.

38. Jorge Pérez-López, *Cuban Studies* (Pittsburgh, PA: University of Pittsburgh Press, 1994), 118.

39. "Hamas Wins Upset Victory in Palestinian Election," Reuters, January 26, 2006.

40. Barron, *KGB*, 76–77.

41. *Soviet Support for International Terrorism and Revolutionary Violence*, CIA Special National Intelligence Estimate, 1981, 23. Released under CIA Historical Review Program.

42. Norman Polmar and Thomas B. Allen, *Spy Book: The Encyclopedia of Espionage* (New York: Random House Reference, 2004) 220.

43. "Moscow's Gold: Soviet Financing of Global Subversion," *National Observer* 40 (Autumn 1999), http://www.nationalobserver.net/1999_autumn_campbell.htm.

44. Oversight Subcommittee, Permanent Select Committee on Intelligence, House of Representatives, *CIA Study: Soviet Covert Action and Propaganda*, February 6, 1980, 13–14.

45. Ibid., 13.
46. Shlomi Elad and Ariel Merari, *The Soviet Bloc and World Terrorism* (Tel Aviv: Jaffee Center for Strategic Studies, Tel Aviv University, 1984), 35.
47. Walter Z. Laqueur, "Guerrillas and Terrorists," *Commentary*, October 1974, http://www.commentarymagazine.com/article/guerrillas-and-terrorists/.
48. Ibid.
49. "German Guilty in '79 Attack at NATO on Alexander Haig," *New York Times*, November 25, 1993, http://www.nytimes.com/1993/11/25/world/german-guilty-in-79-attack-at-nato-on-alexander-haig.html.
50. Speech by Yasir Arafat—identified as Abu Ammar—delivered January 11, 1982, at a poetry recital held by the Palestinian writers and journalists at Beirut Arab University, "Arafat: PLO Revolutionaries in Central America," Voice of Palestine in Arabic, FBIS, Inter-Arab Affairs, January 12, 1982.
51. "A Message for Moscow," *Time*, February 9, 1981, http://www.time.com/time/magazine/article/0,9171,922398,00.html#ixzz18znB1OVQ.
52. Stefan Possony, *International Terrorism: The Communist Connection* (Washington: American Council for World Freedom, 1978).
53. J. Michael Waller, "International Terrorism: The Communist Connection Revisited," June 1, 2002, http://www.opensourcesinfo.org/journal/2007/1/21/international-terrorism-the-communist-connection-revisited.html.
54. Merari, *On Terrorism and Combating Terrorism,* 108.
55. Stephen Segaller, *Invisible Armies: Terrorism into the 1990s* (New York: Harcourt, Brace, Jovanovich, 1987), 126–27.
56. Segaller, *Invisible Armies,* 129.
57. Claire Sterling, *The Terror Network: The Secret War of International Terrorism* (New York: Holt, Rinehart and Winston, 1981).
58. "Soviets Encourage but Don't Inspire Terrorism, Panel Told," Associated Press, April 25, 1981.
59. Ibid.
60. Uri Ra'anan et al., eds., "The International Linkages: What Do We Know?," *Hydra of Carnage: International Linkages of Terrorism—the Witnesses Speak* (Lanham, MD: Lexington Books, 1985), 5–15.
61. Clive Davis, "The Power of Bad Television: The BBC's Bizarre New Documentary on Terrorism and Neoconservatism," October 21, 2004, http://old.nationalreview.com/comment/davis200410211043.asp.
62. Robert M. Gates, *From the Shadows: The Ultimate Insider's Story of Five Presidents and How They Won the Cold War* (New York: Simon & Schuster, 2007).
63. Ibid., 203.
64. Ibid., 204.
65. Ibid.
66. *Soviet Support for International Terrorism*, 6.
67. Ibid.
68. Segaller, *Invisible Armies,* 130.
69. Gates, *From the Shadows,* 206.

Chapter 3: The Wolf at the Door

1. P. K. Rose, "Two Strategic Intelligence Mistakes in Korea, 1950," *Studies in Intelligence,* Fall–Winter 2001, 57–65, https://www.cia.gov/library/center-for-the-study-of-intelligence/csi-publications/csi-studies/studies/fall_winter_2001/article06.html.

2. Ibid.
3. Ibid.
4. Ibid.
5. William Safire, "The C.I.A.'s China Tilt," *New York Times*, July 9, 2001, http://query .nytimes.com/gst/fullpage.html?res=9905E4DB1038F93AA35754C0A9679C 8B63.
6. Boaz Ganor, "Libya and Terrorism," International Institute for Counter-Terrorism, June 1, 1992, http://www.ict.org.il/Articles/tabid/66/Articlsid/699/currentpage /34/Default.aspx.
7. Ibid.
8. Desmond McForan, *The World Held Hostage: The War Waged by International Terrorism* (New York: St. Martin's, 1986), 128.
9. Ganor, "Libya and Terrorism."
10. "Al Mathaba Anti-Imperialism Center," Global Security, n.d., http://www.global security.org/intell/world/libya/mathaba.htm.
11. Ibid.
12. Stephen Ellis, *The Mask of Anarchy* (New York: New York University Press, 2001), 72.
13. Douglas Farah, "Harvard for Tyrants: How Muammar al-Qaddafi Taught a Generation of Bad Guys," March 4, 2011, http://www.foreignpolicy.com/articles/2011/03/04 /harvard_for_tyrants.
14. Douglas Farah, "The FARC's International Relations: A Network of Deception," NEFA Foundation, September 22, 2008, http://www.nefafoundation.org/miscel laneous/FeaturedDocs/nefafarcirnetworkdeception0908.pdf.
15. "Nicaragua Prez Call Gaddafi to Expresses Support," Fox News, February 22, 2011, http://www.foxnews.com/world/2011/02/22/nicaragua-prez-gaddafi-expresses -support/.
16. Ely Karmon, "Hezbollah America Latina: Strange Group or Real Threat?," Institute for Counter-Terrorism, January 25, 2007.
17. "Carlos" and Jean-Michel Vernochet, *L'islam révolutionnaire* (Paris: Editions du Rocher, 2003).
18. "Jackal Book Praises bin Laden," BBC News, June 23, 2006, http://news.bbc.co.uk /2/hi/3022358.stm.
19. John Follain, *Jackal: The Complete Story of the Legendary Terrorist, Carlos the Jackal* (New York: Arcade, 1998), 21.
20. Vladimir Boukovsky, *Jugement à Moscou: Un dissident dans les archives du Kremlin* (Paris: Robert Laffont, 1995). From a letter marked "Secret-confidential/Particularly important/Special file" that was found in the Kremlin archives by former Soviet dissident Vladimir Boukovsky. The date given is April 23, 1974.
21. Bassam Abu-Sharif and Uzi Mahnaimi, *Tried by Fire: The Searing True Story of Two Men at the Heart of the Struggle between the Arabs and the Jews* (London: Little, Brown, 1995), 87.
22. Ibid., 88.
23. Interview published in *Al Watan Al Arabi*, December 7, 1979.
24. Dario Azzellini, "Venezuela: Guerrilla Movements, 1960s–1980s," *International Encyclopedia of Revolution and Protest*, ed. Immanuel Ness (Oxford, UK: Blackwell Publishsing, 2009), http://www.blackwellreference.com/public/tocnode?id=g 9781405184649_chunk_g97814051846491530#citation.
25. Follain, *Jackal*, 26.

26. Sterling, *Terror Network*, 122.
27. Ibid.
28. Follain, *Jackal*, 23.
29. Mark Schreiber, *Shocking Crimes of Postwar Japan* (Tokyo: Yenbooks, 1996), 215–16.
30. "Sandinistas Attract a Who's Who of Terrorists," *Miami Herald*, March 3, 1985.
31. Ibid.
32. Victoria Villaruel, *Los Llaman "Jovenes Idealistas"* (Buenos Aires: Celtyv, 2009), 94.
33. Elizabeth Llorente, "U.S. Senator Bob Menendez Assails Latin American Officials' Show of Support for Syrian Leader," Fox News Latino, October 10, 2011, http://latino.foxnews.com/latino/politics/2011/10/10/us-senator-bob-menendez-assails-latin-american-officials-who-support-syrias.
34. Paula Kaufman, "Woolsey Wary of More Attacks," *Insight on the News*, June 3, 2002.
35. David Brooks, "Saddam's Brain: The Ideology behind the Thuggery," *Weekly Standard*, November 11, 2002.
36. Waller R. Newell, "Postmodern Jihad: What Osama bin Laden Learned from the Left," *Weekly Standard*, November 26, 2001.
37. Spencer C. Tucker, *The Encyclopedia of the Arab-Israeli Conflict: A Political, Social, and Military History* (Santa Barbara, CA: ABC-Clio, 2008), 185.
38. Julio César Jobet, *El Partido Socialista de Chile* (Santiago: Prensa Latinoamericana, 1971), 173.
39. Richard J. Leitner and Peter M. Leitner, eds., *Unheeded Warnings: The Lost Reports of the Congressional Task Force on Terrorism and Unconventional Warfare*, vol. 1 (Washington: Crossbow Press, 2009), 525–26.
40. Ibid.
41. Ibid.
42. Ibid.

Chapter 4: Revolution Makes Strange Bedfellows

1. Tim Rogers, "President Daniel Ortega Isn't a Nice Guy, but Nicaraguans Will Re-elect Him Anyway," *Time*, November 4, 2011, http://www.time.com/time/world/article/0,8599,2098720,00.html#ixzz1teeLeJol.
2. "Nicaragua e Irán, 'Unión Invencible,'" BBC Mundo, June 11, 2007, http://news.bbc.co.uk/hi/spanish/latin_america/newsid_6741000/6741829.stm.
3. Paul Lee, "Unseen Unity: Three Photos You Never Saw," *Michigan Citizen*, October 2007, http://michigancitizen.com/unseen-unity-p5184-106.htm.
4. "Daughter of Che Guevara Meets Hizbullah Leaders in Lebanon," Middle East Media Research Institute, October 26, 2010, http://www.thememriblog.org/blog_personal/en/31429.htm.
5. Amir Taheri, "Tehran's Price for 'Solidarity,'" *New York Post*, October 12, 2007, http://www.nypost.com/p/news/opinion/opedcolumnists/item_ubd6fA2Xym8hXeqCjbzdtL.
6. Ibid.
7. Ibid.
8. Ibid.
9. Jay Bushinsky, "Swiss Probe Anti-U.S. Neo-Nazi Suspected Financial Ties to Al Qaeda," *San Francisco Chronicle*, Foreign Service, March 12, 2002, http://sfgate.com/cgi-bin/article.cgi?f=/c/a/2002/03/12/MN192483.DTL.
10. "Exclusive: Al Qaeda Eyes Bio Attack from Mexico," *Washington Times*, June 3, 2009,

http://www.washingtontimes.com/news/2009/jun/03/al-qaeda-eyes-bio-attack
-via-mexico-border/?page=1.

11. *Der Spiegel,* November 9, 1981, quoted in Bruce Hoffman, "Right Wing Terrorism in Europe Since 1980," Rand Corporation, 1984, 1.
12. Ibid., 2.
13. Ibid.
14. Sterling, *Terror Network,* 38.
15. Milton Meltzer, *The Day the Sky Fell: A History of Terrorism* (New York: Random House, 2002), 198–99.
16. "Propaganda by the Deed," *Workers Solidarity* 55 (October 1998), http://struggle.ws/ws98/ws55_prop_deed.html.
17. "Bin Laden Says U.S. Headed for 'Unbearable Hell,'" *USA Today,* February 1, 2002.
18. Stefan Possony, *International Terrorism: The Communist Connection* (Washington: American Council for World Freedom, 1978), 143.
19. Sterling, *Terror Network,* 28.
20. Paul Hofmann, *That Fine Italian Hand* (New York: Henry Holt), 185.
21. George Michael, *The Enemy of My Enemy* (Lawrence: University of Kansas Press, 2006), 163.

Chapter 5: The Transformation of Neo-Nazi Ideology
1. Eric Geiger, "Germany Bans Islamic Group," *San Francisco Chronicle,* Foreign Service, January 16, 2003, http://articles.sfgate.com/2003-01-16/news/17472100_1_hizb-ut-tahrir-islamic-militants-islamic-world.
2. Ahmed Rashid, "Manhunt to Foil Terrorist Attack at G8 Meeting," *Telegraph,* July 13, 2001, http://www.telegraph.co.uk/news/worldnews/1333867/Manhunt-to-foil-terrorist-attack-at-G8-meeting.html.
3. Jay Bushinsky, "Swiss Probe Anti-U.S. Neo-Nazi; Suspected Financial Ties to al Qaeda," *San Francisco Chronicle,* Foreign Service, March 12, 2002, http://articles.sfgate.com/2002-03-12/news/17533807_1_qaeda-islamic-militants-osama-bin-laden-s-al.
4. *The Middle East* 27, no. 1, Library Information and Research Service (2003): 18.
5. Jessica Stern, "The Protean Enemy," *Foreign Affairs,* July–August 2003.
6. David Duke, "Are You a Racist?" March 12, 2005, http://www.davidduke.com/general/are-you-a-racist_266.html#more-266.
7. David Duke, "Evangelicals Who Serve the Anti-Christ!," broadcast date January 25, 2003, http://www.davidduke.com/general/evangelicals-who-serve-the-anti-christ_100.html.
8. Henry Schuster, "An Unholy Alliance: Aryan Nation Leader Reaches Out to al Qaeda," CNN, March 3, 2005, http://edition.cnn.com/2005/US/03/29/schuster.column/.
9. David Myatt, "Towards the Galactic Empire: Autobiographical Notes, Part Two, a New Strategy: Toward Islam and Understanding Esoteric Hitlerism," http://www.gnosticliberationfront.com/david_myatt2.htm.
10. Ibid.
11. Richard L. Greaves, *Civilizations of the World: From 1800* (New York: Harper & Row, 1990), 985.
12. Jean Lacouture, *Nasser: A Biography* (London: Secker & Warburg, 1973), 47.
13. Chuck Morse, *The Nazi Connection to Islamic Terrorism: Adolf Hitler and Haj Amin al-Husseini* (Lincoln, NE: iUniverse, 2003), 12–13.
14. Ibid., 28.
15. Kenneth R. Timmerman, *Preachers of Hate: Islam and the War on America* (New York: Crown Forum, 2003), 103–4.

16. Ataullah Bogdan Kopanski, "Muslims and the Reich," *Barnes Review,* September–October 2003, 27.
17. Martin A. Lee, *The Beast Reawakens: Fascism's Resurgence from Hitler's Spymasters to Today's Neo-Nazi Groups and Right-Wing Extremists* (New York: Little, Brown, 1997), 128.
18. Timmerman, *Preachers of Hate*, 102–3.
19. Morse, *Nazi Connection,* 73.
20. Roy H. Shoeman, *Salvation Is from the Jews: The Role of Judaism in Salvation History* (San Francisco: Ignatius Press, 2004), 255.
21. Morse, *Nazi Connection,* 29.
22. Mark Falcoff, "Peron's Nazi Ties," *Time,* November 9, 1998, http://www.time.com/time/magazine/1998/int/981109/latin_america.perons_na30a.html.
23. Ronald Newton, *The "Nazi Menace" in Argentina, 1931–47* (Palo Alto, CA: Stanford University Press, 1992).
24. Uki Goñi, *The Real Odessa: Smuggling the Nazis to Perón's Argentina* (New York: Granta Books, 2003), 100.
25. Falcoff, "Peron's Nazi Ties."
26. Larry Rohter, "Argentina, a Haven for Nazis, Balks at Opening Its Files," *New York Times,* March 9, 2003, http://www.nytimes.com/2003/03/09/world/argentina-a-haven-for-nazis-balks-at-opening-its-files.html.
27. Uki Goñi and Rory Carroll, "Last chance to catch Nazis in South America, Aay Campaigners," *The Guardian,* November 28, 2007, http://www.guardian.co.uk/world/2007/nov/28/secondworldwar.rorycarroll.
28. Neal Bascomb, *Hunting Eichmann* (New York: Houghton Mifflin Harcourt, 2009), 91.
29. "Blind Refugee Led Israel to Eichmann," *The Guardian,* January 25, 2002, http://www.guardian.co.uk/world/2002/jan/25/bookextracts.israel.
30. Goñi, *Real Odessa,* 129.
31. Ibid., 100.
32. Ibid.
33. Ibid., 128.
34. Paul Manning, *Martin Bormann: Nazi in Exile* (Secaucus, NJ: Lyle Stuart, 1980), 181.
35. Gonzalo Zaragoza Rovira, *Anarquismo Argentino* (Madrid: Ediciones de la Torre, 1996), 88–90.
36. U.S. Embassy personnel, Buenos Aires, interview by author, August 2008.
37. Christophe Bourseiller, *Extrême-droite: L'enquête* (Paris: F. Bourrin, 1991), 11.
38. Edouard Rix, "Jean Thiriart, the Machiavelli of United Europe," September 8, 2010, http://tpprovence.wordpress.com/2010/09/08/jean-thiriart-le-machiavel-de-la-nation-europeenne.
39. Michael, *Enemy of My Enemy,* 126.
40. Lee, *Beast Reawakens,* 175.
41. Perón, interview by Luc Michel, *La Nation Européenne,* February 1969.
42. "Peron's 'Third World' Dreams," *Patterns of Prejudice,* May–June 1969; and *La Nation Européenne,* May 1967, June 1967, December 1967, January 1968.
43. Gene H. Hogberg, "Interview with Jean Thiriart," trans. Dr. David Wainwright, Counter-Currents Publishing, October 1, 2010, http://www.counter-currents.com/2010/10/interview-with-jean-thiriart-part-5.
44. Lee, *Beast Reawakens,* 177.

45. "Otto Skorzeny, Nazi Commando, Dead," *New York Times*, July 8, 1975.
46. Lee, *Beast Reawakens*, 186.
47. Silvia Sigal, *Le rôle politique des intellectuels en Amérique latine* (Paris: L'Harmattan, 1996), 268.
48. "Argentina: Resurrecting the Swastika," *Time*, September 21, 1962, http://www.time .com/time/magazine/article/0,9171,827543,00.html#ixzz1BA70s6yh.
49. "The Eichmann Kidnapping: Its Effects on Argentine-Israeli Relations and the Local Jewish Community," *Jewish Social Studies* 7, no. 3 (Spring/Summer 2001): 121.
50. Lee, *Beast Reawakens*, 179.
51. "People," *Time*, June 1, 1964, http://www.time.com/time/magazine/article/0,9171 ,875879-2,00.html#ixzz1B9bgK4W5.
52. Lee, *Beast Reawakens*, 179.
53. Bureau of Public Affairs, *Special Report No. 90: Cuba's Renewed Support of Violence in Latin America* (Washington: U.S. Department of State, December 14, 1981).
54. Pablo Calvo, "Ezeiza, una masacre que causó el estallido del peronismo," *Clarin*, June 20, 1973, http://edant.clarin.com/suplementos/especiales/2005/08/28/l-01215.htm.
55. Lee, *Beast Reawakens*, 180.
56. Karmon, "Hezbollah America Latina."
57. Lee, *Beast Reawakens*, 181.
58. Edward Moxon-Browne, *European Terrorism* (New York: G. K. Hall, 1994), 99.
59. Benjamin Netanyahu, *A Durable Peace: Israel and Its Place among the Nations* (New York: Grand Central, 1999), 212–13.
60. "The World," *Los Angeles Times*, December 4, 1985, http://articles.latimes.com /1985-12-04/news/mn-416_1.
61. *Der Spiegel*, July 17, 1981, as quoted in Barry M. Rubin, *Revolution Until Victory? The Politics and History of the PLO* (Cambridge, MA: Harvard University Press, 1994), 243.
62. Rand C. Lewis, *A Nazi Legacy: Right-Wing Extremism in Postwar Germany* (New York: Praeger, 1991), 191.
63. "They Said Our Boss's Name Is Hoffman," *Der Spiegel*, July 13, 1981.
64. Lee, *Beast Reawakens*, 180.
65. William Grim, "Al Qaeda's Neo-Nazi Connections," *Jewish Press*, February 25, 2004.

Chapter 6: The Third Position

1. *Der Stern*, October 29, 1981, as quoted in Yonah Alexander and Joshua Sinai, *Terrorism: The PLO Connection* (Oxford, UK: Taylor & Francis, 1989), 189.
2. *Der Spiegel*, January 11, 1981, as quoted in Bruce Hoffman, "The Contrasting Ethical Foundations of Terrorism in the 1980s," Rand Corporation, January 1988, www.dtic .mil/cgi-bin/GetTRDoc?AD=ADA217004.
3. Netanyahu, *A Durable Peace*, 213.
4. *The German Tribune*, July 3, 1983, as quoted in Hoffman, "Contrasting Ethical Foundations," 12.
5. Peter H. Merkl and Leonard Weinberg, *Right-Wing Extremism in the Twenty-First Century* (London: Taylor & Francis, 2003), 286.
6. Rachel Nolan, "Thor Steinar and the Changing Look of the German Far Right," *Der Spiegel* Online, November 20, 2008, http://www.spiegel.de/international/germany /0,1518,587746,00.html.
7. William Grim, "Al Qaeda's Neo-Nazi Connections," *Jewish Press*, February 25, 2004, http://www.jewishpress.com/pageroute.do/16053/.

8. Waller R. Newell, "Postmodern Jihad: What Osama bin Laden Learned from the Left," *Weekly Standard*, November 26, 2001.
9. Paul Berman, *Terror and Liberalism* (New York: Norton, 2003), 62.
10. Michael, *Enemy of My Enemy*, 149.
11. Ibid., 150.
12. Thomas Joscelyn, "Iran's Proxy War against America," Claremont Institute, October 1, 2007, http://www.claremont.org/publications/pubid.733/pub_detail.asp.
13. Aluma Solnik, "Based on Koranic Verses, Interpretations, and Traditions, Muslim Clerics State: The Jews Are the Descendants of Apes, Pigs, and Other Animals," Middle East Media Research Institute, November 1, 2002, http://memri.org/bin/articles.cgi?Page=archives&Area=sr&ID=SR01102.
14. Michael, *Enemy of My Enemy*, 150–51.
15. Jay Bushinsky, "Swiss Probe Anti-U.S. Neo-Nazi: Suspected Financial Ties to al Qaeda," *San Francisco Chronicle*, Foreign Service, March 12, 2002, http://sfgate.com/cgi-bin/article.cgi?f=/c/a/2002/03/12/MN192483.DTL.
16. Lee, *Terror Network*, 242, 322.
17. Ibid., 183.
18. Ibid., 479–80.
19. Ibid., 480.
20. Andrea Jarach, "Terrorismo Internazionale," *Il Giornale Nuovo*, August 8, 1980, 144.
21. Walter Laqueur, *The New Terrorism* (New York: Oxford University Press, 1999), 168.
22. Brian Crozier, "Libya's Foreign Adventures," *Conflict Studies* 41 (December 1973).
23. *L'Express*, January 25, 1996, as quoted in Elliott A. Green, "Nazis, Communists, Arab Nationalist Terrorists: One Camp, One Kampf," http://www.netanyahu.org/nazcomarnatt.html.
24. David Lee Preston, "Hitler's Swiss Connection," *Philadelphia Inquirer*, January 5, 1997, http://www.writing.upenn.edu/~afilreis/Holocaust/swiss-and-hitler.html.
25. *L'Express*, January 25, 1996, as quoted in Green, "Nazis, Communists, Arab National-ist Terrorists."
26. Ian James, "Chavez Praises Carlos the Jackal," Associated Press, November 21, 2009, http://www.independent.co.uk/news/world/americas/chavez-praises-carlos-the-jackal-1825135.html.
27. Rory Carroll, "Hugo Chávez Courts Outrage with Praise for Carlos, Mugabe and Amin," *The Guardian*, November 22, 2009, http://www.guardian.co.uk/world/2009/nov/22/hugo-chavez-defence-carlos-jackal.
28. Deisy Buitrago and Andrew Cawthorne, "Hugo Chavez Sends Solidarity to Gaddafi, Syria," Reuters, October 1, 2011, http://www.reuters.com/article/2011/10/02/us-venezuela-chavez-idUSTRE7901QW20111002.

Chapter 7: Slow-Motion Revolution

1. Richard Gott, "Hugo Chavez and Venezuela's 'Slow Revolution,'" *Socialist Worker*, February 12, 2005, http://www.socialistworker.co.uk/art.php?id=5826.
2. Saul Godoy Gomez, "El Protosociolismo," *El Universal*, January 17, 2011, http://www.eluniversal.com/opinion/110117/el-protosocialismo. For insight into Gott's point of view, note that he said of Tony Blair: "Like Chamberlain, he is an arrogant and God-fuelled appeaser, the unseemly ally of an unbridled country that presents a global threat similar to Germany in the 1930s." Gott had to resign from the decidedly left-wing British newspaper *The Guardian* in 1994 when a former Soviet spy revealed

that Gott had been an "agent of influence" for the KGB.

3. Arthur Schlesinger, Jr., "The Future of Socialism," *Partisan Review* 29, no. 14 (1947): 231.
4. Laqueur, "Guerrillas and Terrorists."
5. "Charting a Course to Irrelevance," *The Economist*, January 27, 2011, http://www.economist.com/blogs/americasview/2011/01/inter-american_democratic_charter.
6. "Castro's Targets," *Time*, May 19, 1967, http://www.time.com/time/magazine/article/0,9171,840892,00.html.
7. Jose Noguera, "Chávez's Early Ties with the FARC and ELN," *The Americas Report*, March 23, 2008, http://www.centerforsecuritypolicy.org/p16598.xml.
8. Ibid.
9. Ibid.
10. Angela Zago, *La Rebelión de los Angeles* (Caracas: Fuentes Editores, 1992), 78.
11. Brian A. Nelson, *The Silence and the Scorpion: The Coup against Chavez and the Making of Modern Venezuela* (New York: Nation Books, 2009), 122.
12. Joel D. Hirst, "'Revolutionary Brotherhood': 21st Century Socialist Revolution," Council on Foreign Relations, October 13, 2010, http://www.cfr.org/publication/23155/revolutionary_brotherhood21st_century_socialist_revolution.html.
13. "Ortega Calls for Referendum on Renewing His Mandate," AFP/France 24, July 20, 2009, http://www.france24.com/en/20090720-nicaragua-referendum-reelection-ortega-sandinista-constitution-term-limits.
14. Joel D. Hirst, PowerPoint presentation, conference, "Danger in the Andes: Threats to Democracy, Human Rights, and Inter-American Security," Washington, November 17, 2010.
15. Elihu Lauterpacht and C. J. Greenwood, *International Law Reports* (Cambridge, MA: Cambridge University Press, 1994), 749.
16. Christopher Andrew and Vasili Mitrokhin, *The World Was Going Our Way: The KGB and the Battle for the Third World* (New York: Basic Books, 2005), 121.
17. Robinson, *Tell Me How This Ends*, 78.
18. Max G. Manwaring, "State and Nonstate Associated Gangs: Credible 'Midwives' of New Social Orders," *Air & Space Power Journal*, May 2009, http://www.airpower.maxwell.af.mil/apjinternational/apj-s/2009/3tri09/manwaringeng.htm.
19. Ibid.
20. Ibid.
21. "Venezuela Is Promised 'Political Revolution,'" BBC News, February 2, 1999, http://news.bbc.co.uk/2/hi/americas/270790.stm.
22. "Ecuadoran President: Spanish Socialists Were Hired to Help Draft New Constitution," Catholic News Agency, August 11, 2008, http://www.catholicnewsagency.com/news/ecuadoran_president_spanish_socialists_were_hired_to_help_draft_new_constitution/.
23. Ibid.
24. Wesley J. Smith, "Why We Call Them Human Rights," *Weekly Standard*, November 14, 2008, http://www.weeklystandard.com/Content/Public/Articles/000/000/015/823qaarg.asp.
25. "Asesor aconseja a Venezuela, Bolivia y Ecuador seguir en su 'lucha,'" *EFE/El Diario Ecuador*, Febrary 20, 2009, http://www.eldiario.com.ec/noticias-manabi-ecuador/109564-asesor-aconseja-a-venezuela-bolivia-y-ecuador-seguir-en-su-lucha.

26. Alberto Bolívar, *Latin America's Terrorist and Insurgent Groups: History and Status* (Lima: Strategos Institute, May 2006), www.fpri.org/pubs/200605.bolivar.latin americaterrorism.pdf.

27. Carlos Valez, "Castro Urged Ballots, Not Guns, for Bolivia's Populist Revolution, Morales Says," Associated Press, December 30, 2006.

28. Ibid.

29. Ibid.

30. Carlos Sabino, "La Constitución de Chávez," *Venezuela Analitica*, April 11, 1999, http://www.analitica.com/vas/1999.11.4/articulos/06.htm.

31. "Oscar Arias: Last Democrat Standing in the Region?," *The Devil's Excrement*, February 25, 2010, http://devilsexcrement.com/2010/02/25/oscar-arias-last-democrat-standing-in-the-region/.

32. "Voters Reject Chávez's Constitutional Changes," Associated Press, December 3, 2007, http://www.msnbc.msn.com/id/22066948/ns/world_news-venezuela/.

33. "Venezuelan NGOs Fear Restrictions on Foreign Funds," Associated Press, November 25, 2010. http://www.washingtonpost.com/wp-dyn/content/article/2010/11/25/AR2010112503323.html.

34. Aleksander Boyd, "Hugo Chavez Makes an Ass of Himself Again," Vcrisis.com, June 15, 2006, http://vcrisis.com/index.php?content=letters/200606150540; and "Bill to Control NGO's to Be Approved, More Control, More Censorship," *The Devil's Excrement*, Wednesday, June 14, 2006, http://devilsexcrement.com/2006/06/14/bill-to-control-ngos-to-be-approved-more-control-more-censorship/.

35. Salah Uddin Shoaib Choudhury, "Iran: Offensives against the Media," Gatestone Institute, February 26, 2010, http://www.gatestoneinstitute.org/1081/iran-offensives-against-the-media a.

36. Ibid.

37. Ibid.

38. Iranian blogger "Jadi," "NGOs in Iran and the gNGOs," May 29, 2007, http://jadi.civiblog.org/blog/_archives/2007/5/29/2984229.html.

39. Yevgeny Volk, "Russia's NGO Law: An Attack on Freedom and Civil Society," Heritage Foundation Webmemo #1090, May 24, 2006, http://www.heritage.org/research/reports/2006/05/russias-ngo-law-an-attack-on-freedom-and-civil-society.

40. Rory Carroll, "Oxfam Targeted as Nicaragua Attacks 'Trojan Horse' NGOs," *The Guardian*, October 14, 2008, http://www.guardian.co.uk/world/2008/oct/14/humanrights-voluntarysector.

41. Anastasia Moloney, "Ecuador Shuts Down Foreign NGO Operations," AlertNet, August 19, 2011, http://www.trust.org/alertnet/news/ecuador-shuts-down-foreign-ngo-operations.

42. Ibid.

43. Franz Chávez, "Drugs, USAID Complicate Relations," IPS News, June 16, 2010, http://ipsnews.net/news.asp?idnews=51849.

44. "Cuba Accuses US of Creating NGOs to 'Subvert' Island," *EFE/Latin American Herald Tribune*, March 29, 2011, http://laht.com/article.asp?ArticleId=390458&CategoryId=14510.

45. Joel D. Hirst, "Chávez Alters Venezuela's Constitutional Regime," Council on Foreign Relations, December 20, 2010, http://www.cfr.org/publication/23667/Chávez_alters_venezuelas_constitutional_regime.html.

46. Roberto Deniz, "Laws on People's Power Are Set to Nullify Private Entrepreneurship," *El Universal*, December 17, 2010, http://english.eluniversal.com/2010/12/17/en_ing_esp_laws-on-peoples-pow_17A4854613.shtml.

47. "Venezuela Passes Media, Internet-Muzzling Law," AFP, December 20, 2010, http://www.google.com/hostednews/afp/article/ALeqM5hX8P0LZnd4XSj92ygla5HV0raXWA?docId=CNG.5e300c93ec9b464f061edc2145035df7.2a1.

48. Norman A. Bailey, testimony before the Western Hemisphere Subcommittee of the Foreign Affairs Committee, U.S. House of Representatives, July 17, 2008.

49. Ian James, "Venezuelans Protest Chávez's New Socialist Push," AP/*USA Today*, August 6, 2008, www.usatoday.com/news/topstories/2008-08-06-210315117_x.htm.

50. Hugh Bronstein, "Ecuador Referendum Furor Erodes Correa Coalition," Reuters, January 28, 2011, http://www.reuters.com/article/2011/01/28/ecuador-referendum-idUSN2822294620110128?pageNumber=2.

51. "República de Honduras / Republic of Honduras, Constitución de 1982 (Political Constitution of 1982)," *Political Database of the Americas*, Georgetown University, http://pdba.georgetown.edu/Constitutions/Honduras/hond82.html.

52. "Honduras: busca reforma constitucional," *BBC Mundo*, March 24, 2009, http://news.bbc.co.uk/hi/spanish/latin_america/newsid_7961000/7961441.stm.

53. "Ya no era presidente cuando fue detenido," *La Prensa*, July 7, 2009, http://archivo.laprensa.hn/Sucesos/Ediciones/2009/07/07/Noticias/Ya-no-era-presidente-cuando-fue-detenido.

54. Freddy Cuevas, "Backers of Ousted Honduran President Won't Take Part in Elections, Say 'Coup-Mongers' Must Go," AP, http://www.1310news.com/news/world/article/189829--backers-of-ousted-honduran-leader-won-t-participate-in-elections-say-coup-mongers-must-go.

55. Jorge Martin, "Honduras: repression and negotiation defuse the resistance movement," International Marxist Tendency, October 28, 2009, http://www.marxist.com/honduras-repression-negotiation-defuse-resistance.htm.

56. Juan Ramon Huerta, "Dictadura paso a paso," *El Nuevo Diario*, August 5, 2010, http://www.elnuevodiario.com.ni/nacionales/80535.

57. Forrest D. Colburn and Alberto Trejos, "Democracy Undermined: Constitutional Subterfuge in Latin America," *Dissent*, July 2010.

58. Johnson, "Nicaragua's Daniel Ortega Lays Groundwork."

59. Tim Rogers, "Ortega Begins New Term Despite Opposition," *Miami Herald*, January 10, 2012.

Chapter 8: Managing the Media

1. Josh Rogin, "New BBG Chief Wants More Money to Combat 'Enemies' Such as China and Russia," *Foreign Policy*, October 5, 2010, http://thecable.foreignpolicy.com/posts/2010/10/05/new_bbg_chief_wants_more_money_to_combat_enemies_such_as_china_and_russia.

2. Former U.S. ambassador to Venezuela Otto Reich, interview by author at conference titled "Danger in the Andes," November 17, 2010, Washington, DC.

3. David Adams, "Latin America's Balanced/Biased Voice," *St. Petersburg Times*, August 8, 2005, http://www.sptimes.com/2005/08/08/State/Latin_America_s_balan.shtml.

4. Connie Mack, "Mack: New Alliance between Chávez's Telesur and Al-Jazeera Creates Global Terror TV Network," February 1, 2006, http://mack.house.gov/index.cfm?p=PressReleases&ContentRecord_id=fddc76f6-fd8c-42fb-aa21-7c2c81588bea&ContentType_id=8c55a72b-64f8-4cba-990c-ec1ed2a9de24

&Group_id=b3c463ca-96b6-41ff-94e5-a945437bc123&MonthDisplay=2&Year Display=2006 (retrieved October 18, 2011).

5. Humberto Fontova, "Huffington Post Writer a Cuban Agent," Townhall, June 25, 2010, http://townhall.com/columnists/humbertofontova/2010/06/25/huffington _post_writer_a_cuban_agent/.

6. Robert F. Turner, *Nicaragua v. United States: A Look at the Facts*, Institute for Foreign Policy Analysis (London: Brassey's, 1987), 51.

7. Larry Martz, "Next Target: Nicaragua," *Newsweek*, November 14, 1983, 44.

8. Daniel Pipes, "[William Blum and] Al-Qaeda's Leftist Brigade," *New York Sun,* January 24, 2006.

9. David Montgomery, "The Author Who Got a Big Boost from bin Laden," *Washington Post*, January 21, 2006, http://www.washingtonpost.com/wp-dyn/content /article/2006/01/20/AR2006012001971.html.

10. William Blum, *Killing Hope: US Military and CIA Interventions since World War II*, 2nd ed. (London: Zed Books, 2004), 234.

11. Michael Reid, *Forgotten Continent: The Battle for Latin America's Soul* (New Haven, CT: Yale University Press, 2008), 37.

12. "The Vassiliev Notebooks and Soviet Intelligence Operations in the U.S.," video transcript of day 2, Part II at 0:49:00, *Wilson Center on Demand*, May 21, 2009, http:// www.wilsoncenter.org/event/alexander-vassilievs-notebooks-and-the-document ation-soviet-intelligence-operations-the-united.

13. Eva Golinger, "Announcing Venezuela's First and Only English Language Newspaper, the *Correo del Orinoco International*," Postcards from the Revolution, January 21, 2010, http://www.Chavezcode.com/2010/01/announcing-venezuelas-first-and -only.html.

14. Ibid.

15. Kiraz Janicke, "Bolivarian Militias, the Armed People and the April Revolution," *Venezuelanalysis.com*, April 14, 2010, http://venezuelanalysis.com/news/5276.

16. "Country to Change Time Zone by 30 Minutes," Reuters, August 24, 2007, http://www .reuters.com/article/2007/08/24/us-venezuela-time-idUSN2328980320070824.

17. "No More Singing in the Shower: Chavez Urges Venezuelans to Limit Their Wash to Three Minutes amid Water Shortages," *Globe and Mail*, October 22, 2009, http:// www.dailymail.co.uk/news/worldnews/article-1222201/No-singing-shower -Chavez-urges-Venezuelans-limit-wash-minutes-amid-water-shortages.html#ixzz1 EbrDZ87t.

18. Catherine E. Shoichet, "Venezuela Slams Soap Opera Featuring Dog Named 'Little Hugo,'" CNN, January 15, 2011, http://articles.cnn.com/2011-01-15/world/vene zuela.soap.opera_1_televen-soap-opera-colombia-and-venezuela?_s=PM:WORLD.

19. Nelson, *Silence and the Scorpion*, 255.

20. Ibid., 264.

21. Mike Ceaser, "Chavez's 'Citizen Militias' on the March," BBC, July 1, 2005, http:// news.bbc.co.uk/2/hi/americas/4635187.stm.

22. Nelson, *Silence and the Scorpion*, 84.

23. Ibid., 267.

24. Ibid.

25. Organization of American States, "Annual Report of the Inter-American Commission on Human Rights 2006," March 3, 2007, http://www.cidh.oas.org/annualrep/2006eng /Rapporteurship%20for%20Freedom%20of%20Expression.pdf.

26. "Venezuelan Court Seizes RCTV's Equipment for State," *Taipei Times*, May 27, 2007, http://www.taipeitimes.com/News/world/archives/2007/05/27/2003362674.

27. "Chávez Needs Silence of the Media, IAPA Cautions," *El Universal*, November 08, 2010, http://www.eluniversal.com/2010/11/08/en_pol_esp_chavez-needs -silenc_08A4704811.shtml.

28. "Protests in Venezuela; One Hundred High School Students Arrested; Attacks on Media Continue; Bolivian and Ecuadorian Governments Announce Media Crackdown," Human Rights Foundation, May 30, 2007, http://www.humanrights foundation.org/media/mediaShutdown.html.

29. James Suggett, "Venezuelan Government Takes Over Eighth Largest Bank," *Venezuelanalysis.com*, June 16, 2010, http://venezuelanalysis.com/news/5429.

30. "Tras impulsarlas el Gobierno quiere menos importaciones," *El Universal*, May 28, 2010, http://economia.eluniversal.com/2010/05/28/eco_art_tras-impulsarlas-el _1918178.shtml.

31. Suggett, "Venezuelan Government Takes Over."

32. Simon Romero, "Left Behind in Venezuela to Piece Lives Together," *New York Times*, September 18, 2010, http://www.nytimes.com/2010/09/19/world/americas /19venez.html.

33. "Watchdogs Are Muzzled in Latin America," *Globe and Mail*, http://www.the globeandmail.com/news/opinions/editorials/watchdogs-are-muzzled-in-latin -america/article1773929/ (accessed October 10, 2010).

34. Editorial, "Libertad de prensa y democracia," *Clarin*, April 4, 2008, http://edant .clarin.com/diario/2008/04/04/opinion/o-01643113.htm.

35. Helen Popper, "Leading Media Group's Office Raided in Argentina," Reuters, December 20, 2011, http://www.reuters.com/article/2011/12/20/us-argentina-clarin-id USTRE7BJ1LB20111220.

36. Ezequiel Vazquez Ger, "Argentina Joins ALBA in War Against Free Press," Fox News Latino, March 24, 2012, http://latino.foxnews.com/latino/news/2012/03/24 /ezequiel-vazquez-ger-argentina-joins-alba-in-war-against-free-press/#ixzz1tyg CMCIC.

37. Terry Wade, "Bolivia Launches State Paper before Crucial Vote," Reuters, January 22, 2009, http://in.reuters.com/article/idINN2252758620090122.

38. Martin Arostegui, "Morales, Correa Target TV Foes," *Washington Times*, May 31, 2007, http://www.washingtontimes.com/news/2007/may/31/20070531-121115 -7740r/.

39. Ibid.

40. Ibid.

41. *The Declaration of Cochabamba: In Defense of Humanity*, Fifth Conference of Intellectuals and Artists in Defence of Humanity, May 22 and 23, 2007, held in Cochabamba, Bolivia, http://movimientos.org/foro_comunicacion/show_text.php3?key=10251.

42. "Watchdogs Are Muzzled."

43. "Freedom of the Press in Ecuador: A Chill Descends," *The Economist*, July 22, 2011, http://www.economist.com/blogs/americasview/2011/07/freedom-press-ecuador.

44. Nathan Gill, "Ecuadorean Judge Says Correa's Lawyer Wrote Universo Sentence," Bloomberg, February 15, 2012, http://www.bloomberg.com/news/2012-02-15 /ecuadorean-judge-says-correa-s-lawyer-wrote-universo-sentence.html.

45. Arostegui, "Morales, Correa Target TV Foes."

46. Alonso Soto, "Ecuador's Correa Says to Fight Media Corruption," Reuters, May 23, 2009, http://www.reuters.com/article/2009/05/23/us-ecuador-media-idUS TRE54M1L220090523.

47. Douglas Farah and Glenn Simpson, *Ecuador at Risk* (Miami: Inter-American Institute for Democracy, 2010), 13.

48. Roger Miranda and William Ratliff, *The Civil War in Nicaragua: Inside the Sandinistas* (Piscataway, NJ: Transaction, 1993), 91.

49. United Nations Commission on Human Rights, *Observatory for the Protection of Human Rights Defenders Annual Report 2009: Nicaragua*, June 18, 2009, http://www.unhcr.org/refworld/publisher,IFHR,,NIC,4a5f3017c,0.html.

50. James Roberts, "Nicaragua: Daniel Ortega's First Year," Heritage Foundation, January 15, 2008, http://www.heritage.org/research/commentary/2008/01/nicaragua-daniel-ortegas-first-year.

51. Tracy Wilkinson, "Media Critics of Nicaragua Leader Ortega Made to Pay," *Los Angeles Times*, August 2, 2009, http://articles.latimes.com/2009/aug/02/world/fg-nicaragua-media2.

52. Tim Johnson, "Nicaragua's Daniel Ortega Lays Groundwork to Stay in Power," *Miami Herald*, August 17, 2010, http://www.miamiherald.com/2010/08/16/1779031_p2/ortega-lays-groundwork-to-stay.html#ixzz1ERPuMOKA.

53. Will Grant, "Honduras TV Gets Government Order," BBC News Americas, May 25, 2007, http://news.bbc.co.uk/2/hi/americas/6690217.stm.

54. "Zelaya no vestía pijama cuando salió de Honduras," *El Heraldo* (Honduras), January 26, 2010, http://www.elheraldo.hn/Pa%C3%ADs/Ediciones/2010/01/26/Noticias/Zelaya-no-vestia-pijama-cuando-salio-de-Honduras.

55. Frances Robles, "They're Torturing Me, Honduras' Manuel Zelaya Claims," *Miami Herald*, September 24, 2009.

Chapter 9: Managing the Masses

1. Joseph Contreras, "Playing Hardball," *Newsweek* (Latin America edition), December 27, 1999.

2. Alexandra Olson, "Doubts over Touchscreen Tech Choice for Venezuela Recall," Associated Press, July 12, 2004.

3. Tim Golden, "U.S. Investigates Voting Machines' Venezuela Ties," *New York Times*, October 29, 2006, http://www.nytimes.com/2006/10/29/washington/29ballot.html.

4. Richard Brand, "Why Is Hugo Chávez Involved with U.S. Voting Machines?" *Miami Herald*, March 28, 2006, http://www.realclearpolitics.com/articles/2006/03/forget_dubai_worry_about_smart.html.

5. "Venezuela: With Us or Against Us?," *The Economist*, September 11, 2003, http://www.economist.com/node/2054474.

6. Ibid.

7. Helen Murphy, "Chávez's Blacklist of Venezuelan Opposition Intimidates Voters," Bloomberg News, April 17, 2006, http://www.bloomberg.com/apps/news?pid=newsarchive&sid=abASlsAyXgoE&refer=latin_america-redirectoldpage.

8. Ibid.

9. "Venezuela: With Us or Against Us?"

10. Douglas E. Schoen and Michael Rowan, *The Threat Closer to Home: Hugo Chavez and the War Against America* (New York: Free Press, 2009), 59.

11. Michael Rowan and Douglas E. Schoen, "Hugo Chávez and Anti-Semitism," *Forbes*, February 15, 2009, http://www.forbes.com/2009/02/13/Chávez-jews-referendum-opinions-contributors_0215_rowan_schoen.html.

12. Greg Gordon, "Most Electronic Voting Isn't Secure, CIA Expert Says," McClatchy Newspapers, March 24, 2009, http://www.mcclatchydc.com/2009/03/24/64711/most-electronic-voting-isnt-secure.html.

13. Steve Harrigan, report from Caracas on *Special Report*, Fox News Channel, September 27, 2010.

14. Walter R. Mebane, Jr., "Note on the Presidential Election in Iran," June 2009, University of Michigan, http://www-personal.umich.edu/~wmebane/note18jun2009.pdf; and "Preliminary Analysis of the Voting Figures in Iran's 2009 Presidential Election," Chatham House and the Institute of Iranian Studies, University of St Andrews, http://www.chathamhouse.org/publications/papers/view/109081 (retrieved October 19, 2011).

15. "US Embassy Cables: Iran Elections: 'People Are Going to Be Sorry,'" *The Guardian*, November 18, 2010, http://www.guardian.co.uk/world/us-embassy-cables-docu ments/212138.

16. "Venezuelan Military Would 'Not Accept' an Elected Opposition Government," Merco Press, November 8, 2010, http://en.mercopress.com/2010/11/08/venezuelan-military-would-not-accept-an-elected-opposition-government.

17. Thomas Erdbrink, "Mousavi Details Alleged Fraud," *Washington Post*, Foreign Service, July 4, 2009, http://www.washingtonpost.com/wp-dyn/content/article/2009/07/04/AR2009070402685.html, retrieved October 19, 2011.

18. "Venezuelan Military Would 'Not Accept.'"

19. Borzou Daragahi, "Iranian Newspaper Says Opposition Figure Should Stand Trial," *Los Angeles Times*, July 5, 2009, http://articles.latimes.com/2009/jul/05/world/fg-iran5.

20. Erdbrink, "Mousavi Details Alleged Fraud."

21. "Ahmadinejad Says Victory Is Blow to 'Oppressive' World," *The Telegraph*, June 14, 2009, http://www.telegraph.co.uk/news/worldnews/middleeast/iran/5532492/Ahmadinejad-says-victory-is-blow-to-oppressive-world.html.

22. Colin Freeman, "Iran Elections: Revolt as Crowds Protest at Mahmoud Ahmadinejad's 'Rigged' Victory," June 13, 2009, http://www.telegraph.co.uk/news/worldnews/middleeast/iran/5526721/Iran-elections-revolt-as-crowds-protest-at-Mahmoud-Ahmadinejads-rigged-victory.html.

Chapter 10: Managing the Military

1.   Jorge Fernández, *Las FARC en Mexico* (Mexico City: Aguilar, 2008), 8.

2.   Rowland Evans and Robert Novak, "Carter Team at Work; Slap at Argentina Hurts," *Victoria Advocate*, September 7, 1978, http://news.google.com/newspapers?nid=861&dat=19780907&id=v14dAAAAIBAJ&sjid=w1oEAAAAIBAJ&pg=5730,1517440.

3.   Ofira Seliktar, *Failing the Crystal Ball Test: The Carter Administration and the Fundamentalist Revolution in Iran* (Santa Barbara, CA: ABC-Clio, 2000), 49.

4.   Ibid., 50.

5.   Ibid.

6.   Ibid.

7. "Soviet Penetration of the Caribbean," *National Security Record*, Heritage Foundation, June 1980.
8. Ibid.
9. Frank J. Devine, *El Salvador: Embassy under Attack* (New York: Vantage, 1981), 64.
10. Ibid., 45.
11. Ibid.
12. Ibid., 44.
13. As reported in *La Nación* (Costa Rica), June 20, 1990.
14. *La Nación*, October 29, 1992.
15. Sam Dolgoff, *The Cuban Revolution: A Critical Perspective* (Montreal: Black Rose Books, 1996), 28.
16. *Bandera Roja: Voice of the Central Committee of the Peruvian Communist Party* 42 (May 1970), http://www.presidentegonzalo.org/document/p_19740000_brilliante_eng.html.
17. "Avanza una reforma educativa humanística en las Fuerzas Armadas," *Clarin*, August 6, 2007, http://edant.clarin.com/diario/2007/08/06/elpais/p-01201.htm.
18. "Double Standard Prosecuting Political Violence of the Past," *The Economist* (blog), October 6, 2010, http://www.economist.com/blogs/americasview/2010/10/human_rights_argentina.
19. The author served as an expert witness in the extradition trial of Roberto Bravo in 2010.
20. "Do as I Say: The First Couple Plan to Grant Asylum to a Former Chilean Guerrilla Leader," *The Economist*, October 7, 2010, http://www.economist.com/node/17209625.
21. Ibid.
22. Mary Anastasia O'Grady, "FARC's 'Human Rights' Friends," *Wall Street Journal*, July 7, 2008; http://online.wsj.com/article/SB121538827377131117.html?mod=todays_columnists.
23. Michael Radu, "Colombia's 'Revolutionaries' and Their Helpers," *FrontPage Magazine*, January 28, 2003, http://archive.frontpagemag.com/readArticle.aspx?ARTID=20073.
24. O'Grady, "FARC's 'Human Rights' Friends."
25. Ibid.
26. Edward Schumacher-Matos, "Killing a Trade Pact," *New York Times*, March 28, 2008.
27. "Un histórico líder que se tornó sanguinario," *El Nuevo Herald*, January 3, 2008.
28. Tim Padgett, "Refereeing the Colombia Standoff," *Time*, March 6, 2008, http://www.time.com/time/world/article/0,8599,1720012,00.html#ixzz1HAjZOqzU.
29. Ibid.
30. Stephan Küffner, "Ecuador Officials Linked to Colombia Rebels," *Time*, December 15, 2009, http://www.time.com/time/world/article/0,8599,1948040,00.html.
31. Aleksander Boyd, "Chavez New Constituion: Articles 328 and 329," Vcrisis.com, February 11, 2007, http://vcrisis.com/index.php?content=letters/200711020409.
32. D. Romero, "DIM pide catequizar a militares infieles a la revolución," *Tal Cual*, July 19, 2001, 26–27.
33. Ibid.

Chapter 11: Managing the Militias

1. Christopher Andrew and Vasili Mitrokhin, *The Mitrokhin Archive: The KGB in Europe and the West* (London: Gardners Books, 2000), 399.
2. Ibid.

3. U.S. Office of Research and Policy, *Cuba Annual Report*, 212.
4. Manwaring, "State and Nonstate Associated Gangs."
5. "Cristina in the Land of Make Believe," *The Economist*, May 1, 2008, http://www.economist.com/node/11293743.
6. "Bolivia: Unequivocally Condemn Mob Violence; Politically Motivated Attacks Threaten Rule of Law," *Human Rights Watch*, March 12, 2009, http://www.hrw.org/news/2009/03/12/bolivia-unequivocally-condemn-mob-violence.
7. Ibid.
8. "Iran's Bolivia Play," *Americas Forum*, February 28, 2011, http://americasforum.com/content/irans-bolivia-play.
9. "Bolivia Begins Military Training for Civilians; Opposition Warns of Pro-Government Militias," Associated Press, August 5, 2010, http://www.foxnews.com/world/2010/08/05/bolivia-begins-military-training-civilians-opposition-warns-pro-government/.
10. "ALBA to Create Military School to Train Soldiers in the Region," *El Universal*, November 29, 2010, http://english.eluniversal.com/2010/11/29/en_pol_art_alba-to-create-milit_29A4790091.shtml.
11. "Bolivia introdujo en la región a un socio muy peligroso, Irán," *ABC* Digital, February 10, 2011, http://www.abc.com.py/nota/bolivia-introdujo-en-la-region-a-un-socio-muy-peligroso-iran.
12. "'Iran Is Building an Army in Bolivia,' Says Head of Latin American Jewish Congress," Americas Forum, June 1, 2011, http://americasforum.com/content/iran-building-army-bolivia-says-head-latin-american-jewish-congress.
13. Matthew Grace, "Morales Apologizes to Argentina for Bombing Suspect Visit," *Bolivia Weekly*, July 1, 2011, http://www.boliviaweekly.com/morales-apologizes-to-argentina-for-bombing-suspect-visit/2182/.
14. Philippe Naughton and Tony Halpin, "Ahmadinejad Challenger Calls off Tehran Rally to Avert Further Bloodshed," *Times* (London), June 16, 2009.
15. Ian James, "Chávez Says Civilian Militia Should Be Armed Full-Time," Associated Press, October 3, 2010, http://www.washingtonpost.com/wp-dyn/content/article/2010/10/03/AR2010100303313.html.
16. "Protests in Venezuela; One Hundred High School Students Arrested," Human Rights Foundation, May 30, 2007, http://www.humanrightsfoundation.org/media/mediaShutdown.html.
17. Aldo Solari, *Estudiantes y Politica* (Caracas: Monte Ávila Editores, 1968), 33–40, 124.
18. Joseph Maier and Richard W. Weatherhead, "Origin and Philosophy of the Spanish American University," in *The Latin American University*, ed. Mario Gongora (Albuquerque: University of New Mexico Press, 1979), 17–64.
19. Solari, *Estudiantes y Politica*, 124.
20. Daniel H. Levine, *Conflict and Political Change in Venezuela* (Princeton, NJ: Princeton University Press, 1973), 171–74.
21. Ibid., 161–62.
22. Ramón L. Bonachea and Marta San Martín, *The Cuban Insurrection* (Piscataway, NJ: Transaction, 1974), 175–79.
23. Michael L. Smith, "Peru Raids Reflect Frustration; Garcia Seeks Ways to End Insurgency," *Washington Post*, February 15, 1987, http://www.gci275.com/news/post09.shtml.
24. Ibid.

25. Carmen Mendoza, "Sendero de Nuevo en San Marcos," *Peru 21*, June 16, 2010, http://peru21.pe/impresa/noticia/sendero-nuevo-san-marcos/2010-06-16/277636.
26. Liza Gross, "Leftist Students Rule at National Autonomous University of Mexico," *Miami Herald*, September 14, 2008.
27. Ibid.
28. "The FARC in Mexico," Wikileaks, March 28, 2008, released February 13, 2011, http://213.251.145.96/cable/2008/03/08MEXICO886.html.
29. Diego Cevallos, "Rights Groups Protest Killing of Students in FARC Camp," IPS News, March 21, 2008, http://ipsnews.net/news.asp?idnews=41695.
30. Gross, "Leftist Students Rule."
31. "Nicaraguan Cited by Haig Finds Asylum," *New York Times*, March 6, 1982.
32. Juan Tamayo, "Chávez's School Plans Ignite Furor in Venezuela," *Miami Herald*, February 27, 2001.
33. "Hugo Chávez Supporters Attack Parents," Yahoo News, November 8, 2001, http://dailynews.yahoo.com/h/p/ap/20011108/wl/1005259388venezuela_protest_sac103.html (last accessed November 2001).
34. Tamara Pearson, "New Venezuelan Ministry to Be Run by Youth and Students," *Venezuelanalysis.com*, March 14, 2011, http://venezuelanalysis.com/news/6065.
35. Gustavo Mendez, "M28 y Gobierno planifican la toma de seis universidades," *El Universal*, June 11, 2009, http://politica.eluniversal.com/2009/06/11/pol_art_m28-y-gobierno-plan_1426554.shtml.
36. Nicole M. Ferrand, "Venezuela's Tarek El Aissami," *Americas Report*, October 1, 2008, http://themengesproject.blogspot.com/2008/10/venezuelas-tarek-el-aissami.html.
37. Linda Robinson, "Terror Close to Home: In Oil-Rich Venezuela, a Volatile Leader Befriends Bad Actors from the Mideast, Colombia, and Cuba," *U.S. News & World Report*, September 28, 2003, http://www.usnews.com/usnews/news/articles/031006/6venezuela.htm.
38. Phil Gunson, "Chavez Appoints Radicals to Head Venezuelan Passport Agency, Reports of Arabs Obtaining ID Documents," *Miami Herald*, November 28, 2003.
39. Robert Spencer, "Jihad in Venezuela?" *JihadWatch*, November 29, 2003, http://www.jihadwatch.org/2003/11/jihad-in-venezuela.html.
40. Ferrand, "Venezuela's Tarek El Aissami."
41. Robinson, "Terror Close to Home."
42. Gustavo Mendez, "Schools and Universities on Alert for Risk of Indoctrination," *El Universal*, March 17, 2005, http://www.eluniversal.com/2005/03/17/en_pol_art_17A542549.shtml.
43. Neal McFarquhar, "Shadowy Iranian Vigilantes Vow Bolder Action," *New York Times*, June 19, 2009, http://www.nytimes.com/2009/06/19/world/middleeast/19basij.html?_r=2&ref=global-home.

Chapter 12: Exporting the Revolution
1. Richard M. Juang and Noelle Morrissette, eds., *Africa and the Americas: Culture, Politics and History: A Multidisciplinary Encyclopedia* (Santa Barbara, CA: ABC-Clio, 2008), 246.
2. Pan American Union, Dept. of Legal Affairs, General Secretariat, *Inter-American Treaty of Reciprocal Assistance Applications: 1960–1964*, vols. 1 and 2 (Washington: Organization of American States, 1964), 194, http://books.google.com/books?id=LqhAAAAAIAAJ&q=%22This+consisted+in+the+government+of+Venezuela+

lending+$300+million+dollars+to+the+%22&dq=%22This+consisted+in+the+ government+of+Venezuela+lending+$300+million+dollars+to+the+%22&hl=en &sa=X&ei=TXunT6e2NrOf6QH09KTKBA&ved=0CD0Q6AEwAA.

3.   Carlos Bringuier, *Red Friday, Nov. 22nd, 1963* (Delevan, WI: Chas. Hallberg, 1969), 121.

4.   Martin Arostegui, "Cuban Advisers Bolster Venezuelan Regime," *Washington Times*, April 6, 2010, http://www.washingtontimes.com/news/2010/apr/06/cuban-advisers -bolster-venezuelan-regime.

5.   "If Hugo Goes; Raúl Castro Searches for Other Lifelines," *The Economist*, July 7, 2011, http://www.economist.com/node/18928494.

6.   Thomas Joscelyn, "Axis of Subversion," *Weekly Standard*, May 6, 2005, http://www .weeklystandard.com/Content/Public/Articles/000/000/005/575achxn.asp.

7.   Nestor Carbonnell, *And the Russians Stayed: The Sovietization of Cuba; a Personal Portrait* (New York: Morrow/HarperCollins, 1989), 259.

8.   U.S. House of Representatives, "Un-American Activities Annual Report," 1963, 33.

9.   Ibid., 34.

10. "Latin America: Castro's Targets," *Time*, May 19, 1967, http://www.time.com/time /magazine/article/0,9171,840892-1,00.html#ixzz0y3QhdsP1.

11. U.S. Department of State, *Background Paper: Central America* (Washington: Departments of State and Defense, May 27, 1983), 2.

12. Joe Pichirallo and Terri Shaw, "Top Defector Disillusioned by Marxism," *Washington Post*, December 13, 1987.

13. David Brooks, "Latin America Is Not East of Here," *National Review*, March 14, 1986, 33.

14. State Department, *Background Paper: Central America*, 4.

15. Leslie H. Gelb, "Cuban Commander in Nicaragua Post," *New York Times*, June 19, 1983.

16. Nestor Sanchez, deputy assistant secretary of defense for inter-American affairs, speech before American Society for Industrial Security, Washington, December 1, 1982.

17. State Department, *Background Paper: Central America*, 4.

18. *West Watch*, Council for Inter-American Security 6, no. 2 (May 1983): 20.

19. State Department, *Background Paper: Central America*, 16.

20. *Turmoil in Central America: A Special Report by the United States Senate Republican Policy Committee* (Golden, CO: Independence Institute, 1986), 53.

21. *West Watch*, Council for Inter-American Security, special supplement, July 1983, S-2, S-3.

22. Will Grant, "Concern over Cuba's Role in Venezuela," BBC News, June 23, 2010, http://www.bbc.co.uk/news/10344990.

23. "Cubans Mushrooming in Venezuela's Sensitive Sectors," *El Universal*, February 4, 2010, http://english.eluniversal.com/2010/02/04/en_pol_esp_cubans-mushrooming -i_04A3390933.shtml.

24. Grant, "Concern over Cuba's Role."

25. Patricia Rondon Espin, "Ex-general: Venezuela Army Secrets in Cuban Hands," Reuters, April 29, 2010, http://www.reuters.com/article/2010/04/29/us-venezuela-general -interview-idUSTRE63S3CO20100429.

26. Fidel Castro, *Fidel Castro: My Life*, with Ignacio Ramonet (New York: Scribner, 2009), 649.

27. Cuban medical doctor who is a Barrio Adentro defector in Guatemala, interview by author in July 2009 (name withheld because doctor's daughter and family are still living under the Castro regime).
28. Michael Ceaser, "Cuban Doctors Working Abroad Defect to the USA," *The Lancet*, April 14, 2007, http://www.thelancet.com/journals/lancet/article/PIIS0140-6736%2807%2960577-7/fulltext.
29. "Siete Médicos Cubanos Demandan a Cuba y Venezuela por 'esclavitud moderna,'" EFE, February 22, 2010, http://www.noticias24.com/actualidad/noticia/144581/siete-medicos-cubanos-demandan-a-cuba-y-venezuela-por-esclavitud-moderna.
30. Ricardo Matheus, "Abandonados 70% de módulos de BA," *Diario 2001,* July 29, 2007.
31. "Cubans Mushrooming."
32. "Wikileaks Reveal US Concerns on Cuba-Venezuela Ties," BBC News, November 30, 2010, http://www.bbc.co.uk/news/world-latin-america-11883465.
33. Ibid.
34. Arostegui, "Cuban Advisers Bolster Venezuelan Regime."
35. Ibid.
36. "Chávez's War on Free Trade in Peru," *Investor's Business Daily*, June 10, 2009.
37. "Cardinal Cipriani Warns of 'Foreign Meddling in Peru's Internal Affairs' during July 28th Homily," *Peruvian Times*, July 30, 2009.
38. "La homilía de Cipriani tuvo tinte político," *Peru 21*, July 28, 2009, http://peru21.pe/noticia/319953/autoridades-ingresan-catedral-lima-misa-te-deum.
39. "Aymaran Army 'Ponchos Rojos' Behead Dogs as a Threat," *La Razon Bolivia*, November 23, 2007, http://www.latinamericanstudies.org/bolivia/ponchos-rojos.htm.
40. Bailey testimony before the Western Hemisphere Subcommittee.
41. Ibid.
42. Ibid.
43. Tim Rogers, "Nicaragua's Newest Tycoon? 'Socialist' President Daniel Ortega," *Christian Science Monitor*, October 14, 2009, http://www.csmonitor.com/World/Americas/2009/1014/p06s01-woam.html.
44. Ibid.
45. Ibid.
46. Ibid.
47. Tracy Wilkinson and Daniel Hernandez, "Ortega Has Received 'Suitcases Full of Cash' from Venezuela, Leaked Cables Say," *Los Angeles Times*, December 7, 2010, http://articles.latimes.com/2010/dec/07/world/la-fg-wikileaks-nicaragua-20101208.
48. Ibid.
49. Ibid.; "Mayorga under House Arrest in Nicaragua," Associated Press, October 6, 2004, http://sports.espn.go.com/sports/boxing/news/story?id=1896427.
50. Wilkinson and Hernandez, "Ortega Has Received."
51. Ivan Moreno, "Leaked Cables Say Nicaragua Government Took Bribes," Associated Press, December 7, 2010, http://www.washingtonpost.com/wp-dyn/content/article/2010/12/07/AR2010120705736.html.
52. Casey Woods and Gerardo Reyes, "Venezuelan Bribery Stars in Trial over Suitcase of Cash," *Miami Herald*, October 4, 2008, http://www.latinamericanstudies.org/venezuela/bribery.htm
53. Ibid.
54. Ibid.

55. Fiona Ortiz, "Suitcase of Cash Sparks New Scandal in Argentina," Reuters, August 9, 2007, http://www.reuters.com/article/2007/08/09/us-argentina-scandal-idUSN 0943585020070809.
56. John Sweeney, "Hugo Chávez and the Venezuela-Cuba Alliance: Preparing for War against the People," Vcrisis, October 26, 2005, http://vcrisis.com/index.php?content =letters/200510270918.
57. Javier Corrales, *Undermining Democracy: 21st Century Authoritarians* (Washington: Freedom House, June 2009), http://www.old.freedomhouse.org/uploads/special _report/83.pdf.
58. Ginger Thompson and Scott Shane, "Cables Portray Expanded Reach of Drug Agency," *New York Times*, December 25, 2010, http://www.nytimes.com/2010/12/26 /world/26wikidrugs.html?_r=1.
59. "Venezuela: Terrorism Hub of South America?," hearing before the Subcommittee on International Terrorism and Nonproliferation, July 13, 2006, http://commdocs .house.gov/committees/intlrel/hfa28638.000/hfa28638_0.HTM_.
60. Ibid.
61. Clyde D. Taylor, "Cuba Aids Drug Trade, Senate Panel Is Told," *Miami Herald*, May 15, 1985.
62. Larry Rohter, "Former Smuggler Ties Top Officials of Cuba and Nicaragua to Drug Ring," *New York Times*, November 21, 1991, http://query.nytimes.com/gst/fullpage .html?res=9D0CE1DD1530F932A15752C1A967958260&pagewanted=all.
63. Ibid.
64. Samuel T. Dickens, "The Nicaraguan Connection," *San Diego Union-Tribune*, April 22, 1985.
65. Ibid.
66. "Hatred of All Things Yankee Absorbs Lehder," *Los Angeles Times*, May 19, 1988, http://articles.latimes.com/1988-05-19/news/mn-4856_1.
67. Ibid.
68. Andrew and Mitrokhin, *World Was Going Our Way* , 67–70.
69. Marc Lacey and Jonathan Kandell, "A Last Vanishing Act for Robert Vesco, Fugitive," *New York Times*, May 3, 2008, http://www.nytimes.com/2008/05/03/world /americas/03vesco.html?pagewanted=all.
70. Chris Hawley, "Venezuela Drug Trade Booms," *USA Today*, July 21, 2010, http:// www.usatoday.com/news/world/2010-07-21-venezueladrugs21_ST_N.htm.
71. Ibid.
72. "Sierra Leone Drug Bust of Venezuelan Plane with Red Cross Markings," AFP, July 21, 2008, http://afp.google.com/article/ALeqM5jBoomcuMydy9E48JBmu6 bKQZqKqA.
73. Chris Hawley, "New Trend in Drug Smuggling: Secret Trans-Atlantic Flights in Old Jets," Associated Press, November 15, 2010, http://www.cnsnews.com/news/article /new-trend-drug-smuggling-secret-trans-atlantic-flights-old-jets.
74. Ibid.
75. "Extraoficial: Otro familiar de Tarek El Aissami habría sido socio de Makled," *El Informador*, November 16, 2010, http://www.elinformador.com.ve/noticias/sucesos /actualidad/extraoficial-otro-familiar-tarek-aissami-habria-sido-socio-makled/28953.
76. "Venezuelan Minister Hangs Out with Hezbollah," Gatestone Institute, February 11, 2011, http://www.gatestoneinstitute.org/1878/venezuelan-minister-hezbollah.

77. Fabiola Sanchez and Frank Bajak, "The Venezuelan Who 'Knew Too Much,'" Associated Press, January 24, 2011, http://abcnews.go.com/International/wireStory ?id=12748872.
78. Howard Altman, "Mack Wants Answers on Drug-Filled Jet with St. Pete Ties," *Tampa Tribune*, March 21, 2011, http://www2.tbo.com/content/2011/mar/21/212210 /mack-wants-answers-on-drug-filled-jet-with-st-pete/news-breaking/.
79. Sanchez and Bajak, "Venezuelan Who 'Knew Too Much.'"

Chapter 13: The Threat to America's "Soft Underbelly"
1. "Drug Catapult Found at U.S.-Mexico Border," Fox News, January 26, 2011, http:// www.foxnews.com/us/2011/01/26/drug-catapult-mexico-border/.
2. Elizabeth Aguilera, "Controversial Muslim Cleric Caught Sneaking into U.S.," *San Diego Union-Tribune*, January 26, 2011, http://www.utsandiego.com/news/2011 /jan/26/controversial-muslim-cleric-caught-sneaking-into-t/.
3. Department of Justice, Office of Public Affairs, "Two Men Charged in Alleged Plot to Assassinate Saudi Arabian Ambassador to the United States," October 11, 2011, http://www.justice.gov/opa/pr/2011/October/11-ag-1339.html.
4. Uri Friedman, "*New York Times* Leads the Swell of Skepticism at the Iran Plot," The *Atlantic Wire*, October 13, 2011, http://www.theatlanticwire.com/global/2011/10 /new-york-times-leads-swell-skepticism-iran-plot/43624/.
5. Richard Kerbaj, "Top Tehran TV Journalist Wanted by FBI for 1980 Murder in the US," *Times* (London), http://www.timesonline.co.uk/tol/news/world/middle_east /article6820989.ece (retrieved 22 May 2010).
6. Aidan Jones, "Ahmadinejad Chooses Wanted Man for Cabinet," *The Guardian*, August 21, 2009, http://www.guardian.co.uk/world/2009/aug/22/ahmadinejad-appoints -bomb-suspect.
7. William La Jeunesse, "Iranian Book Celebrating Suicide Bombers Found in Arizona Desert," Fox News, January 27, 2011, http://www.foxnews.com/us/2011/01/27 /iranian-book-celebrating-suicide-bombers-arizona-desert/.
8. Chelsea Schilling, "Foreign 'Terrorists' Breach U.S. Border," World Net Daily, May 20, 2010, http://www.wnd.com/?pageId=156441.
9. Tia Ghose, "Threats of Terrorism at Border Overblown," ABC 7 San Francisco, April 26, 2012, http://abclocal.go.com/kgo/story?section=news/state&id=8637619.
10. Louise Shelley, "The Globalization of Crime and Terrorism," America.gov Archive, February 1, 2006, http://www.america.gov/st/business-english/2006/February/200 80608103639xjyrreP4.218692e-02.html.
11. Ibid.
12. Yossef Bodansky and Vaughn S. Forrest, "Narco-Terrorism and the Syrian Connection," report of the Task Force on Terrorism and Unconventional Warfare, U.S. House of Representatives, August 13, 1991, 324.
13. Ibid.
14. Mark Bowden, *Killing Pablo: The Hunt for the World's Greatest Outlaw* (New York: Atlantic Monthly, 2001), 80.
15. "Mexican Cartels 'Working with Afghan Drug Lords,'" *El Pais,* January 5, 2010, http://elpais.com/elpais/2011/01/05/inenglish/1294208447_850210.html.
16. Ibid.
17. William H. Inman, "Southern Border Is the 'Soft Underbelly' of U.S., Officials Say," *Chicago Tribune*, December 5, 1985, http://articles.chicagotribune.com/1985-05 -12/news/8501290622_1_drug-planes-hostile-plane-flying/3.

18. Michael Braun, "Drug Trafficking and Middle Eastern Terrorist Groups: A Growing Nexus?," Washington Institute for Near East Policy, July 18, 2008.
19. Schilling, "Foreign 'Terrorists' Breach U.S. Border."
20. Anthony Kimery, "Iranian Martyrdom Book Found near US/Mexico Border Raises Questions," *Homeland Security Today*, January 28, 2011, http://www.hstoday.us /index.php?id=3400&no_cache=1&tx_ttnews[tt_news]=16501.
21. "FBI Chief Fears Infiltration by al-Qaida," MSNBC, March 9, 2005, http://www .msnbc.msn.com/id/7134185/ns/us_news-security/.
22. La Jeunesse, "Iranian Book Celebrating Suicide Bombers."
23. Charles Kurzman, Panel: "Muslim Diasporas," University of North Carolina, Chapel Hill, International Studies Schools Association, February 17, 2006.
24. Chris Zambelis, "Radical Islam in Latin America," *Terrorism Monitor* 3, no. 23 (December 2, 2005), http://www.jamestown.org/programs/gta/single/?tx_ttnews%5Btt _news%5D=623&tx_ttnews%5BbackPid%5D=180&no_cache=1.
25. Ibid.
26. Nicole Ferrand, "Islamic Terrorism in Latin America," *The Americas Report,* March 12, 2009, http://centerforsecuritypolicy.org/p17937.xml.
27. Darryl Heeralal, "T&T: A Heroin Route to US," *Trinidad Express,* May 29, 2005.
28. Chris Zambelis, "Jamaat al-Muslimeen on Trial in Trinidad and Tobago," *Terrorism Monitor* 4, no. 5 (March 9, 2006), http://www.jamestown.org/single/?no_cache =1&tx_ttnews%5Btt_news%5D=699.
29. "Guyana Man Convicted in Terrorist Plot against JFK Airport," *Newsroom Magazine,* January 16, 2011, http://newsroom-magazine.com/tag/yasin-abu-bakr/.
30. Ronen Bergman, *The Secret War with Iran: The 30-Year Clandestine Struggle against the World's Most Dangerous Power* (New York: Free Press, 2008), 172.
31. David C. Faith, "The Hawala System," *Global Security Studies* 2, no. 1 (Winter 2011).
32. Rex Hudson, "Terrorist and Organized Crime Groups in the Tri-Border Area (TBA) of South America" (Washington: Federal Research Division, Library of Congress, July 2003).
33. Bergman, *The Secret War with Iran*, 173.
34. "Bin Laden Reportedly Spent Time in Brazil in '95," *Washington Post*, March 18, 2003; and "El Esteve no Brazil," *Veja* 1,794 (March 19, 2003).
35. National Commission on Terrorist Attacks, *Final Report of the National Commission on Terrorist Attacks upon the United States* (New York: Norton, 2004), 161.
36. Matheus Machado and Murilo Ramos, "Are the Terrorists Here?," *Rio de Janeiro Epoca*, March 12, 2007.
37. Humberto Trezzi, "EUA pressionam Brasil a colaborar," *Zero Hora*, September 19, 2001.
38. Marina Walker Guevara, Mabel Rehnfeldt, and Marcelo Soares, "Smuggling Made Easy: Landlocked Paraguay Emerges as a Top Producer of Contraband Tobacco," Center for Public Integrity, June 29, 2009, http://www.publicintegrity.org/investigations /tobacco/articles/entry/1439/.
39. Marc Perelman, "Feds Call Chile Resort a Terror Hot Spot," *The Jewish Daily Forward*, January 3, 2003, http://www.forward.com/articles/9036/.
40. Douglas Farah, "Hezbollah's External Support Network in West Africa and Latin America," International Assessment and Strategy Center, August 4, 2006, http:// www.strategycenter.net/research/pubID.118/pub_detail.asp.
41. Ferrand, "Islamic Terrorism in Latin America."

42. "Buenos Aires Bomber 'Identified,'" BBC News, November 10, 2005, http://news .bbc.co.uk/2/hi/americas/4423612.stm.

43. Bergman, *The Secret War with Iran*, 183.

44. Joseph Humire, "Iran's Informal Ambassadors to Latin America," Fox News, February 18, 2012, http://latino.foxnews.com/latino/politics/2012/02/18/joseph -humire-irans-informal-ambassadors-to-latin-america/.

45. Janie Campbell, "Feds Say Men Funded Terror with PlayStations," February 20, 2010, http://www.nbcmiami.com/news/local/Miami-Men-Funded-Terror-With-Play stations-Cops-Say-84855027.html.

46. Farah, "Hezbollah's External Support Network."

47. Horacio Calderón, "Organized Crime and Terrorism in the Triple Border Area," HoracioCalderon.com, August 24, 2007, http://www.horaciocalderon.com/Art iculos/HC_TBA_Organised_Crime_and_Terrorism.doc.

48. "Pleno del Congreso amplía plazo para investigar a las llamadas Casas de Alba," *ANDINA Agencia Peruana de Noticias*, September 4, 2008, http://www.andina.com.pe /Espanol/Noticia.aspx?id=53OYu4+OY6Y=.

49. Naomi Mapstone, "Uribe Ramps Up Tension with Venezuela," *Financial Times*, July 25 2010, http://www.ft.com/cms/s/0/01a671f8-981a-11df-b218-00144feab49a.html.

50. Rep. Sue Myrick, "Myrick Calls for Taskforce to Investigate Presence of Hezbollah on the US Southern Border," letter to Homeland Security director Janet Ann Napolitano, June 23, 2010, http://myrick.house.gov/index.cfm?sectionid=22&itemid=558.

51. Jim Meyers, "Rep. Myrick: Hezbollah Major Threat on Mexican Border," July 15, 2010, http://www.newsmax.com/InsideCover/myrick-hezbollah-mexico-border -terrorism/2010/07/15/id/364796.

52. "Wiesenthal Centre: Hezbollah Plans More Attacks in Argentina," DPA, March, 9, 2010.

53. Juan Antonio Munoz, "Chile: Israeli Expert Discussed Hizballah Presence in Latin America," *El Mercurio*, February 11, 2007.

54. Clinton W. Taylor, "Hezbollah in Latin America," *American Spectator*, November 30, 2006, http://spectator.org/archives/2006/11/30/hezbollah-in-latin-america.

55. Antonio Salas, "Galería de Personajes," http://www.antoniosalas.org/libro/el-palestino /galeria-personaje/darnott-teodoro (last accessed October 2010).

56. Janice Kephart, "Moving beyond the 9/11 Staff Report on Terrorist Travel," Center for Immigration Studies, September 2005.

57. "Boston Street Gang MS-13 Cited as 'True Terror Threat'—Linked to Al Qaeda & Adnan Shukrijumah," Militant Islam Monitor, January 7, 2005, http://www.militant islammonitor.org/article/id/372.

58. Ibid.

59. "Feds Hoped to Snag Bin Laden Nuke Expert in JFK Bomb Plot," FoxNews.com, June 4, 2007.

60. Alfonso Chardy, Juan O. Tamayo, and Jay Weaver, "10 Years after 9/11, Suspected al Qaida Figure Still Eludes FBI," McClatchy Newspapers, September 09, 2011.

Chapter 14: A Potential Failed State Next Door

1. Wikileaks cable no. 08MEXICO886, "The FARC in Mexico," U.S. Embassy Mexico City, March 28, 2008, http://wikileaks.mediapart.fr/cable/2008/03/08 MEXICO886.html.

2. "Mexico Condemns Comment That U.S. Might Have to Send Troops to Fight Cartel 'Insurgency,'" Fox News Latino, February 9, 2011, http://latino.foxnews.com/latino

/news/2011/02/09/mexico-condemns-officials-insurgency-comment-suggesting-crime-groups-topple/#ixzz1EcTGOq4x.
3. Ibid.
4. Teo Molin, "Is Mexico a Failed State?," *Human Events*, June 1, 2009, http://www.humanevents.com/article.php?id=32061.
5. Dick Morris, "Menace in Mexico," *Jewish World Review*, April 4, 2006.
6. Ibid.
7. Ben Conery, "EXCLUSIVE: Hezbollah Uses Mexican Drug Routes into U.S.," *Washington Times*, March 27, 2009, http://www.washingtontimes.com/news/2009/mar/27/hezbollah-uses-mexican-drug-routes-into-us.
8. "Iran Increases its Presence in Latin America," Intelligence and Terrorism Information Center at the Israel Intelligence Heritage & Commemoration Center (IICC), April 19, 2009, p. 36, http://www.terrorism-info.org.il/data/pdf/PDF_09_099_2.pdf.
9. Adam Housley, "Hezbollah Working with Cartels," Fox News, February 21, 2011, http://liveshots.blogs.foxnews.com/2011/02/21/hezbollah-working-with-cartels/.
10. Ibid.
11. Roee Nahmias, "Expert: Hamas, Hizbollah Cells May Be Active in Mexico," YNET, November 2, 2007, http://www.ynetnews.com/articles/0,7340,L-3466854,00.html.
12. Jack Khoury, "Mexico Thwarts Hezbollah Bid to Set Up South American Network," *Ha'aretz*, June 7, 2010, http://www.haaretz.com/news/diplomacy-defense/mexico-thwarts-hezbollah-bid-to-set-up-south-american-network-1.300360.
13. Giles Tremlett, "Hugo Chávez 'Terrorist Link' Sparks Diplomatic Row between Spain and Venezuela," *The Guardian*, March 2, 2010, http://www.guardian.co.uk/world/2010/mar/01/hugo-chavez-venezuela-spain-eta.
14. Anna Mahjar-Barducci, "Basque ETA Terrorists Move to Venezuela, Team Up with Colombia's FARC," Gatestone Institute, January 19, 2011, http://www.gatestoneinstitute.org/1806/venezuela-eta-farc.
15. Tremlett, "Hugo Chávez 'Terrorist Link.'"
16. D. Fernandez, "ETA se repliega en su colonia de Venezuela, que aloja a 47 etarras," *20 minutos*, December 12, 2011, http://www.20minutos.es/noticia/925361/20/eta/repliega/venezuela/.
17. "ETA Suspect Arturo Cubillas Denies Links with the FARC," *El Universal*, October 19, 2010, http://english.eluniversal.com/2010/10/19/en_pol_esp_eta-suspect-arturo-c_19A4626865.shtml.
18. "Spanish Court Prosecutes Five ETA Members Who Supported the FARC," *El Universal*, September 6, 2011, http://www.eluniversal.com/2011/09/06/spanish-court-prosecutes-five-eta-members-who-supported-the-farc.shtml.
19. Edward F. Mickolus and Susan L. Simmons, *Terrorism, 1992–1995: A Chronology of Events and a Selectively Annotated Bibliography* (Santa Barbara, CA: Greenwood, 1997), 407.
20. Larry Rohter, "New Passports Being Issued by Nicaragua to Curb Fraud," *New York Times*, January 28, 1996.
21. Tim Johnson, "Arms Cache Troubles Nicaragua—Chamorro's Real Control Questioned," Knight Ridder, May 25, 1993.
22. Mickolus and Simmons, *Terrorism, 1992–1995*.

Chapter 15: Venezuela
1. Jackson Diehl, "Expose Chavez's Crimes," *Washington Post*, May 18, 2008.
2. Josh Shahrya, "Chavez Caught Red-Handed Sending Gasoline to Iran," PJ Media,

February 22, 2011, http://pjmedia.com/blog/pjm-exclusive-chavez-caught-red -handed-sending-gasoline-to-iran/.

3. Roger F. Noriega, "Hugo Chávez's Criminal Nuclear Network: A Grave and Growing Threat," *Latin American Outlook*, October 2009.

4. Patricia Poleo, *El Nuevo País*, June 11 and 18, 2008.

5. "Treasury Targets Hizballah in Venezuela," June 18, 2008, U.S. Treasury Department, http://www.treasury.gov/press-center/press-releases/Pages/hp1036.aspx.

6. Ibid.

7. Roger Noriega, "Is There a Chavez Terror Network on America's Doorstep?," *Washington, Post*, March 20, 2011, http://www.washingtonpost.com/opinions/is _there_a_chavez_terror_network_on_americas_doorstep/2011/03/18/ABauYU3 _story.html?wprss=rss_homepage.

8. Ibid.

9. Ibid.

10. Ibid.

11. Ibid.

Chapter 16: The Emerging Threats

1. Gordon Thomas, *Gideon's Spies: The Secret History of the Mossad*, 5th ed. (New York: St. Martin's Griffin, 2009), 472.

2. Ibid., 473.

3. Michael Scheuer, interview by Glenn Beck, Fox News, February 9, 2009.

4. "Al Qaeda Eyes Bio Attack from Mexico," *Washington Times*, June 3, 2009, http:// www.washingtontimes.com/news/2009/jun/03/al-qaeda-eyes-bio-attack-via -mexico-border/?page=1.

5. Ibid.

6. Ibid.

7. C. Wergin and H. Stausber, "Iran plant Bau einer Raketenstellung in Venezuela," *Die Welt*, November 11, 2010, http://www.welt.de/politik/ausland/article11219574 /Iran-plant-Bau-einer-Raketenstellung-in-Venezuela.html.

8. Rep. Roscoe Bartlett, "National EMP Recognition Day: The Threat That Cannot Be Ignored," conference held at the Heritage Foundation, August 15, 2011, http://www .heritage.org/events/2011/08/emp-day.

9. Frank J. Gaffney, "Nuke over U.S. Could Unleash Electromagnetic Tsunami," *World Tribune*, December 7, 2005, http://www.worldtribune.com/worldtribune/05 /front2453711.9284722223.html, excerpted from his *War Footing: 10 Steps America Must Take to Prevail in the War for the Free World* (Annapolis, MD: Naval Institute Press, 2005).

10. Joseph Farah, "Iran Military Journal Eyes Nuclear EMP Attack on U.S.," World Net Daily, April 29, 2005, http://www.wnd.com/?pageId=30061#ixzz1FGwYS5r0.

11. Dr. Peter Vincent Pry, "Foreign Views of Electromagnetic Pulse (EMP) Attack," Statement before the United States Senate Subcommittee on Terrorism, Technology, and Homeland Security, March 8, 2005, 4.

12. Ibid.

13. Farah, "Iran Military Journal Eyes."

14. Dr. Ira W. Merritt, "Proliferation and Significance of Radio Frequency Weapons Technology," Statement before the Joint Economic Committee, United States Congress, February 25, 1998, http://www.iwar.org.uk/iwar/resources/senate/merritt.htm.

15. James Jay Carafano, PhD, and Richard Weitz, PhD, "EMP Attacks—What the U.S. Must Do Now," Heritage Foundation, November 17, 2010, http://www.heritage .org/research/reports/2010/11/emp-attacks-what-the-us-must-do-now.
16. Shelby Foote, *The Civil War: A Narrative; Fort Sumter to Perryville* (New York: Vintage, 1986), 800–801.
17. Stephen Coughlin, "To Our Great Detriment: Ignoring what Extremists Say about Jihad," thesis submitted to the faculty of the National Defense Intelligence College, 2007, http://www.aina.org/reports/iwesaj.pdf, 36–37.
18. Janet Napolitano, interview by Cordula Meyer, "Away from the Politics of Fear," *Der Spiegel*, March 16, 2009, http://www.spiegel.de/international/world/0,1518 ,613330,00.html.

Selected Bibliography

Albats, Yevgenia. *The State within a State: The KGB and Its Hold on Russia—Past, Present and Future.* New York: Farrar, Straus and Giroux, 1994.

Barron, John. *KGB: The Secret Work of Soviet Secret Agents.* New York: Reader's Digest Press, 1974.

Brownfeld, Allan C., and J. Michael Waller. *The Revolution Lobby.* Washington: Council for Inter-American Security, 1986.

Cline, Ray S., and Yonah Alexander. *Terrorism: The Soviet Connection.* New York: Crane, Russak, 1984.

Cordesman, Anthony, and Martin Kleiber. *Iran's Military Forces and Warfighting Capabilities.* Westport, CT: Praeger, 2007.

Coughlin, Stephen. "To Our Great Detriment: Ignoring What Extremists Say about Jihad." Thesis, National Defense Intelligence College, 2007.

Cruz, Jose Miguel, ed. *Maras y Pandillas en Centroamerica.* San Salvador: UCA Editores, 2006.

Fishel, John T., and Max G. Manwaring. *Uncomfortable Wars Revisited.* Norman: University of Oklahoma Press, 2006.

Follain, John. *Jackal: The Secret Wars of Carlos the Jackal.* New York: Arcade Publishing, 1998.

Francis, Samuel T. *Soviet Strategy of Terror.* Washington: The Heritage Foundation, 1985.

Gates, Robert M. *From the Shadows: The Ultimate Insider's Story of Five Presidents and How They Won the Cold War.* New York: Simon & Schuster, 2007.

Gold, Dore. *The Rise of Nuclear Iran: How Tehran Defies the West.* Washington: Regnery, 2009.

Halperin, Ernst. *Terrorism in Latin America.* Thousand Oaks, CA: Sage Publications, 1976.

Koehler, John O. *Stasi: The Untold Story of the East German Secret Police.* Boulder, CO: Westview, 1999.

Lee, Martin. *The Beast Reawakens: Fascism's Resurgence from Hitler's Spymasters to Today's Neo-Nazi Groups and Right-Wing Extremists.* New York: Little, Brown, 1997.

Leitner, Richard J., and Peter M. Leitner, eds. *Unheeded Warnings: The Lost Reports of the Congressional Task Force on Terrorism and Unconventional Warfare.* Vol. 1. Washington: Crossbow Press, 2009.

Michael, George. *The Enemy of My Enemy: The Alarming Convergence of Militant Islam and the Extreme Right.* Lawrence: University of Kansas Press, 2006.

Miranda, Roger, and William Ratliff. *The Civil War in Nicaragua: Inside the Sandinistas.* Piscataway, NJ: Transaction, 1993.

Nagl, John. *Learning to Eat Soup with a Knife: Counterinsurgency Lessons from Malaya and Vietnam.* New York: Praeger, 2002.

Schoen, Douglas, and Michael Rowan. *The Threat Closer to Home: Hugo Chávez and the War against America.* New York: Free Press, 2009.

Segaller, Stephen. *Invisible Armies: Terrorism into the 1990s.* New York: Harcourt, Brace, Jovanovich, 1987.

Sterling, Claire. *The Terror Network: The Secret War of International Terrorism.* New York: Holt, Rinehart, and Winston, 1981.

Waugh, Billy, and Tim Keow. *Hunting the Jackal: A Special Forces and CIA Soldier's Fifty Years on the Frontlines of the War against Terrorism.* New York: Avon, 2005.

Wickham-Crowley, Timothy P. *Guerrillas and Revolution in Latin America: A Comparative Study of Insurgents and Regimes since 1956.* Princeton, NJ: Princeton University Press, 1992.

Yallop, David. *Tracking the Jackal: The Search for Carlos, the World's Most Wanted Man.* New York: Random House, 1993.

Index

Aal, Abed Abdel, 192
Abdelaziz Zakkout, Sofian, 201
Abdelnour, Fadi Kabboul, 210
Abu Bakr, Yasin, 193
Abu-Sharif, Bassam, 48
Adams, Barry, "Tyrone Cole," 193
Adolf Hitler Free Corps (Freikorps Adolf
    Hitler), 84
Aflaq, Michel, 53
African National Congress (ANC), 31
Ahmad Barakat, Assad, 196
Ahmad Barakat, Sheikh Akhram, 196
Ahmadinejad, Mahmoud, 1–2, 61, 94, 98,
    138–39, 162, 187, 197, 204
Aissami, Shibli el-, 161
al Diab Fatah, Hakim Mamad, 177
Al Jazeera, 118
al-Gama'a al-Islamiyya, 192
al-Murabitun, 191
al-Mustafa Al-Alam Cultural Institute, 198
Alarcón, Ricardo, 32
Albats, Yevgenia, 24, 26–28
Albrecht, Udo, 84
Alcalá, Oswaldo, 161
Alexander, Yonah, 36
Allende, Salvador, 2, 153
Alo Presidente!, 1, 135
American Muslim Association of North
    America (AMANA), 201
AMIA bombing (1994), 155, 197
Amin, Idi, 94
Andrew, Christopher, 24
Andropov, Yuri, 26–27, 152
Anoun, Rifaat Abul, 47
Anti-Imperialism Center (AIC), 44–45
Anti-Zionist League, 86
Apablaza, Galvarino, 146–47
Arab Nationalist Movement, 47, 88

Arabic Reserve Corps (Hilfskorp Arabien), 82
Arafat, Yasser, (Abu Ammar), 31–35, 44–52,
    72–86
Arabsiar, Manssor, 186
Arellano Felix Cartel, 203
Argentine Arab Home (Hogar Árabe Argen-
    tino), 81
Argentine Israelite Mutual Association (Asoci-
    ación Mutual Israelita Argentina, or AMIA),
    55, 155, 187, 197
Argentine-Islamic Association (Asociación
    Argentino Islámica, or ASAI), 81–82
Argüello, Patrick, 49–50
Arias, Óscar, 107
Armed Forces of National Liberation (Fuerzas
    Armadas de Liberación Nacional, or
    FALN), 48
Armed Revolutionary Nuclei (Nuclei Armati
    Rivoluzionari), 63
Armenian Secret Army for the Liberation of
    Armenia (ASALA), 54
Article 239, 113–14
Artillery of Ideas, 120
Aryan Nations, 68–71
Arzalus, Eusebio, 208
Askapena, 207
Assad, Bashar al-, 52
Assad, Sheik Suhail, 198
Association of Volunteers for Suicide-
    Martyrdom, 60
Association of Young People Loyal to the
    Homeland (Bund Helmattreuer Jugend), 82
asymmetric warfare, 4–9, 100, 185–86, 210,
    216
Atef, Mohammed, 195
Atta, Mohammed, 201
autonomia (autonomy), 156
Ayestaran, José, 206

Baader-Meinhof Gang, 48, 51, 63
Baader, Andreas, 48
Baath Party, 52–53, 73, 161, 210
Baduel, Gen. Raul, 137
Baguazo, 170
Bailey, Dr. Norman, 112, 172
Baldizón, Alvaro, 166
Banco Federal, 125–26
Banco Internacional de Desarrolloa, 172
Bandera Roja, 146
Banna, Hassan al-, 87
Banque Commerciale Arabe, 93
Banque Populaire Arabe, 93
Baralt Avenue, 122
Barbie, Klaus, 93
Barka, Mehdi Ben, 30–31
Barrére, Agustín, 75
Barricadas (Barricades), 130
Barrio Adentro, 10, 168
Bartlett, Rep. Roscoe, 216
Barzini, Luigi, Jr., 65
Basij, 162
Batista, Fulgencio, 157, 164, 167
Battara, Marco, 92
Baxter, José "Joe," 79
Bay of Pigs, 31, 152
Beam, Louis, 69
Berenson, Lori, 208
Berger, Obergruppenführer Gottlob, 68, 73
Betancourt, President Rómulo, 163–64
bin Laden, Osama, 67, 87, 94, 119, 161, 195,
    202, 215
Bitar, Salah ad-Din al-, 53
Black Order (Ordine Nero), 64
Black September, 48–49, 84, 92
Blum, William, 119
Bolivarian Alliance for the Peoples of Our
    America (ALBA), 10, 170, 198
Bolivarian Circles, 122, 124, 131, 155
Bolivarian Continental Coordinator (Coordi-
    nadora Continental Bolivariana), 158
Bolivarian Militia, 2, 155
Borge, Tomás, 45, 119, 208
Borghese, Prince Junio Valerio, 66
Boughader Mucharrafille, Salim, 205
Boyd, Col. John, 7
Braun, Michael, 200, 206
Bravo, Douglas, 48, 99
Brezhnev, Leonid, 26
Briceño, Gen. Gustavo Reyes Rangel, 102
Broadcasting Board of Governors, 117
Brookings Institution, 109
Brownfield, William, 169, 201
Buscaglia, Edgardo, 189
Bush, George H. W., 189
Bush, George W., 7, 68, 161

Cabezas, Hugo, 160–62
Cabezas, Rodrigo, 125
Cablevisión, 127

Cabral, Amílcar, 31
Caggiano, Antonio, 75
Calderón, Felipe, 204
Calderón, Horacio, 199
Caracazo, 100
Cárdenas, Victor Hugo, 153
Caribbean League, 163, 165
Carter Center, 136–37
Carter, Jimmy, 35, 102, 111, 136–44, 166
Casey, William, 36–41
Castro, Fidel, 2, 8, 29–46, 65, 80-87, 100,
    118–27, 140–59, 163–65, 179
Castro, Raúl, 2, 33, 166
Castroite Revolutionary Armed Forces (Fuerzas
    Armadas Revolucionarias, or FAR), 80, 119
Ceauşescu, Nicolae, 77
Center for Arabic Studies (Centro de Estudios
    Arabes), 51
Center for Inter-American Relations, 142
Central Committee of the Communist Party of
    the Soviet Union (CPSU), 23–34
Central Intelligence Agency (CIA), 21, 42–43,
    52, 123, 137, 165, 201, 214
Central University of Venezuela, 156
CEPS Foundation (part of the Center for
    Political and Social Studies), 104
Chain, Paula, 147
Chamorro, Carlos Fernando, 130
Chamorro, Violeta, 130
Chamran, Mostafa, 60
Chapultepec Peace Accords, 144
Chávez, Adán, 99
Chávez, Asdrubal, 135
Chavez, Hugo, 1–2, 8–11, 45–48, 94, 97-216
Che Like Chamran conference, 60
Chedid, Saad, 51
Chepe Fortuna, 122
Chomsky, Noam, 119
Cinchonero guerrillas, 51
Cipriani, Cardinal Juan Luis, 170
Citizens' Councils (*Consejos de Poder
    Ciudadano*—CPC), 131
Clinton, Hillary, 186
Colburn, Forrest, 115–16
Collective Lucio Cabañas, Carlos Marx, and
    Ernesto Guevara (Colectivo Lucio Cabañas,
    Carlos Marx, and Ernesto Guevara), 158
Collera, Dr. José Manuel, (Agent Gerardo), 111
Colombian Communist Party (PCC), 149
Colombian Communist Youth (JUCO), 149
Column 88, 70
Comandante Centeno, 100
Combat 18, 70
Combined Arms Center (CAC), 5
Committee for State Security (KGB), 25–48,
    120, 152
Committee on Foreign Investment in the
    United States (CFIUS), 134
Communist Refoundation Party, 92

Community Environmental Legal Defense Fund (CELDF), 105
Conscience and Freedom (Conciencia y Libertad), 158
Congreso de Chillán, 53
Congressional Task Force on Terrorism and Unconventional Warfare, 54, 188
constitutional subversion, 106-07, 115, 127
Cooper, Rabbi Abraham, 61–62
Correo del Orinoco, 120
Coughlin, Maj. Stephen Collins, 16, 220–21
Courdroy, Robert, 82
Crane, Conrad, 4
Cuarta Urna (fourth ballot), 113–14
Cuban Intelligence Directorate, 164
Cuban Missile Crisis, 18
Cubillas, Arturo, 207
Curiel, Henri, 31,33

Dahrough, Ali Nizar, 197
Dahrough, Mohammad, 196
Darnott, Teodoro (aka Mario Morales Meza and Daniel José González Epieyu), 200
Davison, Ian Michael, 82
dawah, 140
Déby, Idriss, 45
Democradura, 104-7
Democratic Front for the Liberation of Palestine (PDFLP), 49
Department of Defense, 5
Derian, Patricia, 141
Desacato (disrespect), 129
Devine, Frank J., 142
Diehl, Jackson, 209
Diouf, Abdou, 45
Directorate of Military Intelligence (Dirección de Inteligencia Militar, or DIM), 150
Dirty War, 81, 146
disassociation, 141
Dodd, Sen. Christopher, 148–49
Draganović, Krunoslav Stjepan, 74
Duke, David, 69
Dzerzhinsky, Felix, 22

e-Puzzler, 19
Eichmann, Adolf, 74, 79, 93
Eichmann, Horst Adolf, 79
El Aissami Maddah, Amin Obayda, 210
El Aissami, Aiman, 181
El Aissami, Amin Obayda, 181
El Aissami, Firaz, 181
El Aissami, Haifa, 181
El Aissami, Tarek, 160–62, 181, 210
The Brigade Member (El Brigadista), 158
El Palestino, 201
El Salvador: Embassy under Attack, 142
El Silencio, 124
El Universo, 128
Elamsani, Issandr, 52
Electromagnetic Pulse (EMP), 216

Empathic view (of intelligence analysis), 41
Engels, Friedrich, 3, 21, 23
English, Rep. Glenn, 190
Escobar, Pablo, 180, 188–89
Estavanico, "Stephen the Moor," 191
Euskadi Ta Askatasuna; Basque Homeland and Freedom (ETA), 44, 51–55, 172, 189, 206–8
Ezeiza massacre, 81

Fabian Society, 97
Faci, Michel, 86
Fajardo, Manuel, 158
Fallahijan, Ali, 197
Fanon, Frantz, 87
Farabundo Martí National Liberation Front (FMLN), 44–45, 144, 208
Farach, Antonio, 179
Farah, Douglas, 16
Faría, Jesus, 125
Farrakhan, Louis, 87
Faurisson, Robert, 87
Federal Office for the Protection of the Constitution (Bundesamt für Verfassungsschutz), 63
Feltrinelli, Giangiacomo, 64–66
Figueres, José, 178–80
Firk, Michele, 119, 120
Firmenich, Mario, 51
Firuzabadi, Mortaza, 61
FM 100-5, 4
FM 3-0, 4
FM 3-24, 6
Follain, John, 50
Force 17, 82, 93
fourth-generation warfare, 4
Fourth Reich, 78, 86
Fox, Vicente, 192
Fraser, Gen. Douglas, 200
Freedom House, 176
French Communist Party, 119
Freude, Ludwig, 75
Friedberg, Aaron, 43
Front for Student Struggle Julio Antonio Mella (Frente de Lucha Estudiantil Julio Antonio Mella), 158
Fukuyama, Francis, 15

Galeano, Eduardo, 120
Galeria Page Mall, 198
Galimberti, Rodolfo, 51
García, Alan, 157
García, Álvaro, 154
Gates, Robert, 39–41
Genoud, François, 88, 93
German Action Group (Deutsche Aktions-gruppe), 63, 84–85
Giap, Vo Nguyen, 2–3
Globovisión, 125–26, 155–56gNGO, 109
Golinger, Eva, 120–21
Goñi, Uki, 74–76
González-Neira, Emilio, 198

Gonzalez, Sigifredo, Jr., 187
Gott, Richard, 97
Graham, Dr. William R., 219
Green Book, The, 45, 91–92
Grenier, Robert, 206
Grupo Clarín, 127
Guesalaga Fernández, Iraitz, 207
Guevara, Aleida, 60–61
Guevara, Camilo, 60
Guevara, Ernesto "Che," 29–31, 47–49, 60–65, 86, 98, 118, 158–64, 179
Gutiérrez Espinosa, Ligdamis, 159
Guzmán, Abimael, 52, 158
Guzman, Carlos Ariel Charry, 203
Guzmán, Jaime, 146–47

Haas, Monika, 19
Habash, Dr. George, 47, 88
Haddad, Wadi, 26–33, 47–50, 93
Hague Convention for the Suppression of Unlawful Seizure of Aircraft, 23
Haig, Alexander, 35–36
Hamas, 161, 172, 194–97, 206
Handal, Schafik, 45, 144–45
Hanson, Victor Davis, 222
Harkins, Lt. Gen. Paul D., 4
Hassan II, King, 30
Hauptverwaltung Aufklärung (HVA), 20–21
Hausmann, Dr. Ricardo, 136
Hawatmeh, Na'if, 49
Heidegger, Martin, 87
Hezbollah, 9, 16, 33, 60, 81–82, 161
Hezbollah Argentina, 81
Himmler, Heinrich, 71, 73
Hirst, Joel, 101
Hoffman, Karl Heinz, 82–84
Holbrooke, Richard, 141
Holy Land Foundation, 195
Hoskins, Richard Kelly, 69
Housley, Adam, 205
Hoyos, Luis Alfonso, 199–200
Huber, Ahmed, 88–91
Human Rights Bureau, 141
Hungarian Complex, 152
Hussein, Saddam, 9, 44, 53, 86, 109, 161
Husseini, Haj Amin al-, 72, 88, 90, 93

ideological subversion, 152
informational hegemony, 124
Insulza, José Miguel, 132
Inter-American Dialogue, 136
Inter-American Press Association, 128
International Department, 23–25
Iran-Iraq War, 9, 44, 60, 187
Iranian Revolutionary Guard Corps (IRGC), 2, 9, 162, 200–222
Irish Republican Army (IRA), 24
IRNA (Iran's state news agency), 109
Isaacson, Walter, 117
Islamic Liberation Party (Hizb ut-Tahrir), 67

Islamic socialism, 91
Israel-Hezbollah War, 9
Israeli Embassy bombing 1992, 55, 197
Italian Social Movement (MSI), 91
Italy-Libya Association, 91
Iyad, Abu (aka Salah Mesbah Khalaf), 19, 83
Izarra, Andrés, 118, 124
Izarra, Lt. William, 99, 118

Jadi, 109
Jamaat al-Fuqra, 193
Jamaat al-Muslimeen, 193
Jammeh, Yahya, 45
Japanese Red Army, 50, 55
Joundi, Sami al-, 73
Jubeir, Adel al-, 186
judicial warfare, 146, 148
Jung, George, 179

Kabbou Abdelnour, George, 210
Kabchi, Raymundo, 211
Kadir, Abdul, 193
Kahane, Rabbi Meir, 208
Kan'an, Fawzi, 211
Kaplan, Fanny, 21
Kauffman, Carlos, 175
Kayhan, 138
Khalaf, Salah Mesbah (Abu Iyad), 19, 83
Khaled, Leila, 49
Khomeini, Ayatollah Ruhollah, 15, 59, 90–91, 212
Kikumura, Yu, 55
Killebrew, Col. Bob, 4
Killing Hope: U.S. Military and CIA Interventions Since World War II, 119
King Darius the Great, 71
King Hussein, 48–49, 84
Kinzer, Stephen, 129
Kirchner, Cristina Fernández de, 126–28, 146, 175
Kirchner, Néstor, 146
Kolbe, Rep. Jim, 204
Konaré, Alpha Oumar, 45
Koran, 140
Korda, Alberto, 65
Koritschoner, Franz, 22
Kreis, August, 70
Ku Klux Klan, 62, 69
Kühnen, Michael, 84, 86
Küssel, Gottfried, 87
Kyna, Karl von, 82

La Hora, 128
La Hora de los Pueblos (The Time of the People), 78
La Questione Sociale (The Social Question), 76
Laqueur, Walter, 34–35, 77
Lara, Rodrigo, 178
Larraquy, Marcelo, 51
Lawrence, T. E., 6

leaderless resistance, 69
Leahy Law, 148
Leahy, Sen. Patrick, 148
Lebanese Armed Revolutionary Faction
    (LARF), 54
Lehder, Carlos, 178–79
Lenin, Vladimir, 3, 21–24,
Leoni, Raúl, 156
Levin, Shlomo, 84
Lewis, Bernard, 15
Lilley, James R., 43
Linowitz report, 142
Lod Airport, 50
López Díaz, Julián, 166
López Obrador, Andrés Manuel (aka
    AMLO), 204
López Peña, Javier, 207
López Rega, José, 81
López, José Ramon, 126
Lukin, Vladimir, 216

M-19, 44, 105
M-28, 123, 160
Machurucuto, 99, 165
Mack, Connie, 118
Mahdi, Fawzi Salim el-, 82
Maisanta List, 136
Makled, Walid, 181–82, 212
Malatesta, Errico, 64, 76
Malcolm X, 31
Manwaring Paradigm, 102
Manwaring, Max, 6, 102–3, 153, 221
Mara Salvatrucha (aka MS-13), 202
Marighella, Carlos, 64
Mathaba News Agency (aka al-Mathaba or
    AIC), 44–45
McCone, John, 165
McCoy, Jennifer, 136
Medina-Mora, Eduardo, 214
Mein, Ambassador John Gordon, 119
Melli University (National University of
    Iran), 53
Mendizabal, Horacio, 52
Meshal, Khaled, 212
Miceli, Felisa, 175
Mielke, Erich, 19–20
Miguel Reyes Espinosa, José, 201
Military Academy of ALBA, 154
Military Sports Group Hoffman (Wehrsports-
    gruppe-Hoffman), 82–84
Minh, Ho Chi, 2–3
Mini-Manual of the Urban Guerrilla, 64
Ministry of Islamic Liaison, 68. See also Aryan
    Nations
Mirbach, Count Wilhelm, 21
Misión Barrio Adentro (Mission Inside the
    Barrio), 168
Mitrokhin, Vasiliy, 24
Mohammad Shallah, Ramadan Abdullah, 212
Mokhles, Mohammed Ali Hassan, 192

Molotov-Ribbentrop Pact, 77
Monroe Doctrine, 142
Montes, Julio, 175
Montreal Convention for the Suppression of
    Unlawful Acts Against the Safety of Civil
    Aviation, 23
Morales, Evo, 46, 105–111, 127–28, 139, 145,
    153–54, 170–75
Morales, Vilma, 114
Mothers of Plaza de Mayo, 81
Mousavi, Ahmad, 212
Movement for University Transformation, 160
Moynihan, Daniel Patrick, 141
Mubarak, Hosni, 9
Mueller, Robert, 190
Mugabe, Robert, 45, 94
Mughniyah, Imad Fayez, 197
Muhammad, Wali (aka Robert Johnson), 193
Mundaraín, Germín, 136
Munich Olympics, 85
Musawi, Abbas al-, 60
Museveni, Yoweri Kaguta, 45
Mussolini Action Squadron (Squadre d'Azione
    Mussolini), 64
Mutti, Claudio, 91–92
Myatt, David (aka Abdul Aziz), 70–71
Myrick, Rep. Sue, 200

Nafisi, Abdullah al-, 62, 215–16
Nagl, Lt. Col. John, 6
Naim Naim, Kamal, 210
Napoleonic code, 140
Napolitano, Janet, 200, 221
Narváez, Pánfilo de, 191
Nasr al Din, Ghasan Atef Salameh, 210, 212
Nasr al Din, Ghazi, 210–11, 212
Nasr, Jameel, 206
Nasrallah, Hassan, 195–96, 211–12
Nasser, Gamal Abdel, 29, 78–79, 87–90
National Autonomous University of Mexico
    (UNAM), 158
National Counter-Terrorist Directorate (Di-
    rección Nacional Contra el Terrorismo, or
    DINCOTE), 199
National Electoral Council (CNE), 134–35
National European Communitarianism, 77
National Latin Movement (Movimiento Nacio-
    nal Latino), 179
National Liberation Army (Ejército de Liber-
    ación Nacional, or ELN), 148
National Liberation Front, Algeria (FLN), 30
National Liberation Front of South Yemen, 32
National Office of Identification and Immi-
    gration (Oficina Nacional de Identificación y
    Extranjería, or ONIDEX), 161
National Popular Resistance Front (Frente Na-
    cional de Resistencia Popular, or FNRP), 115
National Vanguard (Avanguardia Nazionale), 92
Navarro, Antonio, 105
Nell, José Luis, 79

Nelson, Brian A., 123–24
Netanyahu, Benjamin, 23–24
Neue Rheinische Zeitung, 23
New Order (Ordine Nuovo), 64
New York Tribune, 23
Newsom, David, 44, 141
Newton, Ronald, 73–74
Nidal, Abu, 39, 83
Nixon, Richard, 185
Non-Aligned Movement, 29
Nordic Route, 75
Noriega, Manuel, 178
Noriega, Roger, 210–13
Nosair, El Sayyid, 208
Nujoma, Sam, 45
Nur, Abdul, 193

O'Grady, Mary Anastasia, 147
Observatory for the Protection of Human
   Rights Defenders, 131
Ochoa Sánchez, Arnaldo, 99, 166
Office of Soviet Assessment (SOVA), 39–42
Okamoto, Kozo, 50
Olavarria, Jorge, 106, 133
Open Veins of Latin America, 120
Operation Checkmate (Operación Jaque), 147
Operation No More Lies, 110
Operation Simón Bolívar, 165
Operational Strategic Command, 138
Oqueli, Hector, 119
Organization for Defending Victims of Vio-
   lence, 109
Organization of American States (OAS), 131
Ortega, Daniel, 45–60, 101, 115–16, 129–32,
   165–79
Ortega, Humberto, 179
Organization of Solidarity with the People of
   Asia and Africa (OSPAA), 31
Organization of Solidarity with the People
   of Asia, Africa and Latin America
   (OSPAAAL), 31, 45, 144

Pact of Punto Fijo, 8
Padilla, José, 201
Pahlavi, Reza Shah, 71
Paladin Group, 78
Palestinian Legislative Council, 33
Palestinian Liberation Democratic Front
   (PLDF), 27
Palestinian National Council, 49
Papel Prensa S. A., 126–27
Paredes Ruiz, Francisco, 17
Party of Venezuelan Revolution (Partido de la
   Revolución Venezolana, or PRV), 48, 99
Pastor, Robert, 141
Patrice Lumumba University, 17, 24, 33–35,
   47, 53
Patriotic Revolutionary Movement (Movimien-
   to Patriótico Revolucionario), 81
Paz, Sheik Karim Abdul, 198
PCM-20-2009, 114

Pelosi, Rep. Nancy, 148
Peña, Alfredo, 123
People's Revolutionary Army (Ejército Revolu-
   cionario del Pueblo, or ERP), 80
Peralta, Santiago, 75
Perón, Juan, 51, 74–91
Petraeus, Gen. David, 5–7, 102
Petróleos de Venezuela, S. A. (PDVSA), 135,
   168–75, 210
Popular Front for the Liberation of Palestine
   (PFLP), 26, 33, 88, 93
Phineas priests, 69
piqueteros (picketers), 153
Plan Ávila, 100, 155
Plan Colombia, 148, 150
Plan Patriota, 150
Pol Pot, 52
Poleo, Patricia, 210–11
Ponomarev, Boris, 24, 28–29
Popular Revolutionary Army (EPR), 159
population-centric counterinsurgency (PC-
   COIN), 150
Possony, Stefan, 36–37
Poulsen, Frank Piasecki, 158
Power of Nightmares, The, 38
Practical Guide to Aryan Revolution, 70
Press TV, 117, 186
Prieto, Abel, 128
Protosocialism, 97
Pry, Dr. Peter, 218
Puente Llaguno, 122–23, 139
Putin, Vladimir, 24, 110

Qaddafi, Muammar el-, 8, 35, 43–46, 77, 78,
   91–94, 193
Qasim, Abd al-Karim, 30
Qassemi, Hajj Saeed, 60–61
Quds Force, 186, 197–200
Quebracho, 81, 146
Qutb, Muhammad, 87
Qutb, Sayyid, 87

Rabbani, Mohsen, 197–98
Radio Caracas Televisión Internacional
   (RCTV), 124
Radio Farda, 108
Radio Free Europe/Radio Liberty, 117, 210
Radio Islam, 87
Radu, Michael, 147
Rami, Ahmed, 87
Ramírez Sánchez, Illich (aka Carlos the Jackal),
   20, 33, 46–50, 64, 74–75, 93–99
Ramírez, Sergio, 131
Rangel Silva, Maj. Gen. Henry, 138, 212
Rangel, Domingo Alberto, 157
Reagan, Ronald, 18, 21, 35, 44, 112, 144
Real Odessa, The, 74
Rebel Armed Forces (Fuerzas Armadas Rebel-
   des, or FAR), 119
Rebellion (Rebeldía), 158

Red Army Faction (RAF), 19–20, 39
Red Brigades, 39, 44, 51, 63
The Red Ponchos (Ponchos Rojos), 171
Red Terror, 22
Reid, Michael, 120
Remer, Maj. Gen. Otto Ernst, 71–72
Reporters Without Borders, 128
requerimiento, 140
Revolutionary Action Movement (Movimiento Acción Revolucionaria, or MAR), 17
Revolutionary Armed Forces of Colombia (Fuerzas Armadas Revolucionarias de Colombia or, FARC), 10, 80, 147, 206
Revolutionary Bolivarian Movement (Movimiento Bolivariano Revolucionario, or MBR), 99
Revolutionary Brotherhood document, 101
Revolutionary Coordinating Junta (Junta de Coordinacion Revolucionaria, or JCR), 80
Revolutionary Islam, 47
Revolutionary Left Movement (Movimiento de Izquierda Revolucionaria, or MIR), 80, 157
Revolutionary Nationalist Tacuara Movement (Movimiento Nacionalista Revolucionario Tacuara, or MNRT), 79–80
Rey, Jorge Campos, 157
Reyes, Raúl (aka Luis Edgar Devia Silva), 45–46, 100, 149, 158
Reza Asghari, Ahmad, 197
Rezai, Mohsen, 197
Rezk El Sayed Take El Din, Khaled, 195
Rice, Condoleezza, 148
Richany Jimenez, Aref, 210
Rigobon, Roberto, 136
Risquet, Jorge, 3
Rivero, Gen. Antonio, 167
Robelo, Alfonso, 166
Rodman, Peter, 43
Roeder, Manfred, 84, 85
Rogue State, 119
Rojas, Eugenio, 171
Rose, P. K., 42–43
Rosen, Stephen, 43
Rosenholz Files, 21
Rowan, Michael, 136
Rumsfeld, Donald, 6
Rushdie, Salman, 88
Russia Today, 117, 121

Saab Halabi, Tarek William, 210
Saab Saab, Imad, 210, 212
Sa'ada, Anton, 73
Saavedra, Rubén, 154
Sabbagh, Radwan, 210
Sabino, Carlos, 106
Saca, Antonio "Tony," 145
Safadi, Khaled T., 198
Safadi, Marwan al-, 195
Sakharov, V. N., 24
Salahuddin, Dawud (David Theodore Belfield), 186

Salameh, Ali Hassan "Red Prince," 93
Salas, Antonio, 201
Salinas, Abel, 157
San Marcos University, 157, 158
Sánchez Cerén, Salvador, 208
Sánchez de Lozada, Gonzalo, 153
Sánchez, Arnaldo Ochoa, 166
Sandinistas, 2, 34, 44–59, 101–30, 152, 165–80, 208
Santos, Juan Manuel, 182
Santos, Samuel, 115
Schacht, Hjalmar, 71
Scheuer, Michael, 215
Schlorrmann, Friedrich, 75
Schoen, Douglas, 136–37
Schulz, Carlos, 75–76
Segaller, Stephen, 41
Sejna, Gen. Jan, 24, 29
Seliktar, Ofira, 141
Senate Select Committee on Intelligence, 25
72-Hour document, 102
Sewall, Sarah, 7
Shahid Beheshti University, 53–54
Shakuri, Gholam, 186
Shannon, Thomas A., 115
Shapiro, Amb. Charles, 176
Shariati, Ali, 53, 87
Shariatmadari, Hossein, 138
Sheik Mohammed, Khalid, 195
Shelepin, Alexander, 28
Shelley, Louise, 187–88
Sherman, Brig. Gen. William Tecumseh, 220
Sherman, Rep. Brad, 176
Shevchenko, Arkady, 25
Shibanov, Alexander, 217
Shining Path, 51, 157-58, 171, 214
Shukrijumah, Adnan, 193, 201–2
Simon Wiesenthal Center, 61, 200
Silence and the Scorpion, The, 123–24
Skorzeny, Otto "Scarface," 76–78
Smartmatic, 134–39
Socialist Antifascist Union, 77
Society for Risk Analysis, 190
Solidarité (aka Aide et Amitié), 31, 33
Soliman, Mohammed Ali, 192
Soloviev, Vladimir, 25
Somoza, Anastasio, 34, 49, 130, 165–66
Soros, George, 109
Southern Connection, The, 142
Soviet Military Intelligence (GRU), 23, 36
Squad of the Martyr Patrick Argüello, 50
State Department, U.S., 110
Stavridis, Adm. James G., 204
Stealth NGOs, 145
Sterling, Claire, 37–40
Stern, Jessica, 69
Stigall, Steve, 137
Stone, Oliver, 119
Struggle of the People (Lotta di Popolo), 91
Subcomandante Marcos, 191
Submarine-launched ballistic (SLBM), 217

Sucumbíos, 149
Sufi, Shaykh Dr. Abdalqadir as-, 191
Suitcase EMP, 219
Suleiman Wanked, Abdul Ghani, 211
Swedish National Defense Research Institute, 219
Syrian Social Nationalist Party, 73

Tabatabai, Ali Akbar, 186
Tacuara, 78–81
Tal Cual, 150
Talavera, Ulises, 198
Tarabain Chamas, Mohamad, 198
Tascón, Luis, 135
Taylor, Clyde D., 178
TeleSUR, 117–18, 124
Tenth Chief Directorate, 37
Terpins, Jack, 155
Territorial Militia Troops, 2
Terror Network, The, 37, 39, 40–41
Third Position, 62–64, 85
Third Position (Terza Posizione), 64
Third Reich, 68, 72, 90, 179
Thiriart, Jean-François, 76–80, 91
Threat Closer to Home, The, 136
Tiitinen list, 21
Tilelli, Gen. John H., Jr., 43
Tirado, Victor, 116
Tisserant, Eugène, 75
Tolentino, José Carlos Garcia, 198
Tolkunov, Lev, 34
Transnational Institute, 142
Treaty of Brest-Litovsk, 21
Trejos, Alberto, 115–16
Tri-border Area (TBA), 55, 188–99, 205
Tricontinental Conference, 30–31, 65, 78
Túpac Amaru (MRTA), 157, 171, 208
Turcios, Oscar, 49
Tuti, Mario, 92
21st Century Socialism, 1, 97, 104, 126–32, 133, 155–71, 221
Type II error (false negative), 43
Tyson, Brady, 141

U.S. Agency for International Development (USAID), 111
U.S. Army War College, 4
U.S. Election Assistance Commission, 137
U.S. House of Representatives Subcommittee on Oversight, 25
Ulrike, Meinhof, 48
UN General Assembly Resolution 2625 (XXV), 23
Unified Revolutionary Directorate (Dirección Revolucionaria Unificada, or DRU), 100
United Socialist Young Guard, 77
Urbancic, Frank, 177
Uribe, Álvaro, 147–50, 206
Uriburu, Alberto Ezcurra, 78

Urroz Blanco, Miguel, 167
Urtiaga, Itxaso, 207
Usón, Francisco, 169, 170
Utopia, 161

Vaca Narvaja, Fernando, 51
Vahidi, Ahmad, 155, 187, 197
Valencia-Arbeláez Organization, 181
Valenzuela, Arturo, 210
Vásquez Velásquez, Brig. Gen. Romeo, 114
Vassiliev, Alexander, 24
Velasco, Eloy, 206–7
Venezuelan News Agency (Agencia Venezolana de Noticias, or AVN), 118
Venezuelan Social Television (Televisoria Venezolana Social), 124
Verstrynge, Jorge, 9
Vesco, Robert, 179–80
Vidal, Gore, 119
Vigilantes of Christendom, 69
Villalobos, Joaquín, 140–41
Voice of America, 108
von Leers, Johann (Omar Amin), 88

Waffen-SS Handschar Division, 72
Weinrich, Johannes, 20
Weinstein, Allen, 24
Westmoreland, Gen. William, 3–4,
White, Robert E., 143
Wikileaks, 115, 138, 174, 176
Wilson III, Maj. Isaiah, 5
Wilson, Antonini, 175
Wilton Park, 108
Woolsey, James, 52
Worch, Christian, 86
World Resistance Front Rally, 59
World Revolutionary Center (WRC), 45
World Social Forum, 49
World Trade Center bombing 1993, 192, 208
World Peace Council (WPC), 33–34

Yakuza, 188
Yalá, Kumba, 45
Yale University, 109
Years of Lead (*Anni di Piombo*), 64
Young Egypt (a.k.a Green Shirts), 72
Young Europe, 77
Yousef, Ramzi, 195
Youssef Kourani, Mahmoud, 205

Zapatero, José Luis, 206
Zapatista, 159
Zapatista Army of National Liberation (Ejército Zapatista de Liberación Nacional), 191
Zawahiri, Ayman al-, 214
Zelaya, Manuel "Mel," 101, 113–15, 132
Zetas, 186
Zhou Enlai, 77
Zubaydah, Abu, 196

About the Author

Jon B. Perdue serves as the director of Latin America programs at the Fund for American Studies in Washington, D.C., and sits on the boards of think tanks and foundations in the United States and Latin America. He also serves on the Policy and Economics Council as a consultant to investment professionals on policy and regulatory issues related to Latin America. Perdue has given testimony on Capitol Hill regarding the threat from radical groups in Latin America and served as an international election observer in the historic elections in Honduras. Fluent in Spanish, Perdue lectures widely and has written for numerous publications in English and Spanish in the United States and Latin America, and has been interviewed on radio and television in both languages as well. He lives in Washington, D.C.